32

WAYS *to Be a*

CHAMPION *in* BUSINESS

32 WAYS

to Be a

CHAMPION *in* BUSINESS

EARVIN
"MAGIC" JOHNSON

THREE RIVERS PRESS

NEW YORK

Published in the United States by Three Rivers Press, an imprint of
the Crown Publishing Group, a division of Random House, Inc., New York.

www.crownpublishing.com

Three Rivers Press and the Tugboat design are registered trademarks of Random House, Inc.

Originally published in hardcover in the United States by Crown Business, an imprint of the
Crown Publishing Group, a division of Random House, Inc., New York, in 2008.

Grateful acknowledgment is made to the *Los Angeles Times* for permission to
reprint "Lucky for Us, Magic Has Been Our Gift That Keeps on Giving," by
Bill Plaschke (*Los Angeles Times*, December 25, 2007), copyright © 2007 by
Los Angeles Times. Reprinted by permission of the *Los Angeles Times*.

Library of Congress Cataloging-in-Publication Data

Johnson, Earvin.

32 ways to be a champion in business / Earvin "Magic" Johnson.—1st ed.

p.   cm.

1. Success in business.   2. Entrepreneurship.   3. Leadership.   4. Work ethic.
5. Social values.   I. Title.   II. Title: Thirty-two ways to be a champion in business.

HF5386.J616 2008

650.1—dc22   2008036994

ISBN 978-0-307-46189-6

Printed in the United States of America

Design by Leonard Henderson

10 9 8 7 6 5 4

First Paperback Edition

This book is dedicated to the entrepreneurs who mentored me, to the people and communities we serve, and to all who seek to control their own destinies through hard work and service to others.

CONTENTS

32

WAYS *to Be a*

CHAMPION *in* BUSINESS

While I spent fourteen years in the NBA playing basketball, I always had bigger dreams of building a business empire. My first book, *My Life*, was a 1992 bestseller about my basketball career and my personal life during my playing days. It began with my childhood and wrapped up as I moved into business full time with a company now known as Magic Johnson Enterprises.

I am grateful for my experiences as an athlete. Yet the rewards of my entrepreneurial endeavors have been even more fulfilling. I've learned that creating jobs and providing goods and services to urban communities beats even five NBA championships.

It was not an easy transition, however. I stumbled now and then as I began my business career, just as I stumbled when I tried to host my own television talk show. Still, I've bounced back in all those arenas. I won my first Emmy for my work on *Inside the NBA* with Charles Barkley, Kenny Smith, and Ernie Johnson. And I took home a Grammy Award for my successful audio book too.

In my business career, more than a few skeptics told me that I was wrong to focus on underserved urban communities. Neighborhoods populated by minorities could not sustain the same big brand businesses that had thrived in the suburbs, the doubters said.

They were wrong. Where they saw only problems, I created abundant opportunities. Many of those same doubters didn't think that major investors in private equity funds would support development in urban neighborhoods. Yet our two urban funds have generated more than $2 billion in investments.

Today, Magic Johnson Enterprises is a multimillion dollar company. I promise you that tomorrow we will be even bigger.

Finally, there were many people who felt that my life was over when I discovered that I had HIV. Again they were wrong on all counts. I am grateful to be as healthy, strong, and every bit as energetic as in my NBA days.

As you read *32 Ways to Be a Champion in Business*, I hope you will learn from my experiences and benefit from the lessons I've shared. My goal is to help you fulfill your business dreams while bettering your life and the lives of those around you.

Make no mistake, you will encounter skeptics and doubters too. Tell them that Earvin Johnson says not to bet against anyone with a dream and the determination to go after it.

PART I

BUSINESS STRATEGIES

The Mission

**Each of us can make a difference,
even if it is one street corner at a time.**

My father and other entrepreneurs in my hometown, Lansing, Michigan, were my first business role models and mentors. Later, I got to know major entertainment executives such as Joe Smith of Elektra/Asylum Records and Peter Guber of Sony Pictures because they had courtside Lakers tickets. When we socialized after games, they'd ask me about basketball—and I'd pick their brains about business.

Still, it was J. Bruce Llewellyn, one of the most successful black men in America, who sent me off with a mission on my journey from basketball player to businessman. The son of Jamaican immigrants, he built an empire that includes one of the nation's largest Coca-Cola distributorships, a cable and broadcasting company, and *Essence* magazine.

When we met, I got right to the point.

"I want to be a businessman after basketball," I told him. "I want to make a lot of money like you."

Mr. Llewellyn let me babble on like that for several minutes before he cut me off with a wave of his hand.

"No, Magic," he said; "if money is all you want, there will

never be enough of it and you will never be happy. You've got to be about more than that."

He had my attention. What did he mean?

"You have the opportunity to be a leader who can do great things and change people's lives for the better," he said. "You can be a businessman who is also a catalyst for change."

This great entrepreneur offered me more than I'd bargained for. Since high school, I'd sought out advice from every successful businessperson I'd met. This was the first person who had a bigger vision for me than I had for myself.

A catalyst for change?

That was a role I'd never imagined. I thought you had to be Nelson Mandela or the Reverend Martin Luther King, Jr., to change the world. I learned instead that each of us can make a difference, even if it is one street corner at a time.

I still saw myself as an athlete—a player who performed well on the basketball court and hopefully excited a few fans. I figured once my NBA days were over I'd fade from the public view and focus on building wealth and a family.

God has a way of telling you what you are supposed to be doing. He gets the message out one way or another until you finally pay attention.

That meeting with J. Bruce Llewellyn was a defining moment. He changed my perspective by challenging me to expand my goals as a person and as an entrepreneur.

A few weeks after my talk with him, God sent another messenger by the name of John Mack, who led the Urban League of Los Angeles for more than thirty-five years.

Mr. Mack asked me to join the Urban League. Then he too challenged me.

"You've got to become a leader in this community," he said. "You need to get involved and learn how things work."

Bruce Llewellyn and John Mack opened my eyes and my mind to a much bigger world.

I'd thought I was living large as a member of the Lakers. Yet once I immersed myself in business and joined the Urban League, I realized that an athlete's life offers a very limited perspective.

Over time, I came to understand the vision others had for me. I made the next big step in my manhood when I heeded the advice of those two strong and committed leaders. They refocused my vision for my life, and I resolved to first make a difference in the world and let the money take care of itself.

To accomplish that mission, I went back to school in the classroom of the real world. I was lucky. I had access to brilliant men and women of all races who gave me guidance—from *Black Enterprise* publisher Earl Graves to Lakers owner Jerry Buss and Hollywood superagent Michael Ovitz.

Even with those great minds to guide me, I had a lot to learn. Certainly, I made mistakes, and I will share what I learned from them in the pages that follow. To stay true to my mission, I will share the story of my journey from basketball to boardroom while also providing guidance to aspiring entrepreneurs.

Before we begin, I encourage you, just as Mr. Llewellyn and Mr. Mack encouraged me, to think of yourself and your business as catalysts for positive change in your community. Make a difference, and making money will follow.

CREATING COMMUNITY

One of my greatest pleasures these days is visiting my businesses in South Central. Described as "the soul of Los Angeles," South Central is as diverse and complex as any community in America. It was the scene of the infamous Rodney King riots and the backdrop for many hip-hop music videos. But many intellectuals, musicians, actors, artists, professors, doctors, lawyers, and business leaders call South Central their neighborhood as well.

On South Central's far western edge sits the Ladera Center, a shopping plaza that is home to the first Starbucks that I opened and my Magic Friday's —which is a one-of-a-kind T.G.I. Friday's restaurant. Today there are Starbucks and Friday's throughout urban America. Back then, there were virtually none in minority neighborhoods, until I partnered with those two big brands and convinced them that they were missing out on a huge market.

Some call my target market "urban America" or "emerging markets" or the "inner city." All of those descriptions apply to underserved communities, where my heart lies. I invest in underserved minority communities. My goal is to do well financially while creating jobs and providing goods and services for the people we serve in those areas.

When I pitch that market and my businesses to corporate leaders—whether to Starbucks, Best Buy, Sodexo, or Aetna—I tell them that urban America is the nation's last great frontier for their businesses.

The minority population in this country is growing at seven times the rate of the majority population. African Americans now have almost a trillion dollars in spending power. Latinos are now the nation's largest minority group, constituting 15.1 percent of the U.S. population. They have nearly $900 billion in spending power, and that is expected to be $1.2 trillion by 2012.

Blacks and Hispanics combined will have more than $2 trillion in spending power, according to the Selig Center for Economic Growth at the University of Georgia.

No business can afford to ignore that kind of consumer market. Minority populations are growing, and they spend at rates above those of mainstream consumers. The median age of African Americans and Hispanics is considerably younger than that of other consumer groups, and more of them are millionaires than ever before.

Minority Americans are aggressive producers of goods and services too. According to the U.S. Census Bureau, the rate of growth for minority-owned businesses ranges from more than

25 percent for Asians and 31 percent for Hispanics to 45 percent for blacks, compared with 10 percent for all U.S. businesses.

When I tell corporate leaders about the opportunities to serve and work with minorities in urban America, they listen because my partners and I have proven that investing in minority communities makes financial sense.

Still, what I love most about visiting the Ladera Center has nothing to do with finances. I'm just amazed by the sense of community we've created there. Nearly any time of day, any day of the week, you can walk into my Starbucks at the Ladera Center and find men and women of all ages working on laptops, reading books and newspapers, or laughing and socializing.

When you step outside to the back patio, you will find something that amazes me and warms my soul every time I visit. This Starbucks serves as a home away from home for Susan Guillyard, Lonnie Neal, Joseph Lloyd, Eugene Krank, and Donald Bolt. You will find these avid speed-chess players "snappin' pieces" every day of the week.

Joseph Lloyd, seventy-four, comes as often as five days a week because it is a place where he feels safe and welcomed.

"The operative word for me is 'safe,'" Joseph says. "If you can't go somewhere and be safe, why go? And I have camaraderie here with the other regular chess players who like to exercise their minds and do positive things."

Joseph, who is a musician and poet, gathered for years with fellow chess players outside Fifth Street Dick's, a famed South Central jazz club. When their longtime hangout shut down, the speed-chess crowd had nowhere to go until I convinced Starbucks to break the suburban model by putting picnic tables on the patio, giving these great customers a new place to congregate.

Now chess players from around the world—even masters from Russia—come to *our* Starbucks to challenge the home team. Some of them are doctors, lawyers, and professors. Others are wage earners and retirees. They've even drawn young recruits such as a college student and aspiring entrepreneur, Donald Bolt, twenty, who lives more than twenty-five miles away.

"I used to play at a place in Long Beach near my home, but I heard there was tougher competition at the Magic Starbucks, so now I come here every day of the week," said Donald. "I was a little intimidated the first time I came to play. It was a trial by fire because most of the players are older than me, and I thought if I didn't win, they wouldn't want me around. Luckily, I won my first two matches and one of them said, 'We need you to come back.' Now I feel like I belong here."

Across the street, my T.G.I. Friday's draws male and female motorcycle clubs, Saturday singles, and families who come in after church in their Sunday best.

My name is on the buildings, but you better believe that the customers have taken ownership of both businesses. If there is a menu change, an overflowing trash can, or a moved table, they don't call the corporate offices of T.G.I. Friday's or Starbucks; they call Magic Johnson Enterprises—and we are glad to hear from them.

The fact that our customers consider our businesses to be *theirs* too gives me more satisfaction than all the basketball trophies at home. I want you to have that same feeling about whatever business you go into.

The urban American market was not an easy sell initially. The corporations behind the big brands had their own proven business models, and they targeted the suburbs. They knew they could make money in sprawling, outlying areas populated mostly by middle- and upper-income white families. They were slow to grasp the economic viability of investing in places such as Harlem and South Central.

I heard it all. *Urban neighborhoods won't support a cineplex. Blacks and Hispanics won't pay for premium coffee.* I had to convince a lot of skeptical white executives—the same people who lived mostly in suburban communities—that the inner-city market was ripe and ready.

My celebrity status as a former athlete got me in the door. Yet most of them did not take me seriously. They'd hand me a basketball and ask for an autograph, but they did not want to hear my pitch for investing in neighborhoods populated by blacks, Latinos, Asians, and other minorities.

Back then, I had to overcome the skepticism of bankers and corporate leaders. They seemed to think I was just a jock playing around in a new game. So in my early ventures I had to take most of the financial risk.

You will face your own challenges as you chase your entrepreneurial dreams. Know that as long as you build your business around your passion and make solid business decisions, you can find a way to make it happen. If you believe in what you are doing, others will pick up on it and support you.

There will always be someone trying to shoot you down. Yet if you are passionate and work hard, you will turn doubters and skeptics into believers.

It took me a while to unload the baggage of my athletic career. I made mistakes too. Now, however, my business team is on a roll and investors and political leaders are eager to talk to me about opportunities in the urban market.

Political leaders come to us now. Our quiet revolution provides jobs and increases tax revenues while revitalizing communities from within. We are doing it in Harlem, South Central, and other neighborhoods across the country.

We aren't just building businesses, we are building dreams. More important, we build *futures*. We do this both at Magic Johnson Enterprises, which is the umbrella company for all of my business ventures, and at the Magic Johnson Foundation, which encompasses all of my charitable and nonprofit ventures.

Magic Johnson Enterprises, formed in 1987, serves as a catalyst for community and economic empowerment by providing high-quality entertainment and brand-name products and services for residents of multicultural urban communities. We bring into those communities major players, including Starbucks, Best Buy, Aetna, Abbott, SodexoMAGIC, 24 Hour Fitness, Magic Workforce Solutions, and AMC Theatres.

My partnerships provide urban residents like Joseph Lloyd and Donald Bolt places where they can feel safe shopping, relaxing, and enjoying themselves. Building and running urban developments is a business—a big business. Thankfully, it has been very profitable for both me and my partners. Yet, just as Bruce Llewellyn, John Mack, Earl Graves, and others have repeatedly told me, let me tell you again: to be a successful entrepreneur—and a successful person—your business has to be about much more than making money.

Whatever you do—whether it is running a fast-food franchise, a dress shop, or an online enterprise—should be more than a job for you. It should be a passion and a mission. In the long run, that is what makes it all worthwhile.

Don't get me wrong; making money is not only a good thing, it is necessary for the survival of your business, and I'll offer plenty of advice on that in this book. Still, if you are going to invest all of your talent, time, and energy in an endeavor, your heart should be in it too.

Developing businesses in urban neighborhoods for the benefit of underserved communities—our communities—is a mission with deep meaning for me and for the more than twenty thousand people who work for me. Our motto is "We are the communities we serve."

That isn't a catchy phrase designed to impress people. It is from the heart. Our mission frames everything we do.

Before I became a basketball player and a familiar face to sports fans, I grew up in a big family in the small community of Lansing, Michigan. I have nine brothers and sisters, but despite the size of our family, blacks were a minority in our hometown.

Still, we shopped, got our haircuts, and ate our meals at businesses owned by African Americans.

As a kid, I looked up to those neighborhood entrepreneurs. I worked for two of the biggest—Joel Ferguson and Greg Eaton—in high school. Their holdings included commercial developments, banks, apartment complexes, television stations, janitorial services, and car dealerships. I cleaned their office buildings at night. Now and then I'd take a break from emptying trash cans and running the vacuum cleaner to sit at their desks, imagining that I was the boss: large and in charge.

One night Greg Eaton caught me doing that in his office.

"Earvin, what are you doing at my desk?" he asked.

"Just seeing how it feels," I said. "One of these days, I'm going to be a businessman and have my own."

Wilt Chamberlain and Bill Russell were my sports heroes. Yet Joel Ferguson and Greg Eaton were more real to me. Self-made multimillionaires who truly cared about their community, they were my business role models and mentors. They were respected for creating more than thirty thousand jobs through their businesses. These two socially conscious entrepreneurs also built affordable housing for low-income and elderly residents.

Years later, while traveling from city to city with the Lakers, I was struck by a different side of black America. Something had changed. Once close-knit and thriving black neighborhoods had imploded for a wide range of social, political, and economic reasons.

I observed the deterioration firsthand. Most NBA teams play their games in inner-city arenas. Riding in the team bus to the arenas in Chicago, Detroit, and other cities, I'd see boarded-up storefronts and houses where black businesses had once operated and where hardworking black families had once lived. Poverty, crime, and hopelessness had driven them out and taken over.

Despair dominated every block. I'd see young men my age going through trash in Dumpsters and hassling women on street corners, all of their talents and energy wasted. The lost lives and empty buildings made no sense to me. *How did urban America deteriorate so quickly? Where did the black store owners and shopkeepers go? When did the beauty parlors, the clothing stores, and the restaurants shut down?*

Time after time as we drove through those desolate city landscapes, I'd think, *Someday, I'm going to do something about this. Someday, I'm going to come back here and help rebuild these neighborhoods.*

That thought and those sad images stayed with me. They helped determine my mission as a business leader, and they drove me to succeed. Now I am in a position to erase those sad images from the map of urban America. That's my mission, and I'm working on it one street corner at a time.

Guiding Vision

**Create a guiding vision of where you want to go
and what you want to do with your life.**

My father worked at least three jobs while I was growing up in Lansing. His primary job was welding in an automotive factory. He'd come home from his split shifts with holes burned in his shirt and pants from the sparks flying onto his clothing. Whenever we'd ask about those holes and the scars they left on his back, stomach, and chest, he'd tell us we needed to stay in school and work hard because he wanted us to have better jobs and maybe start businesses of our own someday.

Dad also had his own trash-hauling company. My brothers and I worked for him on weekends and during summers. I helped him while also holding down a job as a stock boy at the Quality Dairy convenience store. Dad expected us to work hard. He didn't care if I'd scored forty points the night before; I had to be up at six o'clock Saturday to help him. I wasn't real enthused about hauling trash for my father—especially on cold winter mornings before the sun came up.

The first time I went out with Dad on a winter trash run, all I could think about was staying warm. I'd jump out of the truck, grab the garbage cans or barrels, throw the trash into the back of the truck, and then scramble back into the cab and try to crawl inside the heater vents.

Dad had a little different vision of the job, which he shared with me. On one of my first cold-weather trash runs, I did my usual mad dash out and back. Before I could get my gloves off and both hands on the heater vents, Dad snatched the passenger door open from the outside and dragged me out of the truck into the snow-packed alley.

"You forgot something, didn't you, Junior?" he asked, using my family nickname.

This isn't going to go well, I thought between shivers.

Dad escorted me to the rear of the truck and pointed a gloved hand at newspapers, old soup cans, plastic bottles, and other trash frozen in the snow around the trash barrels I had just emptied.

"Didn't I tell you to clean up?" he said.

"But that trash is frozen to the ground," I said.

"Were you going to leave it here until the spring thaw?" he asked.

I didn't have an answer. He did.

Dad grabbed a shovel out of the truck. It wasn't a snow shovel for scooping. It was an ice shovel for chipping. He gave me a brief demonstration on how to chip trash out of ice and then handed me the shovel.

"Never leave a job unfinished," he said.

When I finally scrambled back into the warm truck cab, Dad had a few more words for me.

"Always remember that your job is to take care of the customer, so that the customer gets what he is paying for," he said. "The money they pay us is for our good service, and that money feeds our family."

I'd thought I just had a job. My dad gave me a vision for that job; a purpose and a reason for doing it right every time. He showed me that his trash-hauling business was not only a service for his customers but also a means of support for our family.

Once I understood that vision, Dad never had to tell me again. When I learned to see beyond the job and the paycheck to larger goals, I became a better worker. It was no longer just about getting a job done and getting home; it was about taking care of family.

That was one of my first lessons in the importance of having a greater vision for whatever it is you do. Later, my basketball coaches talked about vision in another context: they told me to envision each game as a step toward our goal of winning the championship.

My basketball coaches also stressed the importance of seeing the whole court, of knowing where I was in relation to every other player and understanding how each player would respond to my actions on the floor. It is important to have "court vision" in basketball so that you are fully aware of every opportunity on defense and offense as the game progresses.

The same holds true in business and in mapping out a career: I encourage you to create a guiding vision of where you want to go and what you want to do with your life. This vision should give your business or your career—anything you do—purpose and meaning beyond paying the bills and putting a big screen in the family room. Dad taught me that his trash-hauling business served the greater purpose of supporting our family and allowing us to stay together and pursue our individual goals.

It wasn't about the money, it was about *my family*.

CREATING A VISION

How does having "a guiding vision" translate in the real world of building a business or starting a career? That's something I didn't get right away. Some people never get it at all. Yet a guiding vision can transform your life by injecting it with passion and purpose.

What happens when you don't have a well-defined vision for your business or your career? To see an example of that, I suggest you stop by one of the Magic 32 stores, my national sporting goods chain.

Or not.

The Magic 32 retail chain, which was launched in 1990 in the Baldwin Hills district of L.A., offered an assortment of licensed sports paraphernalia: clothing, shoes, and accessories. This was my first big retail venture. As I was the first NBA player to obtain a merchandise licensing agreement with the National Basketball Association, my goal was to sell top-quality NBA-branded clothing and sporting goods in a national chain of stores.

We never made it beyond the first store. Looking back, I can give you a whole list of reasons why this start-up flopped. The major factor was our crazy main buyer, who ordered clothing *he* liked rather than stocking up on what our customers might buy.

Did I mention that *I* was the main buyer? Big mistake. I knew what I liked in sportswear. Yet I didn't have a clue what our customers would buy or could buy. There were other factors, but what really killed the Magic 32 retail chain was my lack of vision for it.

There was some talk about building our brand. Still, I never asked the question "What is the larger vision for these stores?"

I had my share of turnovers and bad games as a player, but nothing humbled me as much as failing at that first business. I poured several hundred thousand dollars down a deep, dark hole. Still, what hurt was not the lost money so much as the nagging sense that I'd missed something really important.

What was it?

Sometimes you don't know what you've done wrong until you get something else right. In this case, I did not understand what went wrong with the Magic 32 concept until I saw what went right with our Magic Theatres.

THE BIGGER PICTURE

In 1993, shortly after I had to shut down the Magic 32 store operation, I got a call from Ken Lombard, the executive vice president of the Economic Resources Corporation, a nonprofit corporation that promoted business development in the South Central neighborhood.

The ERC had purchased the 1949 landmark Baldwin Theater at La Brea Boulevard and Rodeo Drive in South Central. At one time the Baldwin was the only black-owned first-run movie house in the country. Yet, like the neighborhood around it, the theater had fallen on hard times.

Run-down and neglected, the Baldwin was also a crime-scene cinema. Gangs and violence in the neighborhood made going to the theater a risky venture. The owners had installed metal detectors at the entrance to keep out knives and guns.

Ken had hoped to restore the Baldwin as part of a national group of inner-city theaters, but a planned partnership with a theater chain fell through. Initially, Ken pitched us on buying the theater and reviving it. I was intrigued, but there was a major problem: the Baldwin was losing money.

I wondered why a movie theater in a densely populated neighborhood was struggling and whether it could be revived. Before I met with Ken, I asked two of my most trusted business and financial advisers, Warren Grant and Corey Barash, to help me answer those questions. They are with Grant, Tani, Barash & Altman, a Beverly Hills business and financial management services firm. Warren and Corey have been my go-to guys for business advice for many years. Warren took the lead in this case. I told him that I loved the idea of giving kids, couples, and families in South

Central a place where they could get away from their troubles and enjoy themselves.

As we discussed it, my mind flashed back to the Michigan Theater, an Art Deco movie house in Lansing where I'd seen fun movies such as *Cleopatra Jones, Superfly,* and *Shaft.* I can still smell the buttered popcorn. Of course, when my dad went with us, he enforced his "one-treat rule": "You can each have either one popcorn or one candy or one soda. You can't have popcorn *and* soda or soda *and* candy or candy *and* popcorn."

As family ringleader, I found a way around Dad's "one-treat rule": we would each order a different drink or type of candy, and then we'd all share. That way we'd all get at least a little bit of everything we wanted. There were ten of us kids, so we didn't get to take a lot of family trips or fancy vacations. Going to the movies was a big treat, and some of the movies I saw as a boy sparked the dreams I've pursued as an adult.

BUILDING DREAMS

From the start, this opportunity to open a movie theater was more exciting than the Magic 32 stores—because a vision based on a passion was forming. This wasn't just about me selling something and making money. The Baldwin project was about entertaining people and providing something of value to the community; *something that had been lost.*

The sense of mission and the larger vision came to me slowly as this deal unfolded. Later I realized that this deal appealed to me so much because that vision and sense of mission drove me to find a way to make a movie-theater project work.

Something very interesting happens when you have a strong vision for your business: it becomes contagious. My enthusiasm grew the more I thought about creating a safe, fun place where families in Baldwin Hills and other South Central neighborhoods could buy buttered popcorn and watch great movies. My business advisers picked up on my enthusiasm, so they did their best to help me make it work. It didn't take them long to figure out one of the major reasons the old Baldwin Hills Theater wasn't making money: it couldn't get first-run films.

That's not a good thing when you consider that most of the major Hollywood movie studios are just a few miles away. When you can see tomorrow's movies being made down the street, the last thing you want is yesterday's movies on the screen in front of you.

The Baldwin Theater had been converted into a three-screen movie house. Movie distributors would not release first-run films to theaters unless they had six screens. The old movie house just wasn't big enough. Still, I told my business adviser Warren Grant that the theater business intrigued me. Based on my own experiences and those of my family and friends, I thought South Central and Baldwin Hills residents would support a modern, safe, clean movie theater with first-run films.

CHECKING IT OUT

I needed help to make my vision become reality, since my cinema expertise was limited mostly to watching movies and eating popcorn. It's one thing to talk about bringing top-quality movie theaters to urban neighborhoods; others had been talking about it for years, including some of the big players in the business. I was determined to see this vision become a reality, and that meant getting serious and doing our homework. Ken Lombard, who had first approached me about the Baldwin Theater, and I put our heads together and went to work. We figured out what we needed to know about the movie-theater business so that this dream made financial sense too.

We had a vision and we had enthusiasm, but you can't build

a business on a dream cloud. I'd learned a lesson with the Magic 32 stores. I thought we'd done our homework with that concept, but the problem was that I didn't know what I didn't know about the retail business. I wasn't going to make the same mistake twice.

Ken and I set out to determine what area residents wanted in a movie theater. I drove around the neighborhood and saw them lining up to buy fast food, so I knew that those franchises had done their homework. They'd figured out that residents would buy their burgers, tacos, and pizza, and so they'd invested in Baldwin Hills. It seemed to me that they'd line up for a safe and modern movie theater too.

One of the first things we did was look at the numbers—always a good idea. I learned that African Americans make up just over 12 percent of the U.S. population but 25 to 35 percent of the nation's movie audiences. That was a good sign. It was also true that many fans had been priced out of the ticket market for Lakers, Rams, Dodgers, and other increasingly expensive sports venues, so going to the movies was one of their affordable entertainment options.

The more we looked at this opportunity, the more I liked it. Warren gave it the thumbs-up too. What really appealed to us was that we weren't just starting a new business venture; we were providing something of great value to the people of Baldwin Hills. It wasn't just an excellent "theatrical entertainment experience," it was where families, couples, and friends of all ages could go to escape the pressures of the daily grind and to relax and have fun. From a business perspective, we realized early on that the movie theater could serve as a building block, a stimulus for other retail stores, restaurants, and offices in the area.

We learned more in the months that followed as we studied the ins and outs of this business. Still, it made sense for us to look for partners who knew how much butter to put on the popcorn and how many seats to put in each row.

I'd met Peter Guber, the former head of Columbia Pictures who'd become CEO of Sony Pictures, during my playing days, when he'd had a seat on the floor. I'd told him I wanted to learn more about business, and he became one of my mentors. He'd tried coaching me on basketball too, but I found his business expertise more useful. We went to Peter with the idea of partnering with Sony Retail Entertainment, and he was receptive. We entered the business just as a wave of mergers was hitting, so it got a little complicated.

In 1994, my company, Johnson Development Corporation, formed a partnership with Sony Retail Entertainment. Then Sony made a merger move that created Loews Cineplex Entertainment. I met with Lawrence Ruisi, the Loews CEO, and told him about my research. Despite statistics showing that blacks were major moviegoers, there were few modern theaters in African-American neighborhoods. I told him that residents of South Central and other urban communities were driving thirty minutes or more to see first-run movies because there were no theaters in their own neighborhoods.

We discovered that this particular South Central neighborhood had a per-household income of nearly $50,000. There were nearly 2 million potential customers in a four- to five-mile radius. I noted that it was cheaper to buy or rent property in urban neighborhoods and that even in tough times residents there go to the movies to forget their troubles and relax. I also explained that our movie theaters would become community centers that would serve as building blocks for surrounding commercial development.

SELLING THE VISION

The Loews executives got it. Larry understood that this was a great, unmined market for them. He also understood that I could help his people better understand and serve the people living in the urban market. "Combining our expertise in how to run and operate a theater and Earvin's ability to get community support was how it got started," he later told a reporter.

Of course, Loews expected me to put skin in the game too. I put in well over a few million dollars to become a full partner, so that I was sharing in the risk. Both partners had to agree on the locations and timetables for each theater complex. We shared the handling of day-to-day operations. Still, it was my job, as head of Johnson Development Corporation, to work with local government officials and to build community support.

Our partnership worked so well that we built theaters in Los Angeles, Atlanta, Houston, Cleveland, and New York City's Harlem. In early 2006, Loews merged with AMC Entertainment, forming one company under the name AMC Development Corporation.

Though those mergers were complicated, the behind-the-scenes drama was worthy of Hollywood. When we made the initial announcement with Sony, the skeptics bet against us. They never thought we'd make money with a movie theater in a neighborhood such as South Central. Even some community leaders said that residents had become so accustomed to going to "safer" neighborhoods for their shopping and entertainment that it would be difficult to change those habits. The theater-chain executives told me that they'd often talked about locating cineplexes in urban neighborhoods such as South Central but they weren't sure they'd be welcomed. It had to make economic sense for them.

This wasn't a charity move. We intended to make money, and

we knew there was potential. I'm happy to say that the critics and skeptics were wrong. Our first Magic Johnson Theatre became one of the top-grossing movie theaters in the country. Even better, it revitalized the entire neighborhood.

Just building the theater provided 850 construction jobs, and once it opened there were more than a hundred permanent jobs inside. Even more jobs were created because the success of the movie theater brought more tenants, including major brands that had been reluctant to locate in urban areas before.

What matters to our customers is that Magic Johnson Theatres are great places to watch a movie. They offer anywhere from ten to fifteen screens, seating as many as five thousand people. We do our best to provide a safe, clean, and welcoming environment with employees who cater to our customers' needs.

Later in the book, I'll get into how I did some serious "Magicizing" on the standard cineplex model—and how I made sure my customers would feel safe and secure. First, however, I want to share with you the moment when I realized that we'd fulfilled our vision for the movie theater.

On opening night so many thoughts and reflections were running through my mind. Being a micromanager, I went early, of course, to make sure that fresh popcorn was being popped and everything else was ready. When I got there, the line of movie fans waiting to get in stretched around the block. What a beautiful sight! There were mothers and fathers with their kids, teenagers by themselves, young and older couples, people of every age. I was a kid again, going to the movies with my own family.

I got so excited! Then I started thinking about all the skeptics and doubters who'd said that this neighborhood would never support a movie theater. Tears welled up in my eyes at those thoughts. More than once I had to stop and wipe my eyes as I walked up and down the line of our customers waiting to get into *our* first-run, state-of-the-art South Central movie theater.

I shook the hand of every one of them. I might have shaken a couple hands twice. It was a wonderful night that I will never forget because it was the night I saw my vision become reality! I hope that one day you enjoy the same thrill when your business dreams become realities.

Entrepreneurial Passion

**To reap the rewards of business, you have
to jump into the game and pursue it passionately.**

I first met Lori Carter while I was speaking at one of our Magic Johnson Foundation Community Empowerment Centers in Los Angeles. During a question-and-answer session, she introduced herself as the winner of a business-plan competition for young entrepreneurs. She then asked me if I thought her plans for a chain of smoothie and fresh juice bars would work in urban America. I loved her enthusiasm as much as her concept. I encouraged her to pursue her vision and to stay in touch. She did.

Lori, twenty-six, called my office a few days later and told me that she was preparing to open her first smoothie juice bar in Carson, where she grew up. This industrial city of about 100,000 just thirteen miles south of Los Angeles is one of a growing number of towns in the United States in which the black population has a higher median income than the general population. Diversity is another hallmark of Carson, where Latinos, Filipinos, and Samoans have a strong presence along with whites and African Americans.

Lori's enthusiasm was contagious, and she had done her homework. She had received a $25,000 grant for winning the business-plan competition, put on by Recycling Black Dollars, an organization that I respected greatly. This Los Angeles nonprofit was created by a great man, Muhammad Nassardeen, to support black economic development. Muhammad, who died in 2007, was a true grassroots champion of economic development in urban communities. He didn't just talk about it, he made it happen. I admire his organization and all of the good work it has done. It invested in Lori, and I wanted to do my part to help her get her business up and running.

A few weeks after my speech, I met her at the retail space she was negotiating to lease for her first smoothie bar. She gave me the address, but I drove right by it the first time because it was surrounded by palm trees. When I turned around and found it, Lori was waiting out front. The street-level space she was considering was in a mixed-use building with apartments for low-income residents above it. She gave me a tour of the inside and told me all of her plans for fixing it up. I listened, admiring her energy and ambition.

Then I asked her if she had driven around the surrounding neighborhoods to check out whether residents appeared to have the sort of disposable income that would support a smoothie juice bar. Lori had grown up in Carson, but I was asking her to look at it in a fresh way, from the perspective of a businessperson studying a potential market.

Next I asked her if she'd scouted out the competition in the area. She said there were no smoothie or juice bars but there were at least three ice cream places in the area.

"Let's take a look at them," I said.

We drove three blocks before finding an ice-cream place, which looked as if it had been in the neighborhood for a long time. I pulled the car into a parking space and told Lori to go in to see if it offered smoothies or yogurt or any of the other products she planned to sell.

She came back to the car with a price list and said that it offered several of the same items.

We then drove back to the place she had hoped to rent and took another look around. After walking through the interior, we stood in the front doorway talking for fifteen minutes or so before I asked Lori another question that threw her off.

"Have you heard any car horns honking?" I said.

"I don't know. What do you mean?" she replied.

"Well, this is Los Angeles. I'm pretty well known around here. Wherever I go, people see me and honk their car horns and say hello. Even though I'm six feet nine inches tall and pretty hard to miss, nobody has honked the whole time we've been out here. Why do you think they haven't honked?"

Lori looked around sheepishly.

"Maybe because they can't see us with all the trees around us?" she said.

"That should tell you something about this location," I said. "People driving by can't even see the building because of all the trees. That's not a good thing. On top of that, the people living in the apartments may not be smoothie customers and they have to park their cars on the street, which means potential customers will have a hard time finding a place to park. That's especially troubling since you have some established competition just a few blocks away that is selling products for a dollar less than you plan to charge, and it has better parking."

I told Lori that one reason Starbucks had been so successful in its early years was that the company had made a science of choosing its locations. Its real estate team had developed a method of identifying the absolute best building in the absolutely best neighborhood in a city, and it's been reported that average store sales soared and practically doubled over a year. Between 1992 and 1997, only two of its 1,500 sites closed. More recently, when Starbucks strayed from that strategy toward overall aggressive growth, some of their locations were subsequently closed.

Lori got the picture. She told me that she was still negotiating her lease on the retail space but she would reconsider whether she should locate her smoothie bar there. She thanked me for helping her. The following Monday, she called me and told me that she'd decided to scout for another location.

Lori's $25,000 grant from Recycling Black Dollars was a one-time deal—and one mistake in the use of that grant could be very, very costly. If she had opened her smoothie bar in the little place in the palms, she very likely would have blown through her start-up money quickly and then gone out of business. She would not have had the money to start a second one. So it was critical that she get her first business up and running by making sure it was the right thing for her, in the right location, with the right pricing, in the right market.

I'm happy to say that Lori found a better location where she is doing very well. I stop in from time to time to check in with her and enjoy a smoothie at Juice C Juice in Carson. The great thing is that Lori also created her own nonprofit program to encourage teens to learn about entrepreneurship by opening smoothie bars in area high schools.

Lori and I share the belief that too many people of all ages talk about getting into the game of business but never get off the bench. She is offering teens the opportunity for hands-on experience, and I applaud her for that and for being a great role model as an entrepreneur in an urban community.

OPEN FOR BUSINESS

Now that I've had some success in business, I get requests for advice from many athletes, former athletes, and other celebrities and aspiring business owners. I'm glad there is so much interest because, as Earl Graves and the other pioneers in black business will tell you, for a long, long time many minorities just didn't get it.

For years, black business leaders were frustrated because

young African Americans weren't getting in the game. Even many of those who made a lot of money in sports or entertainment failed to invest it in their own business enterprises. When I was with the Lakers, I used to beg Kareem Abdul-Jabbar and other teammates to invest in businesses with me, but most of the time they weren't the least bit interested. Some of them laughed at me for trying to "play" businessman, as if it were something that only rich white college graduates could do.

Most players then were happy to do a few endorsement deals and some commercials to pick up extra money, but I wanted to be a business owner, so I was always looking for opportunities. When we traveled to other cities for games, I'd set up meetings with local business leaders to talk about opportunities. When we went to Atlanta to play the Hawks, I'd meet with Coca-Cola the day before the game. If it was Minneapolis and the Timberwolves on the schedule, I'd have my agent set up a meeting with Target's top people there. I figured as long as the Lakers were flying me around the country for free, I might as well get some business done.

Like a lot of my teammates, I did promotions for a Los Angeles radio station, but I also bought in to two radio stations in Colorado. This was a great deal because there were special incentives for minorities to get into broadcast ownership. I went around to several of the Lakers players, trying to get them to invest with me, but none of them would.

The one friend who immediately jumped at the opportunity was Isiah Thomas, who has always shared my interest in business ownership. Then we convinced our friends and fellow NBA players Mark Aguirre and Herb Williams to invest too. We bought the first radio station for a low seven figures, and it turned out to be a lucrative deal. We had six acres of land and two broadcast towers on our property. When we converted the station from AM to FM, we moved the towers closer to the station and then sold off the land where they'd been—for a significant return. Then we sold the station after a couple years and walked away with a $2 million profit.

That deal provided another good lesson in business: one opportunity often leads to another.

LISTEN AND LEARN

For many years it was tough to get my teammates to invest in serious business deals. Now, though, it's a whole lot different. I get calls every day, and when I'm in the office I meet with at least two or three people a week who are looking for opportunities or advice. NBA player Grant Hill, most recently with the Phoenix Suns, has spent time working in our office for two straight summers, soaking up all he can. I've also talked business with Yankee Alex Rodriguez and former Padre and Yankee Dave Winfield, Shawne Merriman of the San Diego Chargers, Charles Woodson of the Green Bay Packers, Terrell Owens of the Dallas Cowboys, boxer Oscar De La Hoya, Shaquille O'Neal, and the actress and singer Queen Latifah.

The biggest question they usually have is how to get started and what sort of business to choose. I'm glad to help out because I benefited from the hard-nosed advice of my friends and business advisers Warren Grant and Corey Barash. For a long time, I was the only professional athlete they would work with. Others had asked for their help, but too often they had refused to follow their professional advice. Many wanted their brothers or mothers or best friends from high school to run their businesses.

Corey and Warren told me that at the time I got started in business I was one of the only athletes who had come to them who were willing to actually listen to their advice and learn from them. That's not to say we didn't have our disagreements. They claim they are going to write their own book one day about all of the deals they had to talk me out of doing. One of their top ten is my continuing efforts to get into the boxing business. I've tried for years to promote professional boxers and their fights because I love the sport. Warren and Corey do not love it. So far, they've won every round.

EGO VERSUS PASSION

I tell athletes, celebrities, and aspiring entrepreneurs the same thing that Corey and Warren told me when I first came to them: you have to take your ego out of the equation when it comes to starting and running a business. It took a while for me to get this, so I understand why it is difficult for other people to grasp.

A business venture has to make financial sense above all else. You can't let your ego take you places that your bank account won't cover. My ego told me that since I liked $1,500 leather jackets I should stock them in my Magic 32 store. The financial reports later told me that my tastes were too expensive for my customers.

So checking your ego at the door is critical when starting a business, but it is equally important that you remain passionate and fully engaged while being open to opportunities that may take you outside your comfort zone.

I have never been a coffee drinker, yet I became the first person to partner with Starbucks. Between 1998 and 2008, I became co-owner of more than a hundred Starbucks around the country. So where does passion come into play in my Starbucks deal? Our venture allowed me to put Starbucks coffee shops into the communities that I am dedicated to serving.

My passion is to better the lives of men and women and children in underserved communities and neighborhoods. I do that by bringing movie theaters, health clubs, and top-brand restaurants and retail stores to them. I also work to provide jobs and careers for them. What really gets me excited is creating opportunities that will better the lives of people who have been neglected in the past. I enjoy giving them fun things to do, safe places to gather, and jobs that give them greater security.

When you are looking at what sort of business or career to pursue, put your passions into play and don't be afraid to think long term. Give yourself plenty of room to keep growing your businesses over time. Build your life around something that you love to do, and then keep building.

If a business is "just a job" for you, you probably won't have the drive and determination necessary to get it started, keep it running, and grow it over the years. Hopefully, you will be living with this business for a long time, so it's like being married or having a roommate—it's a lot easier if you really like each other and enjoy each other's company.

As you might imagine, my business success creates all sorts of opportunities. Every day I hear pitches from people wanting me to invest in, buy, or start businesses they've envisioned. I refuse to consider proposals that do not bring value to urban America and the people who live there. Any business I am involved with must provide valued goods and services for those neighborhoods and create jobs for residents.

A few years ago, I was visiting my 24 Hour Fitness center in Oakland when I met a woman who started crying as she spoke to me. She told me that before our fitness center opened in her urban neighborhood, she'd had nowhere to work out. She'd joined on the first day even though she had to come in with the aid of a walker because she weighed 260 pounds.

That day when I met her, she tearfully told me that she'd lost 95 pounds. Her husband was standing there with me as we talked, and he was crying too.

"You helped me get healthy again," she told me.

My association with 24 Hour Fitness centers has been so successful financially that I've helped pave the way for several of my friends, including Shaquille O'Neal and Derek Jeter, to start their own franchises. There is no better payoff than knowing that my businesses are changing lives for the better. Providing jobs and opportunities in urban neighborhoods may just be the greatest reward for getting off the bench and into business. Dreaming is not doing. Talking about what you might do "someday" is only talk.

Conquering Fears

Get past fears and insecurities by understanding that the feeling is usually worse than the reality.

Dad was sleeping in the living room, trying to get some rest between his morning and night shifts at the factory, when my brother Larry and I came running through the front door scared out of our minds.

"What's going on?" Dad said as he rose.

"We got off the junior-high bus and these gang members jumped us," I said. "They chased us all the way home."

Dad went to the front window. Sure enough, four of them were still standing in the yard, yelling for us to come out. My father then turned and glared at us.

"Come here," he said.

We walked forward, and as we did, he opened the front door and pushed us out. Then he locked the door behind us.

His message was clear. *You can't keep running. Sooner or later, you have to stand and fight.*

Times were different then, of course. When I was a teenager, guns and knives were not as prevalent as they are today. A father today would likely advise his sons to steer clear of gang members, and rightfully so. In my school days and in my neighborhood, fights were settled with fists, not weapons. Still, it was my first serious fight, and it seemed to go on forever. The four of them came at us, and we just started swinging. I did a lot of windmilling since I had a height advantage. I got in some lucky punches. I think they finally realized that we weren't going anywhere. One by one, they gave up and walked away.

Dad stepped onto the porch after the last one limped off pinching his nose to stop the bleeding. Larry and I crumpled to the grass, bruised and exhausted but proud that we'd held our own against the four of them.

"They won't bother you anymore," Dad said. "If you run, they'll keep chasing you. Yet if you stand and fight, they'll learn to leave you alone."

FEAR FACTOR

We were lucky to have a father around—most of the gang members did not have that kind of support. We were even luckier that my dad took time to offer lessons about the importance of hard work, education, family, and facing our fears. Larry and I still talk about that day. It was a step toward manhood for both of us. We held our heads a little higher after that. The gang members never again bothered us. In fact, they became our supporters and defenders at basketball games and around school.

The fear is worse than the fight. I carried that thought with me in my basketball career too. Going to the hoop is often seen as a test of courage for players because that is where you are likely to get banged up by bigger players. Still, if you want to be respected as a scorer, you have to face those fears of injury and take the ball to the basket.

I learned to face my fears and move past them on the basketball court and, later, in business too. I'd feel a knot in my stomach before important presentations to investors or negotiation with bankers. They were usually white, well educated, and far more experienced in business than I was. The old fears would come welling up: Am I smart enough? Will I be able to get the words out? Will they take me seriously?

No matter how many NBA trophies or magazine covers in frames there were at home, when I stepped into the business realm I carried the baggage of a black man from a blue-collar family. We all have our insecurities. Luckily for me, my father pushed me out the door and taught me that the fear of what might happen is often worse than the reality.

Now I am holding the door open for you to step through. Every entrepreneur endures sleepless nights. Blacks, Latinos, and other minorities are often hampered by a lack of financial resources, educational opportunities, and networking resources. Their challenges have created an entrepreneurial "racial gap" that sociologists and economists have studied for decades.

Blacks traditionally are less likely to be self-employed than whites. About 15 percent of working white Americans are self-employed, compared with 6 percent of working African Americans, according to the National Bureau of Economic Research. The U.S. Commerce Department reported that more than 1.57 million Hispanic-owned firms were operating in the United States in 2002. Those Latino firms were growing at a rate of 31 percent, which was three times the national average of 10 percent. Still, only 1.8 percent of Hispanic-owned firms had receipts of $1 million or more.

Education, financial resources, and a strong business network are certainly assets for starting a business, but lacking some or even all of those benefits does not block you from getting into the game. Only fear can do that. The good news is that fears can be overcome.

If you dream of owning your own business but can't seem to get it going, maybe your fears are holding you back. In later chapters, I'll tell you about all of the resources and opportunities that are out there waiting to be tapped. Still, before you can reach out, you have to look within. Be honest: Are old fears and insecurities blocking your path toward success and the future?

FEELINGS VERSUS REALITY

When Larry and I got off the school bus that day back in Lansing, the gang members came at us. It was fight or flight. We chose flight. Looking back, there was no reason for us to run even though we were outnumbered two to one. Larry and I were both bigger than any one of the four stalking us. Truth is, we were probably stronger too. Despite those facts, our fears got the best of us and we ran.

That's the thing about fears; they are usually based on feelings rather than reality. As kids we know the boogeyman isn't really under the bed and the scratching on the bedroom window is just a tree branch, but we let ourselves get scared anyway. As adults, we tell ourselves we can't chase our dreams because we are afraid of failing, but what is the reality of failure? Everyone fails at some point. If you understand that and know that failure is just part of the learning process, you can always get back up and try again.

Fears come at us in many forms. Fear of failure is common; so is fear of success. Some people never make a move because they are afraid that they will get what they want and then somehow blow it or not know what to do next. Others feel undeserving of success, so they run from it. There are aspiring entrepreneurs who are afraid of starting a business that might put the spotlight on them, making their friends jealous or bringing criticism. Still others are afraid to reach higher because they might have to let go of where they are. They don't want to leave the comfortable and familiar to strive for something greater.

When you see fears described on the page like this, they seem insignificant, even silly, don't they? Yet when they plant themselves in our mind, they take on more power. We give them that power. We can take it away. That's why it's important to recognize them for what they are. Fears are emotions. They are not real. You can walk right through them if you just make yourself take that first step, and keep moving.

LOOK FOR INSPIRATION

If you feel yourself backing off from your dreams of starting a business because of your fears, look for inspiration by seeking out entrepreneurs in your neighborhood and community. I have been fortunate to have so many business mentors and role models in my life, even back in Lansing. These days nearly every town has associations for African-American, Latino, Asian, and other minority business owners. Many of them have mentoring and role-modeling programs. Magazines such as *Black Enterprise, Hispanic Business, Minority Business Entrepreneur,* and *Entrepreneur* offer many stories of men and women of every race and income level pursuing their dreams. There are also scores of Web sites that offer information and encouragement for minority entrepreneurs; including www.blackenterprise.com, www.mbemag.com, Entrepreneur.com, HispanicBusiness.com, and www.naaap.org, the Web site of the National Association of Asian American Professionals.

GO STEP BY STEP

After you face your fears, and move on, do a little victory dance. Then go after your dream. Figure out what it is you need to do, and do it. Take it one small step at a time. If you aren't making progress, figure out smaller steps and take them until you find your momentum again. Write down your goals, and then keep a daily record of what you have done to go after them. Celebrate your accomplishments, but keep going.

Continue to break it down step by step until you have a task that you know you can accomplish. Keep a list of every small achievement. When you find yourself mentally reviewing the things you have not done, stop yourself and read the list of things you have done. Stay positive and on track.

BUDDY UP

I keep moving past my fears and toward my goals by surrounding myself with friends from similar backgrounds who encourage and support me. As a young player in the NBA, I spent many hours in the off-season talking about my dreams of owning a business with Isiah Thomas, who had the same ambition. We talked on the phone, over dinners, and on vacations about one day controlling our own destinies. We tried some crazy things too.

Isiah and I were talking one day about a *Forbes* magazine story that listed Bill Cosby as the second-highest-paid black celebrity, earning more than $60 million a year. This was back when *The Cosby Show* was a hit television series. We'd read other stories about what a smart investor and businessman he was, so, on a whim, we decided to go talk to him. We called a mutual friend, who set it up. Then we got on a plane and went to the Cosby house for dinner.

Bill and his wife, Camille, were warm and welcoming. We laughed until my face hurt from smiling so much. Still, Bill got very serious at one point and warned us about handling our money wisely and not throwing it away on luxuries.

"Young men, it is important that you take care of the money you make as athletes," Bill Cosby said. "Do not waste it. Put it to work so that it keeps making more money for you even after you are done playing."

We laughed at his jokes that night, but we took his serious statements to heart too. Isiah and I both began putting our earnings into real estate and other long-term investments, and we have reaped the benefits ever since.

Another one of my fear-fighting friends is Eric Holoman, now the president of Magic Johnson Enterprises. He shares my vision not only for our business endeavors but for our lives. Eric has been a business owner and banking executive, so he knows the ins and outs of entrepreneurship. We help each other overcome our fears not only by encouraging each other but by talking things through and finding ways to reduce risk.

KEEP MOVING

One of the things that Eric and I agree on is that success is not some goal that lies at the end of the road. Success isn't being ahead at the final buzzer. Success is being in the game. It's working to build something meaningful, something that provides for your family, something that makes life better for your customers and clients, something that will continue after you've stepped aside.

To me, the definition of personal success is to take on new challenges, to keep stretching and growing, and doing some good for others along the way. We all have our fears, but as long as we are able to face them and move forward, we can't be stopped. Going to the hoop in basketball means driving toward the goal even though you know you are going to meet opposition and maybe get bruised and battered. Successful entrepreneurs must have the same sort of focus and drive to get past their fears and the competition.

Focus on Strengths

Build on your strengths and you will overcome your weaknesses.

In 1994, Michael Jordan failed at a baseball career. Four years later, I struck out as a late-night talk-show host for *The Magic Hour* television show.

Michael and I both made the mistake of trying to build on weaknesses instead of sticking with our strengths. In our failures, we proved that you can do only so much with your natural weaknesses. Rarely can you turn a weakness into a strength. Greatness is achieved by building on strengths and managing your weaknesses so they do not matter.

In 1997, executives at Fox suggested that I try a talk show. I was feeling good because the success of our movie theaters was bringing in a lot of other opportunities. As the Fox executives pointed out, I'd been a popular guest on other talk shows. Arsenio Hall and Jay Leno liked to have me on, and they made hosting seem so easy. I had so much fun on their shows that I'd go home thinking, *I could do that.* I didn't stop to think that cracking jokes and making smooth conversation came naturally to them. It played to natural strengths they'd built upon doing stand-up comedy in clubs for years and years.

Once *The Magic Hour* was on the air, television critics and viewers were all too willing to point out that I was much better at dribbling than talking. I got out there in front of millions of people and tried to be something I'm not—a comedian. No matter how much I rehearsed, it didn't come naturally. In fact, the more I rehearsed and the more the show's producers tried to fit me into their box, the worse I got.

WEAK SIDE PLAY

My attempt at a late-night television talk show had ego written all over it. That's where many entrepreneurs go wrong. They tend to think that success in one area is a guarantee of success in another. Take it from me, that is not how it works.

I was seduced into doing the show also by the fact that the initial concept fit what I'd already done with the Magic Johnson Theatre. The show was aimed at the same audience. Executives at the Fox network spotted a void on late-night television after Arsenio's show went off the air, and they figured my career in basketball and business would translate well to a talk show.

Boy oh boy, were they wrong. The concept was good, but the show was terrible, especially the host. It didn't help that my movie theaters and other business ventures were taking off around the same time that I was trying to do five shows a week. I was stretched thin, and the chain always breaks at the weakest link.

The Magic Hour was canceled after eight weeks. It was a mercy killing. Yet, as bad as it was, good things came of it. For one thing, I worked on my public speaking and got much more comfortable standing in front of crowds and cameras without a basketball in my hands. More important, I realized that I had to refocus and get back to my strengths.

KNACK ATTACK

The Magic Hour was one of my most spectacular flops, but it wasn't the only time I messed up by straying from my strengths. I didn't exactly tear up the league during my short-lived stint as coach of the Lakers either.

In March of 1994, I stepped in as coach late in a tumultuous "rebuilding" season and led my former team to a dismal 5–11 record. I should have known that coaching wouldn't work out when I showed up for work on my first day at 7 a.m. and couldn't get into the offices at the Forum. I didn't have a key yet, and there was no one to let me in that early in the day!

Just as it had never been my dream to be a talk-show host, I had never aspired to be an NBA coach. Our strengths and our interests usually go hand in hand. So the first step in determining what your own marketable strengths might be is to think about those activities and areas you are naturally drawn to—the things you enjoy doing because you have a knack for them.

Let's try a little "Knack Attack." What were your favorite classes in school? Did you get your best grades in mathematics? English? Science? Engineering? Is there something that comes easy for you, such as working with tools, writing an essay, or playing an instrument? What gets you motivated? Your answers to these questions should help you define and focus on building your strengths and then building your career around those strengths.

But you don't want to ignore your weaknesses entirely. My weaknesses as a basketball player were my foot speed and my long-range shooting. I worked on both of those weaknesses in practice. They never became strengths, but I never let them become liabilities either. Still, when it came to crunch time, I went to my strengths—my ability to run the offense, make key plays, and get the ball to open teammates.

Building on your strengths puts you in a positive and proactive frame of mind so that your weaknesses become irrelevant. There is no better example of that than the Wild Thing himself. Dennis Rodman loved to do outrageous things on and off the court, whether it was dyeing his hair orange, wearing a wedding dress, or head butting a referee. Still, the remarkable thing about him was the way he built upon his strengths to become such a force that even his official NBA bio notes that he was "one of the few players in basketball who could change the course of a game without taking a shot."

Despite his cross-dressing skills, Dennis was not the most well-rounded NBA basketball player. He didn't play much at all in high school, and even though he eventually became a star in college, it was for a small NAIA school, Southeastern Oklahoma State. Yet after being drafted in the second round in 1986, he became a star, first with the Pistons and later with the San Antonio Spurs and the Chicago Bulls.

Dennis accomplished this even though some would contend that his weakness was that he had virtually no outside shot; and he rarely scored from more than ten feet away from the basket. Yet he thrived for many years at the highest level in the NBA because he developed his strength—his uncanny knack for getting rebounds—to remarkable levels. Dennis was often much shorter and less bulky than the defenders guarding him. Yet he led the NBA in rebounds per game for seven years and played on five NBA championship teams before retiring.

HONOR YOUR STRENGTHS

I saw it on the basketball court during my athletic career, and now I see it in business. There are two basic mistakes that send both players and businesspeople down the wrong path:

1. They spend too much time trying to improve their weaknesses.
2. They don't focus on their strengths.

How many times has Tiger Woods modified and adjusted his swing or his putting stance, trying to build on his accomplishments as a professional golfer? He understands that when you try to eliminate your weaknesses, the best you can usually do is bring them to a mediocre or middle level. When you focus on building on your strengths, you can achieve excellence.

When my playing career ended and it was time to focus fully on my businesses, I did not have an in-depth understanding of accounting, statistics, management, marketing, finance, and business law—all the things you learn in business school. I certainly encourage anyone who wants to become an entrepreneur to get a business degree or an MBA if possible. I didn't go to business school because I decided to go to my strong side rather than the weak side. I didn't have "book" knowledge, but I had access to an incredible real-world education in entrepreneurship. Many of my "business teachers" had seats around the basketball court at the Forum.

By the time my playing career ended, I'd spent years picking the brains of some of the smartest and most successful businesspeople on the planet. I learned directly from business leaders such as *Black Enterprise* publisher Earl Graves, real estate financier Victor MacFarlane, entrepreneur J. Bruce Llewellyn, Lakers owner Jerry Buss, superagent Michael Ovitz, and Sony CEO Peter Guber.

ACKNOWLEDGE YOUR WEAKNESSES

It was Earl Graves who helped me develop what became one of my greatest strengths. It wasn't an easy lesson to learn, but the good ones often come the hard way. Earl became a driving force for black economic development and a pioneering entrepreneur after serving as a captain in the U.S. Army. Later, he was one of the first undercover federal drug agents in Harlem and an administrative assistant to Senator Robert F. Kennedy.

When he launched the first business magazine for black professionals and entrepreneurs in the 1960s, Earl had to fight for every ad. In those days, most major brands and corporations were run by white males who had no idea that a black middle or professional class even existed. Earl had to educate them before he could sell them. He built his empire on business smarts and determination, earning such respect that he has served on the boards of Aetna, American Airlines, DaimlerChrysler, and Federated Department Stores, among others.

In 1990, Earl asked me to join him as a partner in the Pepsi-Cola distributorship that served the mostly black residents of Prince George's County, Maryland. NBA Commissioner David Stern had recommended me to Earl because he knew I was interested in business. I already had ties to Pepsi as a spokesperson in its advertising and marketing campaigns, so it seemed like a natural fit. Michael Ovitz helped me put the deal together and acted as an adviser.

This was my first major business partnership, and it quickly became apparent that I had a lot to learn. At that point, I had more than ten years with the Lakers and we had won five NBA championship titles. Still, my basketball accomplishments didn't mean a whole lot to Earl. He felt I had a lot to learn when it came to business, and he was right. He put me to work learning the Pepsi operation from the ground up. I met with bankers and made sales pitches to potential clients, from the owners of mom-and-pop groceries to top executives at Marriott and other major buyers.

The Pepsi experience opened my eyes to how much I still needed to learn about business. The most important thing I learned was that there was so much more that I did not know. This may sound funny, but one of the greatest strengths you can develop is the ability to acknowledge your weaknesses. You have to know what you don't know so that you can open yourself to listening and learning from those who can help you.

How will you know that you have a weakness in your approach to business? You will feel frustration because you don't have the skill or the knowledge to get where you want to go. Frustration is a useful emotion if you respond to it the right way. Consider it a warning. It is telling you that you need to change your focus. Go to your strengths.

It didn't take long for me to get frustrated in my Pepsi partnership with Earl. He was frustrated with me too. We both knew that I had a lot to learn. He wanted to teach me, and I was willing to do the necessary work. Still, at that point in my life, I simply did not have the time that it would have required.

Earl and I agreed that I wasn't the partner that either of us wanted me to be—and that I didn't have the time to hold up my end of the operation. So we dissolved the partnership in 1992. We remained friends and, in fact, have become even closer over the years. I rely on Earl's guidance and experience now more than ever. He has been instrumental in several of my more recent business deals. I still count on him to let me know what I don't know.

I've already proved I'll never be Leno or Arsenio. No matter how hard I might try, I'll never be Warren Buffett or Bill Gates, either. Yet I have been able to attain my own brand of business success by focusing on my knowledge and credibility in urban markets. I plan to build on that strength. How can you build on your strengths?

Seizing Opportunities

Always be prepared to jump on business opportunities.

After eight years with the Lakers, I *finally* earned my first season's Most Valuable Player Award from the NBA in the 1986–1987 season, and then we beat the Celtics for the championship. It had bothered me that Larry Bird already had three MVP season awards. I eventually caught up with him in that category, but I trailed him in another area. I discovered that Larry's Celtics jersey and T-shirt merchandise sales were number one that year. My Lakers shirts were number two.

When I heard that, I wasn't really concerned about Larry being number one. I was more interested in where the profits were going. I called my agent, Lon Rosen, and asked, "How much are the checks from all of my T-shirt and jersey sales?"

"What checks?" he replied.

After some research, we learned that the NBA Players Association had sold the rights to license products with our names and numbers to the NBA for $150,000. Royalties were distributed evenly among the players, no matter whose shirt sold the most. I didn't mind sharing the wealth, but the league was making millions of dollars from those licensing rights and we were each getting just a few thousand dollars. That didn't make sense to me.

I talked to Larry Bird, who felt that there probably wasn't much we could do about it. Still, I thought it was worth a try, so I asked for a meeting with NBA Commissioner David Stern.

My research revealed that the manufacturers licensed by the NBA to use our names and images had sales of $173 million in 1986–1987. Thanks to the exploding popularity of the league, they were expecting sales to exceed $1 billion during the 1991–1992 season. At our initial meeting, I told David Stern that it was not right for the league and its owners to be reaping millions off licensing our names while we got only nickels and dimes by comparison.

"Let me think about it," Stern told me.

I knew what that meant. It was the sort of thing parents tell kids when they hope they'll just forget about the pony or the go-kart they want.

Stern wasn't going to get rid of me that easily. I had come prepared with my own plan. I told him that I was going to form my own T-shirt company and that I wanted the rights to license products in my own name, with my own jersey number.

The NBA realized I was not going to forget about this. So, after some long negotiations, it agreed to "grant" me a small licensing deal with the understanding that if my business did well, I would be able to come back for a bigger deal. I became the first active NBA player to have my own licensing deal. Initially, my license allowed me to manufacture and sell shirts with only my likeness and number, and I could do it in only three styles.

I worked with my agent to set up a manufacturing deal with a T-shirt company in Tennessee. Magic T's was born. As luck, and maybe a little skill, would have it, the Lakers won the NBA championship again in the 1987–1988 season, this time over the Detroit Pistons. I picked up my second MVP season award and my third NBA Finals MVP Award. Magic T's manufactured and sold play-off and championship shirts with my name and image on them. I wore one of my own T-shirts during our victory parade through downtown Los Angeles. We sold 120,000 T-shirts in four days!

Our initial licensing deal with the NBA required that my company finish the season among the top fifteen licensees in sales. We were seventh and growing faster than any other NBA licensee in history! Even today, I tell my team at MJE that the key to our success is to overdeliver on all of our deals. When you overdeliver, as we did with the T-shirt company, it creates even more opportunities.

That success allowed us to go back and get a better licensing deal from the NBA. We took advantage of that opportunity to become the first licensed sports apparel company to make "belt" T-shirt prints in which the design extends all the way around the shirt.

Not only did we overdeliver by outselling our competitors, we also overdelivered by introducing innovative fashions. That style of T-shirt became very popular and spurred even greater profits. My Lakers team lost to Detroit in the 1988–1989 championship finals. My consolation prize was that I got my third MVP season award—and we quadrupled our T-shirt sales!

Over the next several years, Magic Johnson T's expanded with licenses for the NCAA, the NFL, the NHL, and other sports. For fifteen years, we made some serious money with our T-shirt business, all because I saw an opportunity, jumped on it, and kept riding it.

Selling T-shirts required a lot of time and effort. I had to approve every design and color. That little business turned big profits, and I had a great time teasing the other players on the court about my business off the court. Once we got rolling, we had licenses to make T-shirts for nearly seventy players and teams, selling them for $25 and more. The best part was the reaction from my rivals when they learned that my business was profiting from their success—even if they beat me on the court!

When we played the Chicago Bulls in the 1991–1992 NBA finals, Michael Jordan asked me to be a guest on a play-offs show that he was hosting for CBS. The Bulls beat us 4–1 in that series, but I managed to pull off a good one on Michael when I presented him with one of our Magic Johnson T's with his image and number on it—along with mine.

"How can you make T-shirts with me on them?" Michael asked.

"I'm the first player to become a licensee of the NBA," I said. "And I want to thank you for playing so well, because whether we win or lose, I'm going to make a lot of money off you."

Michael laughed at that while we were on the air, but as soon as the cameras stopped rolling he called his agent and demanded his own licensing deal with the NBA! It was too late. We had Michael on more shirts than any other player. And he was the championship series MVP that year, so I was very happy for him and for me too! That year, the Foot Locker sports apparel chain alone ordered $2.4 million in T-shirts from my company.

OPPORTUNITIES KNOCK

I always stay on the alert for new business ideas. Most natural-born entrepreneurs have a sixth sense for spotting opportunities where other people see only problems—or nothing at all. Entrepreneurs are as diverse as any other population group. They run one-man shops, franchises, corporations, and business empires that include all of the above. Yet they all share the ability to see opportunities and then act on them. Often the businesses they create open up even more opportunities.

We named our Starbucks joint venture Urban Coffee Opportunities, not only because that deal itself was a great opportunity for both parties but also because we felt it would open up other opportunities—and it did. The Starbucks deal brought us a new level of business credibility and introduced Magic Johnson Enterprises to new markets.

In the chapters that follow, I will walk you through many of the opportunities that have spawned businesses for me, jobs for others, and economic development for urban communities. Some of these businesses have been solo endeavors. Some have been partnerships. Some have been joint ventures. Others have been franchises. Still others have involved buying existing businesses and taking them to another level. All of them have become reality because I saw opportunities and I jumped on them.

Not every opportunity is golden. Still, you never know until you make the effort to check it out. You have to believe in your abilities and trust your entrepreneurial instincts. I believe every opportunity is a good one until proven otherwise. That optimistic spirit, combined with a lot of hard work and thorough research, has made me hundreds of millions of dollars, but more important, it has helped me in my mission to help others.

Even the opportunities that did not work out taught me something, and many of those that didn't pan out initially led to better deals down the road. The important thing is to always be alert for business opportunities and to do whatever it takes to check them out before jumping on board.

I've put together these tips for spotting and capitalizing on opportunities to help fine-tune your sixth sense as an entrepreneur. I will describe how they worked for me in greater detail in later chapters.

TIPS FOR SEIZING OPPORTUNITIES

1. Find opportunities in problems

When the home mortgage market experienced turmoil in 2007–2008, I joined forces with K. Robert Turner of Canyon Capital Realty Advisors to create our third Canyon-Johnson Urban Funds investment fund. We raised $1 billion to build, buy, and refurbish affordable apartment developments because the problems in the housing market meant that renting made more sense than owning for millions of urban residents.

When gasoline prices soared above $4 a gallon in 2008, it created huge problems for many businesses and consumers. Yet rising oil prices created opportunities too. Tomorrow's billionaires will include entrepreneurs who develop alternative fuels and vehicles that run on them. There will also be successful entrepreneurs who seize the opportunity to create car-pooling services, kick-start a motor scooter dealership, or peddle a bicycle delivery service.

The economic downturn in 2007–2008 hurt many businesses and put a lot of people out of work. Yet it also created new opportunities for businesses that help people with financial challenges like foreclosures and bankruptcies. Some entrepreneurs launched liquidation businesses that buy and resell business furniture and equipment. Others provide services tracking and pursuing accounts receivable for businesses, including hospitals, whose patients have been hard hit by job losses and rising medical care costs.

When one door closes because of a shift in the economy, another opens. Opportunity awaits you on the other side.

2. Find a need and fill it

My T.G.I. Friday's restaurant in the Los Angeles neighborhood of Baldwin Hills is one of the most successful in the entire national chain. This venture began when a woman told me there was no place in her neighborhood for her to get a decent salad. "Maybe you can build us a restaurant next," she said to me one day after church. It was a straightforward request, and I took it seriously. We checked out the neighborhood, and she was right. There were few family restaurants—no major brands—in the community. The long lines at my movie theater proved that residents in Baldwin Hills would patronize a high-quality, safe business in their neighborhood. That success helped me convince T.G.I. Friday's that there was a lucrative opportunity in South Central, and together we launched a very profitable business and created dozens of jobs while serving a need in the community, and for one salad-loving lady in particular.

3. Find a partner

Joining forces with Starbucks, 24 Hour Fitness, Sodexo, Adecco, and other partners has helped build my business and my brand much faster than I could have done on my own, so I encourage you always to look for opportunities to form partnerships, joint ventures, and strategic alliances.

4. Find a niche

Sodexo is one of the world's largest food and facilities management companies. Adecco is a global leader in human resource services. Yet both of these dominant companies were missing out on opportunities for contracts designated for minority businesses in their industries. I joined forces with those two companies to serve those niches and to create even more opportunities for minorities in those fields.

There are niche opportunities in every neighborhood, in every industry. It's simply a matter of searching for them, knowing them when you see them, and finding ways to serve them.

5. Find the future

Whether it is the next great thing in cell phone software or global positioning system technologies, personal security devices, health spas, or home entertainment, business opportunities are being created with each new trend, twist, and turn in the culture and the economy. Magic Johnson Enterprises has entrepreneurial opportunity scouts who go to industry conventions and other networking events. They also monitor Web sites, blogs, wikis, and other online sources for the latest trends and technologies.

Everyone within my company is tasked with understanding trends. For example, Doug Melville is the vice president of marketing and business development and looks for ways to create new revenue streams for the brand. Chris Morrow, marketing and business development associate, implemented our new constituent relations management database. This type of information is crucial to make sure my team is armed with the correct tools to be on top of the latest twists and turns in popular culture, the cutting-edge technologies, and the hottest spots for networking. Because global business is becoming more and more important, business models and new brand development and activity are key to success. Tomorrow's exciting ideas are being developed today, so focusing on the future is an important role within the company. These scouts patrol the leading edge for us, looking for opportunities to create new revenue streams for the brand.

6. Find time to listen

An entrepreneur's "sixth sense" for finding opportunities is closely connected to one of the regular five senses: your sense of hearing. Even if you aren't a natural-born entrepreneur, you can train yourself to listen for opportunities in your everyday conversations. My mother, like many other mothers, was fond of telling us that God gave us two ears but only one mouth, so we should listen twice as much as we talk. Many athletes and entrepreneurs tend to forget that motherly advice. Knowing it all means you never learn much.

I am approached all the time by people who have ideas for business opportunities, and I never blow them off. I am just naturally curious, and I have this innate desire to learn as much as I can about everything I can. We were on a Christmas family vacation in 2006 when another dad with his own family sitting nearby struck up a conversation. We'd been there a couple days, and his kids and his wife had been talking with mine, so we were like any other dads enjoying a day on the beach.

At first we talked about our children and sports, and it was the second or third day before the subject of business came up. He asked what sort of businesses I was involved with, and I told him about our core mission to lead economic development and opportunities for minorities and their communities. I could see that this interested him, and after a while he said, "I could use your advice. I'm the CEO of my company, and one of our biggest challenges is finding qualified minorities to work for us and to serve as our suppliers."

I could see that he was very concerned about this and that he'd done a lot of research. At that point, I didn't know much about the staffing industry, so I listened and I learned. That conversation on the beach two years ago led to the creation in 2008 of an alliance between Magic Johnson Enterprises and Adecco. I expect Magic Workforce Solutions to become a wildly successful billion-dollar business that will finance even more of our efforts for economic development in underserved urban areas.

Risks and Rewards

Smart entrepreneurs don't avoid risks, they manage them.

I was approached one day in a Florida hotel lobby by Rick Barry, the legendary basketball player and father of four other professional players. He invited me to participate in a charity poker tournament with several other former NBA players in Las Vegas. I told him I would be glad to make a contribution but that I don't gamble—for fun or for business, either.

Entrepreneurs are often portrayed as risk *takers,* but to be successful in business, you have to be a risk *mitigator.* When you start a business, you put your money and your reputation on the line. In most businesses, you are betting that customers or clients will want to buy your product or service.

You can't avoid risk in business. Without it, there is no reward, but you should always work to minimize or mitigate your risk by doing your homework and understanding every aspect of every deal, backward and forward, inside and out.

Managing risk is a continuous consideration. You should be thinking about minimizing risk at every stage of the game including when you decide what sort of business to get involved in, how you structure the company, how you'll finance it, where you will locate it, who you will hire, who you will partner with, and how you will grow it. At Magic Johnson Enterprises, we are very focused on risk mitigation. It is incorporated into every aspect of our operations.

As our business has grown and gained leverage, we have stepped up our risk-mitigation efforts. We minimize risk, in part, by partnering only with major brands or "best-in-class" businesses that are recognized and respected by urban consumers and that already have a successful infrastructure and back-of-shop systems in place. Before we enter into any partnership, joint venture, or other working relationship, we mitigate risk by understanding the company, its market, its competition, its finances, and any past, present, or pending legal challenges.

Every entrepreneur and business owner must determine what level of risk is acceptable. Some may feel that the more success they have, the more risks they can take. Yet, it is also true that the more you achieve, the more you have to lose. When building a business or a brand into a valuable asset, you certainly don't want to put your personal finances at risk. Sometimes, though, that is unavoidable.

I had to put my own money on the line in the early days of my career, when other forms of financing weren't available. Most entrepreneurs tell similar stories of taking out second mortgages, tapping credit cards, or borrowing from friends and family to get their businesses going. Your level of risk will change over the years, but that doesn't mean you should not always do whatever you can to minimize your exposure. That is just smart business.

Managing risk is a fine art. You never want to take unnecessary risks, but you don't want to miss out on opportunities due to "paralysis by analysis" either. Those who manage risk thoughtfully tend to be the most successful in their business dealings because risk is a consideration in every venture, no matter how big or small your company may be.

When I discussed forming a partnership with Loews Cineplex Entertainment Corporation, risk was a major part of the equation for both of us. Lawrence Ruisi, who was then the president and CEO of Loews, told reporters that partnering with me was a way to manage his company's risk because of the strength of my brand and reputation in urban communities. "We wanted the community to accept and welcome the theater that we were bringing to the market," he told a reporter. Larry credited my ability to build community support as a key factor in bringing the theater to the neighborhood.

But Loews also wanted me to invest cash in this joint venture so that I would be sharing the risk. My contribution was more than a few million dollars, which Loews saw as part of its risk reduction because it made me a full partner in the deal and showed my commitment to the project. Loews's involvement, in turn, provided the expertise and resources that reduced the risk to manageable levels for me and my company.

RISK REDUCTION 101

The key to managing and mitigating risk is thoughtful, thorough planning. That is one reason a well-done business plan is so important. It forces you to go step by step through every aspect of an endeavor so that you consider the risks involved. When you write a business plan, you have to examine the risks inherent in your market, your financing, and your operations.

You evaluate *market risk* by determining the demand levels for your product or service. Is the market big enough now to generate enough cash flow to cover your investment and a profit too? Is the market growing? How much competition is there? Are there new or emerging technologies that will impact your market? What sorts of government regulations can impact your market? Is your market local, national, or international?

These are all questions you need to ask in order to reduce market risk before you put anything on the line. You also need to look at *financial risk* by running the numbers. You have to get a good handle on revenues and costs and the factors that impact your ability to meet expenses and make a profit. How much will your labor costs be? Will you buy a building or rent it? How much will you have to pay for health and business insurance? How will you price your product or service?

Finally, you also need to look at your *operations risk,* which covers the day-to-day nuts and bolts of getting your product or service to your customers or clients. You will need to understand and constantly evaluate whether you have enough employees to get the job done, whether you should outsource or subcontract some of the work, and whether you have the best technology and delivery systems available within your financial means.

RISK REDUCERS

To help manage risk in my businesses—and yours—I've developed a list of *risk reducers* that you may want to review during every phase of your business development. I will cover some of these in greater depth elsewhere in the book, but this list will serve as an overview of protecting your investment and your brand reputation.

1. Develop impulse control

Entrepreneurs are often confident, action-oriented, optimistic go-getters. We can also be impulsive because we get passionate about our ideas and opportunities. Entrepreneurs tend to think that success in one area makes them "golden," and as a result of that overconfidence they sometimes jump into other businesses without giving them enough thought and research. Fortunately, I have strong impulse control, which comes from growing up in a family where resources were stretched thin. I get excited by and even obsessed with opportunities, but I look before I leap. I break down business deals and examine them from all angles. Before I complete my analysis, my team and my backup teams do their own.

2. Create a system of checks and double-checks

Magic Johnson Enterprises has a solid executive team, and we have both formal and informal processes for evaluating the potential risk of business ventures under consideration. Yet in the biggest deals, we may also bring in trusted advisers and experts to double-check and confirm our risk-management conclusions. We pay for those outside consultations, but if you are just starting out you may be able to tap the expertise of an informal board of advisers, mentors, or business leaders.

3. Plan ahead for worst-case scenarios

You can protect your investment and your brand from risk by planning for worst-case scenarios in your market, finances, and operations so that when something goes wrong, you have a course of action in place. You can't predict the future, but looking ahead and anticipating what could go wrong will help keep you alert for signs of trouble so that you can react quickly. This is especially important when planning for cash-flow emergencies, which should be done for at least six months to a year from your start-up date.

4. Stay focused on your strengths

I had a tendency to get excited about all sorts of possible ventures early in my business career. I pushed my advisers to let me get involved in everything from boxing to music production and nightclubs. Fortunately, I listened to them when they told me to stay focused on economic development in urban communities. You need to develop a set of criteria for identifying new opportunities and stick with it. Staying with your strengths reduces risk by keeping you focused so that you can build on what works and

expand your network within your area of expertise. If you stray
from what you know, you run the risk of hurting your brand and
draining your financial reserves.

5. Be a smart partner

One of the main reasons for forming partnerships and joint
ventures is to reduce risk for both sides. Magic Johnson Enterprises provides a brand that is trusted, admired, and deeply invested in urban communities. Starbucks, Burger King, 24 Hour
Fitness, and other partners see my company as a risk-mitigating
factor because our brand is so respected. Those companies, in
turn, help reduce my risk by providing expertise, products, and
infrastructure. Still, it has to work for both sides. I've been offered deals that, at first glance, seemed very attractive and lucrative. Yet on closer inspection, it became clear that I was being
asked to invest more money and take on more risk than the potential partner was. In some cases, I have pushed for a better deal
that reduced my risk and increased profits. In other cases, I have
walked away from deals that were loaded with too much risk. You
have to be willing to do both.

6. Don't scrimp on lawyers, financial advisers, or industry experts

I hire the best legal and tax and finance experts I can find because they reduce risk dramatically. Their experience and expertise will protect you from problems that you may not know exist.
In other cases, I've hired independent industry experts to analyze
deals offered to me. The expense of hiring them proved to be
well worth it when they showed me potential risks in the deal that
I never would have seen without their expertise.

7. Use your smarts instead of your money

Marketing and advertising costs can drain your profits and
add to the risk of doing business. Most start-ups operate on a

tight budget. You can reduce costs and risk levels by finding creative ways to promote your business without paying for print or television ads. Bookstores do this by inviting big-name authors to talk about their books. Investment advisers and real estate agents put on free seminars. Landscape architects, nursery owners, fitness trainers, and even doctors and lawyers write advice columns for local publications or do guest spots on local television shows. Creating a blog on your Web site is another way to attract attention to your business without cutting into your business profits. Before you dig into your earnings, pick the brains of other entrepreneurs for their guerrilla or underground marketing ideas.

8. Use free resources available to entrepreneurs

Many communities and colleges now have entrepreneurial centers and small-business incubators that offer free assistance for start-ups with limited finances. Government agencies such as the Small Business Administration (www.sba.gov) and the Minority Business Development Agency (www.mbda.gov) have Web sites that offer a wide range of services at no charge. Reduce your risk and minimize your start-up costs by tapping in to those resources.

9. Prime the pump

You should start marketing your business and its products and services before you open the doors. Having customers or clients lined up and ready to do business will reduce the initial risk and get the cash flowing. Satisfied customers and clients will also help market your business, which will help reduce the need for expensive advertising and marketing campaigns.

10. Run lean

Even if your start-up is a huge success, resist the temptation to risk its future by spending your limited funds on fancier furnishings or more employees for at least the first year. Things can go sour quickly in a new business, so you want to keep that cash in reserve in case you need to invest in more inventory or new technologies to keep the business pumping through the hard times that will inevitably come.

Mitigating risk should be part of every decision you make as an entrepreneur. The more you grow your business, the more important managing risk becomes because you have more at stake. You certainly cannot expect your business partners and suppliers to shoulder all the risk, but it is your responsibility to protect your company by minimizing your risk as much as possible, in every way possible.

Creating a
Strong Business Plan

A good business plan is money in the bank.

agic, it's me, Derrick! You know me, man. C'mon. This time I've got the perfect idea. Hear me out.

I get that a lot.

Derrick and I ran in the same social circles in my early days in Los Angeles. I'd see him at parties now and then, and we got to know each other casually over the years. Initially, we talked about basketball and cars, but once I started having some success in business, Derrick would pitch his moneymaking ideas to me.

It's crazy the way things have changed. For many years, most of the people who approached me wanted to talk about the Lakers and maybe get an autograph. Nowadays, nearly all of them want to talk about their business ideas and maybe get my signature on a check.

Derrick was very persistent. He kept calling and wearing out my assistant. Finally, she set up an appointment. Derrick came into the office to make his pitch, but without a business plan. He was lugging a gym bag instead.

As he launched into his spiel, I felt as if I were auditioning a comedian instead of listening to a business proposal. Derrick's presentation was funnier than most *Saturday Night Live* skits. He had my entire staff rolling in the aisles.

"Okay, Magic . . . Earvin . . . okay, so you know how when you're driving on the freeway and stuck in traffic or stopped at a light and you see a good-looking woman in the car next to you that you want to meet, but, like, you can't communicate with her over the traffic noise?"

"Derrick, is this a business pitch or a joke?" I asked.

"No, man, I'm serious as a heart attack. Listen up. So she's sittin' there in traffic, you're sittin' there in traffic, and time is short. You gotta make a move before the light changes or the traffic jam clears. But how do you let her know that, you know, you want to get to know her?"

"I give up, Derrick. How do I do that?" I said.

"With this!"

Derrick reached into his gym bag and pulled out—I kid you not—one of those cardboard fans on a stick—the kind that they pass out in southern churches on hot Sundays so the people in the congregation don't pass out from heat exhaustion during the preacher's long sermon. Yet this fan lacked the usual excerpt from the Bible. Instead there was a message written in letters with black Magic Marker.

It said, "Hi, I'm Derrick! What's your cell number?"

I nearly lost it when I saw that. Derrick was so proud of his creation that I didn't want to discourage him, but finally I had to ask him, "Derrick, how is she going to tell you her number?"

"That's the point, Magic. We're going to sell her a fan too. We're going to sell them to everybody who has a car! I'm telling you, this is going to be bigger than big!"

Derrick didn't have a business plan, and he didn't have a clue. He wanted me to put up *all* the money so that he could mass-produce cardboard fans on sticks that men and women would use to pick each other up on freeways.

That may be the craziest business proposal brought to my door, but I get a lot of people who come knocking, wanting just to throw out an idea and take home a check. The real kicker is that often the person who wants me to finance a business doesn't have anything invested in it other than the time it took to dream it up.

If I've heard 1,000 pitches, probably 950 of them have called for me to put up all the money. I do not invest in ventures with people who aren't confident enough to put up their own money too. That isn't fair to me, and it isn't fair to you. Stakeholders are much more motivated. They work harder because they have something at risk. I'm all for that. People with money at stake are more careful about what sort of businesses they get into.

I can't tell you how many young athletes come into my office because they want to discuss starting either a record label or a sports bar. I usually spend the first half hour or so telling them why those are two particularly tough and highly competitive businesses that take a lot more work than they are probably inclined to put into it. "Oh no," they'll say, "I'm going to have my cousin/brother/uncle/sister run it. I'm just letting them use my name."

I have seen so many of those deals fail that I refuse to go anywhere near them. Of course, I had to learn these lessons the hard way. I had interests in both a record label and sports bars at one time. Neither one of them added a dime to my retirement fund. I also seem to be the potential financier of choice for everyone pitching hair extension and hair products businesses. Without fail, these aspiring entrepreneurs come in without business plans but with the expectation that I'm going to finance the entire operation.

"Magic, it's only gonna cost $500,000, and you don't have to give me all the money right away. Just $100,000 today is fine!"

I don't like to squash anyone's dreams, so it's hard for me to say no. But I'm getting a lot better at "no," especially when someone comes to me looking for an investment without taking the time or making the effort to put together a serious business plan.

You can't get a banker or a venture capital investor to talk to you without a business plan, and it should be the same way when you approach any potential adviser, partner, or funding source—especially if the person is a friend or a family member.

Why? Because a properly done business plan shows that you have done *your* homework. It also provides the starting point for your business. I enjoy helping other people get started as entrepreneurs, but before I take the time to answer their questions, I want them to be able to answer *my* questions. Have they carefully researched their market? Do they know what the competition is doing? Do they have a pricing plan that takes into consideration all of their costs and market considerations? Do they have a five-year plan? An exit strategy?

Even if someone comes to me with a really well done business plan, I tend to ask the same tough questions, just as a bank or a venture capital firm would ask. You can bet that if I am seriously considering putting money into a business, the questions are going to get even tougher. I don't want to lose money, and just as important, I don't want the other person to lose any either.

I am glad to be seen as a go-to guy for other entrepreneurs. Still, I always tell people that if they are serious about starting a business, they need a solid, professional business plan. This is a document that describes your business, its goals, the people involved in leading it, your funding needs and sources, market analysis, and its prospects for short- and long-term growth. There are many helpful and free Web sites that lay out the step-by-step process for doing a business plan.

You can build a basic model online at the U.S. Department of Commerce Minority Business Development site (www.mbda.gov) or download a business plan template for free at the Web site of SCORE, a nonprofit partner with the U.S. Small Business Administration: www.score.org/business_toolbox.html.

With these and most business plans, the format is very basic. Doing it right takes research, no-nonsense mathematics, and careful consideration. Yet when a business plan is done thoroughly and creatively, it can launch your entrepreneurial career. A strong business plan is an essential part of your presentation to bankers and potential investors or partners.

SLAM DUNK

One of the best business plans to come my way was handed to me by a talented and creative marketing ace I was trying to hire. I didn't want him to start his own business; I wanted him to work for me. Aaron Walton had impressed me while he was helping us work on marketing strategies in 2005. A business administration graduate of Babson College, Aaron became the point man for corporations looking to connect their marketing campaigns and brands to entertainers and musicians.

After college, he joined Pepsi-Cola, where he became a brand manager for Pepsi's sponsored tours for Miami Sound Machine, Tina Turner, and Michael Jackson. Then, after working on Michael Jackson's fourteen-month international tour, Aaron was assigned to help other Pepsi-Cola companies identify artists who would make good partners. Feeling that he had established his own identity in business, Aaron left Pepsi and created Aaron Walton Entertainment (AWE), where he worked with major brands such as AT&T, Banana Republic, General Motors, and Gap Inc. He did so well that Omnicom bought AWE in 2006. Aaron was working for Omnicom when I met him.

I liked Aaron's creative energy. We worked well together. I thought he'd be a great addition to our team, but before I could entice him to join us, Aaron told me that he and another Omnicom star, Cory Isaacson, were looking at creating their own company. Cory had also joined Omnicom after being a partner in his own entertainment marketing business. He had played matchmaker in some very successful marketing campaigns, partnering

Hanes Hosiery with Tina Turner, Kodak with the House of Blues, Burger King with the Backstreet Boys, and Budweiser with the Rolling Stones.

I could see that these two very smart young executives were fired up about starting their own marketing firm, so I told them to let me know if they needed any investors for the start-up.

A few weeks later, I was traveling by private jet to a speaking engagement with Aaron and my chief operating officer, Kawanna Brown. They were seated behind me, and I overheard Aaron tell Kawanna that he and Cory had put together a killer business plan for their new venture.

"Do you have it with you?" I asked.

He had a copy on his laptop, so I took a look, and it blew me away. It was the most exciting business plan I'd ever seen and the easiest decision I've ever made about investing in a new company. The business plan for their marketing and advertising agency mapped out exactly what they wanted to do and how they were going to do it. They wanted to create a new model for their industry. Aaron and Cory had put their hearts and souls into their business plan. You could feel their passion and sense of mission.

They weren't just starting a new creative company; they wanted to build "the planet's most interesting agency." And they already had clients lined up. Even better, they knew exactly how much investment capital they needed—and they told me they would return my initial investment within eighteen months. (They did it too!)

SECRET INGREDIENTS

Business plans are not complicated. In fact, the simpler they are, the better. Those who read your business plan—bankers, investors, potential partners, clients, employees, and suppliers—don't want to read your life story. They want to learn quickly about your proposed business so they can decide whether they want to be part of it.

Aaron and Cory's business plan had the basic ingredients:

- Mission Statement
- Industry Review
- Key Challenges
- Solutions
- Core Disciplines
- Partner Background
- Five-Year Plan
- Financial Analysis
- Next Steps

Aaron and Cory created a business plan that included all of the necessary elements, then they tossed in their own secret ingredients of passion and vision. Of course, these two veterans had an advantage in putting the business plan together. Entertainment marketing was their turf. They were proven, battle-tested, award-winning innovators in that field.

When they announced that their goal was to create the planet's most interesting agency, it was not empty boasting. I had no doubt that they would do it. They had been on the leading edge for most of their careers. Aaron and Cory were already plugged in to the marketing matrix. They knew everybody they needed to know to do what they said they were going to do.

Even if they'd been rookies fresh out of business school, their passion and sense of mission would have captured my attention. Those ingredients are critical to any business plan, no matter what sort of business it is.

Cory and Aaron called their marketing agency Walton/ Isaacson. They've allowed me to share their mission statement with you:

w/i is a marketing agency that builds Fortune 500 brands through innovative marketing campaigns. w/i will capitalize on industry trends by leveraging the intellectual capital of the world's best and most diverse marketing and brand talent. w/i combines industry-leading creative and strategic thinking with "best" execution. This dynamic team will provide:

- Smarter campaigns for our partners
- An inspiring and fueled culture (& benefits) for our employees
- Agility and speed that will define the "new agency model"

The two creative geniuses threw in a few unique twists. Their proposal also came with a three-part brand promise:

1. Everything we do will be stimulating, exciting and new for the sole purpose of creating impact for the partners we represent.
2. The people we employ will be forward-thinking, leaders in their field and offer something unique to our culture.
3. A real-time approach—the most responsive and adaptive group in the industry ("Navy SEALs of Marketing").

Another unique feature was their map of their "Agency DNA":

- Passionate
- Creative at the core
- Strategic
- Tech savvy
- Respectfully aggressive
- Hip and young

- Entrenched in pop culture
- Style with sway

WALKING THE TALK

Cory and Aaron did their homework by distilling critical findings from their research. They looked at where their industry was going and targeted marketplace opportunities being created by trends in pop culture, media, and entertainment. Their in-depth research and the informed conclusions they drew while creating their business plan propelled their business onto the leading edge. Their new company hit the streets as the next wave; an innovative and dynamic agency, immediately distinguished from old-school competitors.

As veteran insiders from the highest level of the creative and volatile world of marketing and advertising, they saw that the old agency model was not working in the modern marketplace. Aaron and Cory instinctively realized that the best way to manage change was to create it.

The masterstroke of their business plan was their decision to walk the talk by creating their own products from scratch. This move put them into the game as entrepreneurs themselves. It made them brothers in arms with their clients, and it gave them the power to say, "Look what we did on our own; imagine what we can do for you!"

By creating and marketing their own products they came up with the perfect response to prospective clients who might say, "How do you know what works?" The idea of developing their own products had come when they reflected on the story of the investor who asked his stockbroker, "If you're such a smart stock picker, why don't you invest your own money?"

That got them thinking, *If we are so good at building brands, why don't we build our own?* And so, to prove themselves, they did just that with successful and critically praised campaigns for Right Gin and Kübler Absinthe. Cory and Aaron helped conceive and create both brands from conception to launch. They invested their own money as well as their ingenuity. Once they had those products on the shelves, their marketing and advertising campaigns were recognized across the industry. Big-brand clients were soon knocking on their door.

CREATIVE BURST

After I bought in to their business plan and offered to help finance Cory and Aaron in their new venture, they told me something that I could hardly believe at first: they had written their masterful business plan in just one day! Still, they had been planning it for years. They were totally immersed in the advertising and marketing business. Over the years, they each had given a lot of thought to creating how they would do things if they were to one day start their own cutting-edge marketing agency. They had also spent many hours talking with each other about what they wanted to do and how they wanted to do it.

So when it came time to actually sit down and write a business proposal, they were more than ready. Since I happened to be the co-owner of over 100 Starbucks stores at the time, I'm very happy to report that Cory and Aaron got together at a Starbucks on Rush Street in Chicago to create their masterpiece while the coffee flowed in a long, inspired session.

"It was eight hours of caffeine and a lot of conversation," Aaron told me. "The first things we talked about were the kind of company and environment we wanted to create and the kind of talent we wanted to attract. We talked in big, global terms, like we were looking down from thirty thousand feet in the air. We agreed that we wanted to change the industry."

Their goal was to be able to hand their business plan to people who had no background in brand and entertainment marketing, let them read it, and inspire them to become just as passionate about their vision as they were. When I read their business plan, I was also struck by the thought that these two creative minds must have had fun putting their ideas on paper.

"It was a daunting task, and I know this sounds weird, but as we were doing it, I kept thinking of the old Dick Van Dyke television show where they were TV writers sitting in a room, drinking coffee, and tossing jokes and ideas back and forth," Aaron said.

They did it word by word, debating and collaborating, shaping their ideas and passions into a business according to their shared vision. Three years after I first read what Aaron and Cory had put together, Walton/Isaacson has more than twenty-five employees with offices in Los Angeles, Chicago, New York, and Tokyo. In January 2008, it was named the African-American agency of record for Lexus.

In early 2008, Aaron and Cory helped roll out Burger King's "Late Night Ambassador" campaign with Sean "Diddy" Combs and director Spike Lee to promote later hours on Thursday through Saturday. They also helped launch Apple Fries with the Jonas Brothers' North American "Burning Up" tour and worked on Unilever's "Degree Girl" launch with Ashley Tisdale. Dove, Axe, and Whirlpool are also clients.

Walton/Isaacson is meeting and even exceeding the projected financial goals that its creators laid out for me. Aaron and Cory will tell you, and I will confirm, that much of their success is due to a great business plan that has stood the test of time and has continued to serve as both a practical and an inspirational guide.

PART II

BUSINESS PLAYS

Mentors and Role Models

**Know what you don't know and
listen to those with the knowledge you seek.**

I was six feet nine inches tall when I first walked into the office
of Hollywood superagent Michael Ovitz.

By the time I walked out, I was about five-two.

I went to Michael in the summer of 1987 with four NBA
championships on my résumé. I was being offered all kinds of
sponsorships, partnerships, movie roles, television appearances,
and other deals. I wanted him to help me build my brand as a serious businessman, not just as a celebrity athlete who signed autographs and endorsed other people's products.

Michael was known as the most powerful man in the entertainment business. He had created Creative Artists Agency (CAA),
the talent agency that dominated the industry. His firm represented the biggest stars and made them the best deals. Everyone
told me that he was one of the smartest businessmen in the country. I'd also heard that he was tough, but I had no idea just how
tough.

I'd already made some inroads into the business world with
my radio station purchase in Colorado, but I still felt like a rookie
in this other game. I was sent to Michael by Sony Pictures CEO

Peter Guber after a crazy moment in a Lakers game. It was an easy game, and we were way out in front. I'd been thinking a lot the day before about the financial struggles of my teammate Kareem Abdul-Jabbar—he had entrusted the wrong people who made bad investments on his behalf.

As I was passing the ball inbounds on a play late in the game, I saw a pair of big-time entertainment executives sitting together: Peter Guber and Joe Smith of Elektra/Asylum Records. They were huge Lakers fans and my friends too, so the question popped out of my mouth as I stood on the court near them: "How do I get into business?"

I don't recommend doing that as a way to impress your basketball coach. Still, I was hungry for information and guidance. I knew what I didn't know, and I didn't mind asking anyone and everyone for help. I was confident in my basketball skills at that point, but I knew they would carry me only so far.

Fortunately, one of the nation's most successful entrepreneurs, J. Bruce Llewellyn, agreed to give me an introductory course in business when I was still playing for the Lakers. I wanted to learn from him because he had started with nothing and built a multimillion-dollar empire that provided thousands of jobs in urban America. He also champions economic development for minority communities.

"Business is the emancipator," he told me. "The trick is to get your hands on the levers, on the money, to get the guy off your back. That's the real world, and that's the plight of the black community—they don't have the leverage."

Mr. Llewellyn is the son of Jamaican immigrants who owned a restaurant in White Plains, New York. After serving in World War II, he opened his first retail store in Harlem while attending the City University of New York. He got his bachelor's degree and kept studying until he got two graduate degrees and a law degree.

He worked a number of government jobs before pursuing a business career in 1969. After mortgaging his home and selling nearly everything he had, he got a $3 million loan to purchase a chain of ten supermarkets in the Bronx. He turned it into the largest minority-owned retail chain in the country, with nine hundred employees in twenty-nine stores and annual sales of $100 million when he sold it.

In 1983, Mr. Llewellyn formed an investors' group to buy shares of the Coca-Cola Bottling Company of New York. His fellow investors included former NBA star Julius Erving and Bill Cosby. In 1985, Mr. Llewellyn and Julius Erving joined forces to purchase the Philadelphia Coca-Cola Bottling Company.

Three years later, Mr. Llewellyn became the company's chairman and majority stockholder. He kept building that business into one of the largest in the Coca-Cola family. In 2008 it had sales of more than $500 million. He also owns a number of television and radio stations and cable systems.

When I went to him for guidance, Mr. Llewellyn was patient with me. Still, he quickly lost me when he started talking about ROI (return on investment) and build-to-suit leases (when a landlord builds to a tenant's specifications).

I didn't want to waste his time, so I confessed, "Mr. Llewellyn, if you were talking about the Xs and the Os on a basketball court, I'd be able to pick apart everything you said, but I don't have a clue what you are talking about right now."

It was a humbling moment—one of many I had while making the transition from basketball to business. I am grateful for these sometimes embarrassing experiences. They changed my thinking processes. They made me not only a better businessman but also a better person.

HUMILITY HELPS

Today, when other athletes and aspiring entrepreneurs ask me
what tools they need to get into business, I always tell them: "Hu-
mility." They usually think I'm joking, but I'm not. I can't tell you
how many times top businesspeople such as Peter Guber, Joe
Smith, J. Bruce Llewellyn, and my other mentors have commented that the reasons they were willing to help me were that:

1. I asked for advice.
2. I listened to it.

I didn't go to them for money or favors. I asked for guidance,
and when they took the time to offer it, I paid attention. Still, I
admit I didn't always like what I heard—especially from Michael
Ovitz at that first meeting. Peter and Joe suggested that I get him
to represent me as a business adviser because of his incredible
network. So I requested a meeting, and his assistant told me to
come at the appointed hour to the landmark I. M. Pei building
on Wilshire Boulevard that Michael had built for his agency.

On our meeting day, I was ushered into his huge office. He
was there, groomed like a Hollywood power player, wearing a
business suit that fit like Under Armour.

After we shook hands, I said, "I'd like you to represent me because I want to get into business."

Michael studied me but didn't say anything. I was expecting
the usual talk about the Lakers because I knew he was a fan, but
there was nothing. In fact, he looked a little annoyed.

After several minutes of just staring at me like some unwanted
package that had arrived in his office, he finally spoke.

"I've got enough clients and enough money, why do I need
you?" he said.

Then he told me that most athletes who came to him did not

want to hear what he had to say. "What makes you any different?" he asked.

Before I could answer, Michael said that he'd once had a meeting with other professional athletes and it had not gone well.

"So let me think about this," Michael said.

Then he basically kicked me out of his office: he picked up a document and studied it. I took the hint that our meeting was over. It was a humbling experience, and I'm sure that was his objective. He was letting me know that business was a tough game and that being an MVP in the NBA didn't carry much weight in his world.

Of course, I figured all that out later. At the time, I was shocked. I hadn't gotten a cold shoulder like that since the third grade—and she was a whole lot cuter than Michael Ovitz. I told Peter Guber what had happened, and he laughed. Then he told me to call Michael's assistant and ask for another appointment.

To my surprise, he agreed to meet with me again.

"I checked you out, and everybody said you are different from most athletes and that you are serious about business," he said.

Then he threw a curveball: "Tell me about your family."

I gave him a quick rundown of growing up in Lansing with my mother and father. I told him how my dad had worked two shifts and had his own business. He listened intently as I talked about working for my father and for Joel Ferguson and Gregory Eaton, the entrepreneurs who had provided so many jobs in our town. I told him that I had always dreamed about being a businessman and being in a position to help people in the same way.

"I am going to go against everything I said I would not do in our first meeting," he said. "I do not represent athletes as a rule, but people tell me you are special."

Before I got to feeling too special, Michael threw in some homework.

"What's the first thing you read in the morning?" he asked.

"The sports section," I said.

"Wrong answer!"

With that he reached back to a pile of magazines and newspapers and slammed them on his massive desk. Somewhere in South Central, there was a report of a sonic boom. His assistant came running, but Michael waved him away.

"I want you to start reading *The Wall Street Journal, The New York Times,* the business section of the *Los Angeles Times, Forbes,* and *BusinessWeek,*" he said. "I'm going to tell you the things you have to do if you are going to be serious about business. When I tell you to do something, you need to do it. When I tell you to be somewhere, I want you there on time."

Michael broke it down and laid it out. Then he tested me. If he told me to meet him at noon for a business lunch, I was there by 11:20 a.m. He always commanded the biggest table in the center of the restaurant so that everyone could see the steady stream of people coming to greet him and pay their respects. "When you are successful and doing the right things, this will happen to you, and you want everybody to see it," he told me.

MENTORS MATTER

Michael took me places I never would have gone and introduced me to people whom I never would have known without him. Just being seen with him gave me access to a whole new world because it gave me credibility as a businessman. Sure, he was my business adviser, but he was in charge. It was business boot camp. He tore me down to build me back up.

A student of Eastern philosophy and martial arts, Michael was extremely confident. He always seemed to be thinking twenty steps ahead of everyone else, and he urged me to be "forward-thinking."

Michael has a reputation for being a tough man in a tough business, but I've spent many, many hours with him. I've been to his kids' bar mitzvahs and birthday parties. I've sat in on meetings with him at all hours of the day. I know him as well as you can know a person, and I love the guy. As my business adviser, he put me in several major deals but never took a fee.

"I don't want your money," he said. "There is nothing you can give me. I'm doing this because I love you and because you thrill me every time you get on the basketball court."

My day job as an NBA player gave me access to many of the best business minds in the country, no doubt about it. The guidance I got from Jerry Buss, Peter Guber, Michael Ovitz, J. Bruce Llewellyn, Earl Graves, and many others was worth fifty MBA degrees. Still, none of them came to me and offered their services. I had to ask, and then I had to prove that I was willing to listen and to learn. Even more important, I had to let them know that I was committed to a dream before they would buy in to it.

You don't have to be a sports star or a celebrity to find mentors and role models. Passion, however, is required. Enthusiasm is contagious. It attracts people to your cause. They buy in to your dream. Then you have to show them that you are willing to put in the work and the time.

Shortly after Earl Graves and I took over our Pepsi distributorship, I shocked a lot of people by announcing that I was going to ride on delivery runs with our drivers, who start at about 5 a.m. each day. It wasn't a publicity stunt. I wanted to learn the business. What they didn't know was that I'd done the same thing in grade school with an earlier mentor.

Jim Dart was the husband of my fifth-grade teacher, Greta Dart. When the sixth-graders started their own basketball team, my classmates decided we had to have a team too. We drafted Mr. Dart to be the coach of our team, and he turned out to be a great coach and a wonderful early mentor for me. He and Mrs. Dart were like a second set of parents to me, and they were the first white adults I got to know well.

When I wasn't helping my father with his trash-removal business, I worked with Jim. Like my dad, he had a couple of side businesses along with his day job. He owned several rental houses on the west side of Lansing, and my buddies and I cut the grass and painted and cleaned them. He paid us, but the benefits were better—lunch at the Dart house and trips to basketball games at Sexton High School and Michigan State University. Jim sent me to my first basketball camp when I was in seventh grade. It was held at Michigan State and run by the university's assistant basketball coach, Gus Ganakas, who always had tickets for me.

Jim liked that I was willing to work, so he sometimes took me along on his day job. Jim drove a truck for Vernors, a Michigan ginger ale company. I helped Jim deliver cases of Vernors to supermarkets, mom-and-pop groceries, and convenience stores. He taught me about the importance of shelf positioning and displays so that later, when I became involved in a Pepsi distributorship, I had a foundation for understanding that part of their business.

REACHING OUT

Jim Dart, my dad, and Lansing's leading black entrepreneurs, Joel Ferguson and Gregory Eaton, were my early business mentors. I was so lucky to have them within reach and willing to help. They showed me that success was attainable for someone of my race and background.

Look for your mentors in your family and neighborhood and communities. Ask your teachers for suggestions. Big Brothers and Big Sisters groups are great for providing mentors for young people. So are Boys and Girls Clubs and Junior Achievement. I also recommend you check to see if there is a Magic Johnson Foundation Community Empowerment Center in your area by checking our Web site at www.magicjohnson.org. I'll tell you more about these later, but they can be a great place to get started in your business career.

For those in college or just out, there are campus organizations for most professions and career fields, all sorts of young entrepreneurs groups, and organizations such as the Center for Entrepreneurial Leadership.

For those who are already in the workplace, most big companies, corporations, and professional organizations have mentoring programs. Harvard business administration professor David Thomas has done extensive research on corporate mentoring programs. He found that the minority managers whose careers advanced the farthest were generally the beneficiaries of the best networks of mentors and "corporate sponsors" who provided support. Mentors in a corporation can serve as guides who help you understand both how things are supposed to work and how they really work. They can also watch your back and provide you with someone to vent to when you get frustrated.

If you are an aspiring entrepreneur or already in business for yourself, I'd suggest that you put together either a formal or informal board of advisers made up of mentors who have your best interests at heart but are not afraid to tell you when they think you are doing something wrong.

Mentors are not a luxury. They are a necessity. I need them. You need them. My mentors taught me many practical and invaluable things. They shared their experiences, their knowledge, and their contacts with me. They set me straight when I needed it. I try to do the same now by reaching back to pull others ahead. I try to do at least a little mentoring every day to honor those who mentored me.

Often professional athletes or entertainers ask for business guidance because they've seen what I've done. I also get daily requests for mentoring assistance from employees, college students, high-school students, and even grade-school kids. I'm glad to do what I can for them, but aspiring entrepreneurs need to understand that often the best mentors and role models are their own parents, coaches, and people in their neighborhoods and communities. Reach out to them. Share your dreams and goals with them. Show them you are committed and willing to get your hands dirty and break a sweat. You will be rewarded.

ROLE MODEL

Your best bet for a close-up mentor is a regular, reachable person like Jim Dart, someone you know who buys in to your potential and is willing to spend time with you, sharing knowledge, encouraging you, and helping you make connections. Role models can also be helpful. These may be successful people whom you don't know personally but who serve as an inspiration. One of my role models as a young basketball player and then later as an aspiring businessman was Dave Bing, one of the first NBA stars to make it big in business after basketball.

Dave has a classy, low-key personality. He is so unassuming that a sports magazine once nicknamed him "Mr. Unsung-About." He never became a big celebrity even though most sports fans hailed him as one of the greatest players in NBA history. Dave, who had a twelve-year NBA career, was a Detroit Piston from 1966 to 1975, back when I was still living in Michigan and allowed to be a Piston fan.

As a kid playing basketball, I'd pretend I was Bill Russell, Wilt Chamberlain, or Dave Bing. As it turned out, Dave was the player I most resembled in my style on the court. I've followed a similar path to his in my business career too. Even though he's not someone I talk to or see regularly, he's been a great role model. I don't think I've ever told him this, but I've often been in situations in business or in a community leadership role where I'll ask myself, "How would Dave Bing handle this?" That is the value of role models. They lead you by example even when they aren't close at hand.

Like me, Dave grew up in a close-knit blue-collar family that had everything but a lot of money. His dad was a bricklayer and building contractor in Washington, D.C. His mother was a maid. He was an All-American at Syracuse University, where he earned degrees in economics and marketing. A six-foot-three-inch guard, he was picked second in the NBA draft. During his career, he averaged 20.3 points a game and was named to the All-Star team seven times. He was known as a great all-around player, one of the highest-scoring guards in NBA history, a team leader, and a man who always had serious goals.

There weren't many NBA players back then—or now—who work in the off-season as bank-management or auto-dealership trainees. Dave did both. After he retired, he was offered a job in public relations by Paragon Steel in Detroit. I love what Dave did when they offered him that job. He saw that they just thought of him as a marketing tool, a former NBA star who could serve as a figurehead. Dave was more ambitious than that. He turned down the job and told them that he wanted to be taken seriously as a businessperson. He entered the company's management training program instead.

Two years later, he started his own company, Bing Steel, which cut steel to size for auto-manufacturing clients. Dave was a pioneering black businessman who had to fight both racism and the misconception that great athletes cannot be great business leaders. He landed a contract with General Motors and built a business empire. His Bing Group has grown to include ten companies with 1,400 employees. Its annual sales have exceeded $350 million in recent years.

Even more impressive, Dave is looked to as a community leader in Detroit. Concerned that his workers had to drive long distances to find affordable homes, Dave built forty houses near his Highland Park manufacturing plant. He also teamed up with

Ford Motor Company to build a training center for minority workers in his community.

I hope to be as good a role model and as honorable a man as Dave Bing. I encourage you to look for your own close-up mentors and your own role models too. Share your dreams with them. Show them you want to learn. Most of all, listen to what they tell you.

Building a Brand

Your brand is your greatest business asset.

The first Magic Johnson Theatre was more than a business venture. It was my statement to corporate America and financial institutions that underserved minority communities in urban areas were the next frontier.

Major retailers with stores on every corner of suburbia were still wary of urban markets. So were the bankers, venture capitalists, and investment funds whose money built those stores and the shopping centers around them. I was out to prove them wrong.

My greatest tool was the value of my *brand*. That word gets thrown around a lot in business schools and in the corporate world. *Brand value* is not just a catchphrase. My brand has been through it all, good times and bad. Thanks to very hard work and a little luck, we have built what is recognized as one of the most valuable brands in America.

BUILDING A BRAND

My image and reputation—my personal brand—were developed over the course of my NBA career. Still, many felt that all of the goodwill and respect I earned over those first twelve years was severely damaged, if not wiped out, when I announced in November of 1991 that I was leaving basketball after discovering that I had HIV.

Back then, some considered it a death sentence. Scientists were still trying to determine the source of HIV and AIDS. They did not know for certain how it was spread. There was still a widespread public perception that HIV and AIDS were strictly "gay diseases."

After my announcement, some NBA players expressed fears that they could get HIV if my sweat got on them. Others thought that even if I didn't soon die of AIDS, I would have to just go off somewhere and live in seclusion for the rest of my life.

"The marketing companies whom Johnson represented faced a potentially explosive dilemma: one of America's most well-loved sports heroes had contracted the virus that causes one of the most feared and stigmatized of diseases," said a case study by a researcher at Harvard Business School.

Prior to making my announcement in November 1991, I had endorsement deals with several major companies such as Converse and Nestlé. My income from those endorsement deals was nearly $12 million a year. I ranked behind only Michael Jordan in my Q-rating, a measure of the popularity and appeal of professional athletes conducted each year by Marketing Evaluations, a marketing company. Q-ratings are important because companies use them to help determine which athletes or celebrities will make the best endorsers or partners.

Five minutes after the HIV announcement, I probably had the lowest Q-rating in any sport. I lost most of my endorsement deals within a few weeks or months. I'd been with many of the companies a long time, so I won't tell you that it didn't hurt. Yet I understood that they too were trying to protect their brands.

I was focused on my wife, Cookie, and our family and not

thinking about the reactions and repercussions from the outside world at the time. There were people in business who were already counting me out.

"Advertisers Shying from Magic's Touch," read a *New York Times* headline in January 1992. The story quoted an Associated Press report in which a Pepsi-Cola spokesman said a new promotional campaign featuring me was no longer "on the front burner." The story also noted that except for Converse, "most Johnson ads have already been pulled and most of the [other endorsement] companies are going to walk."

I lived in the spotlight as a Laker, so my private life was a matter of public interest. I understood that. I accepted it. When this challenge arose, I did not run from it. Certainly, there were moments when I wanted to hide in humiliation. Yet I am not much for wallowing in self-pity. I had a wife and family who needed me to be strong. It is simply not my nature to give up.

Instead, I owned up to my mistakes, apologized to those who deserved apologies, and then started fighting back. I became an advocate and a champion for those with HIV and AIDS. I am a competitor. I was determined to learn all I could about the disease so I could beat it.

I told everyone that I was going to fight it and that I planned on sticking around a long time. I made some mistakes early on in my public statements. I wasn't always as sensitive as I could have been. This was a new role for me. I was learning on the run. Mostly, I did what comes naturally to me: I moved forward, staying true to the values that always have guided my life.

FIGHTING BACK

That seems like a long time ago now. We have come far in our understanding of HIV and AIDS, even as the fight continues for millions of people around the world. I learned that HIV is not a death sentence, and I've made it my mission to give others hope as well as the information they need to survive.

Along the way, I rebuilt my life, strengthened my relationships, and, despite all predictions, regained the trust and the respect of the public and created an even more powerful brand in the marketplace.

Brands are built on values. They begin with who you are as a person. Your personal brand is what my parents used to refer to as "our good name." We were taught to protect the integrity of our family name by striving never to embarrass our parents or ourselves. That lesson holds true when building and protecting your business brand too. Tiger Woods dominates the world of professional golf because of his focus on excellence as a player. At the same time, he has built a brand that has come to represent the highest levels of performance in the business world.

In 1997, when Tiger was emerging as a dominant force in professional golf, he visited with me while I was doing a photo shoot. We talked about the importance of personal values and brand building. Like me, Tiger benefited from strong parents who had instilled in him the values he needed. My only advice was that he stay true to them.

"Be yourself, not who anyone else wants you to be," I said.

When your values are strong, it is not difficult to build a brand, but it is not always easy to protect and maintain it. Your company brand, like your good name, is a valuable commodity that you have to protect. The good news is that if you build a strong brand upon solid values, it will be resilient.

Just a few months or so after I announced that I had HIV, after most of my endorsement deals and partnerships had fallen apart, a representative from American Express contacted me. He said that American Express wanted to partner with me for an advertising campaign that would be introduced at the All-Star Game in February 1992. It was a six-month campaign with my image in print and television ads and on billboards across the country.

Next came a call from 24 Hour Fitness for a similar endorsement deal. Then Dick Ebersol of NBC asked me to do the NBA Game of the Week and the play-offs. I will always be grateful to American Express, 24 Hour Fitness, and Mr. Ebersol. They were among the first to see that I was the same person with the same business values and that I was going to come back stronger than ever.

I made some big mistakes on a big stage, and I went through a humiliating and humbling period. There was no grand plan for rebuilding my public image. Healing my relationships and fighting for my life were bigger concerns. I simply held true to the values that had brought me success in the first place, and everything else took care of itself.

My Q-rating today is higher than it ever was. My corporate brand is considered to be one of the strongest in the country. In 2008, a report by the consumer research company Yankelovich found that nearly 57 percent of the African Americans and Hispanics polled in states where we do business were likely to purchase from businesses associated with my Magic Johnson brand.

I also was named number one in appeal to corporate executives among all active and retired athletes in a 2007 business survey of more than two hundred marketing executives by TSE Sports & Entertainment, New York. My score was 99.85 out of 100. We've learned from these and other polls and studies that people appreciate that I've created jobs in underserved communities, and they know that when I bring a business to the community, more economic development follows.

Like most competitors, I welcome all challenges as motivation. Anyone who still sees me as a basketball player runs the risk of missing out on a business opportunity.

BANKING ON THE BRAND

With the success of the first Magic Johnson Theatre, we had momentum. I wanted to build the brand by making another big statement in the urban market. So I asked a question: What do people in underserved urban communities need in their neighborhoods?

Our theaters offered entertainment, but they weren't really places where people could come and spend a lot of time socializing. In driving around the suburban areas and upscale neighborhoods of L.A., Atlanta, and other cities, I'd noticed that there were always black and Hispanic customers in line at the Starbucks cafés.

Curious, I stopped and visited with some of those customers. I asked how far they'd driven to get their Starbucks coffee. Some worked nearby, but quite a few said they had driven five, ten, even twenty or thirty miles because Starbucks offered not only good coffee but also a quiet place where they could meet, talk with friends, read the newspaper, or work on their laptop computers.

Some said they went to Starbucks four or five times a week. It dawned on me that Starbucks CEO Howard Schultz was selling more than premium coffee. He was selling an environment that was welcoming, safe, and highly social. Yet he wasn't selling it in most black neighborhoods.

I decided to see if I could change that. I set up a meeting with Mr. Schultz and his leadership team at the Starbucks headquarters in Seattle. After describing the success we'd had with our Magic Johnson Theatres in urban markets, I told the Starbucks executives about my field research at Starbucks cafés around L.A., Atlanta, Houston, Cleveland, and other cities. I said I'd been impressed with the fact that many black and Hispanic customers were driving so far to visit his stores.

"You have built a loyal customer base in suburbia and affluent city neighborhoods. Let me help you build your business even more by taking you into minority communities," I said. "We are willing to pay for premium coffee and a comfortable place to meet, and we love to hang out."

Howard Schultz noted that he'd grown up in Brooklyn, so he was no stranger to urban neighborhoods. "We thought we would eventually move into those markets," he said.

I offered to help him speed up the process. "Our brand is trusted in the urban market. People know we create secure and welcoming environments. They respect our theaters. They will do the same if we partner with you. We can also help you recruit good employees and show you how to better market your products to minority customers."

I laid it all out there, but I wasn't naive. I knew that Starbucks had never partnered with any other company or individual for one very good reason: it didn't need partners. It was hugely successful. Still, I figured we had nothing to lose in making the pitch.

I could tell that Howard Schultz thought there was merit in the proposal, but he would have to sell it to his board of directors.

"Why don't you come to L.A. and take a look at what we've done in South Central?" I asked.

This is where "brand value" becomes so critical in the business world. We built a beautiful theater. We did whatever it took to make our customers feel safe and welcome. Then we reaped benefits that we never could have anticipated.

Howard Schultz came to visit on a Friday when our Magic Johnson Theatre was showing a new movie: *Waiting to Exhale*. This was a groundbreaking movie aimed directly at the urban market. Based on Terry McMillan's bestselling book, it focused on four well-to-do black women. These were characters cut from real life portrayed by a cast that included Whitney Houston, Angela Bassett, Lela Rochon, and Wesley Snipes. The movie was directed by Forest Whitaker, with the sound track by Kenneth "Babyface" Edmonds.

Waiting to Exhale was the perfect movie for us to be showing that night.

When Howard Shultz arrived to check out the Magic Johnson Theatre, there must have been more than a thousand women lined up to buy tickets and another thousand moving through the doors. It was a sellout crowd, and they were wound up.

They'd been waiting months to see this film. Most had read the book at least once, and they were excited to see it on the big screen. When the movie began, the ladies in the audience jumped right in. They were talking to the characters, cheering them on and offering advice.

"Dump his ass, girlfriend!" was one of the more memorable audience comments of the night.

When Howard and I walked out after the movie, he was smiling. "I've never had a moviegoing experience quite like that," he said. "Your customers were having a great time."

Once the lobby cleared out, I gave him a tour of our "Wall of Fame," where we saluted people in the community alongside black movie stars and celebrities. I also showed him the "Walk of Fame" bearing the names of our patrons.

"This is their theater, and they enjoy it," I said.

Howard went back to Seattle with a new appreciation for the vitality of the urban market. He also saw that the Magic Johnson brand was trusted and respected in that market. Howard measured the value of the brand that I'd fought so hard to build and protect and he convinced his board of directors to agree to the first—and only—partnership deal ever done by Starbucks.

We agreed to a joint partnership for as many as 125 Starbucks shops, most of them in urban neighborhoods. This was a huge deal financially, but it meant even more symbolically. The success of Magic Johnson Theatres led to the Starbucks partnership. We called that partnership Urban Coffee Opportunities, because the goal was to create job opportunities as well as social centers in urban neighborhoods. My association with Starbucks catapulted my business to an entirely new level. It legitimized everything we'd done and everything we'd said about urban America. It has meant hundreds of millions of dollars to my business ventures, but more important, it has put us into a position to keep growing and expanding while providing jobs, services, and products and building wealth in areas that had long been neglected and underserved.

That, my friends, is the *true* measure of brand value.

Brand Maintenance

Zealously protect and build your brand.

They say the best offense is a good defense, so in the spring of 1995, early in my business career, I sat down face-to-face with the leaders of the Crips and the Bloods in South Central L.A.

I asked "a guy who knew a guy" to set up the meeting. Every banker I'd talked to had refused to finance my portion of the movie-theater project because of gang violence in the area. They could not see beyond that threat to the untapped market for movies in the neighborhood.

The money men weren't alone. Everyone I talked to—from snack and soda vendors to neighborhood merchants—wanted to know: "What are you going to do about the gangs?"

Earlier I told you how the Magic Johnson Theatre chain fit my vision for creating a greater sense of community in urban neighborhoods. The vision led me to the movie-theater concept, but it was the strength of my brand that got it built and made it successful.

Skeptics and doubters told me I was crazy for even thinking about putting a sixty-thousand-square-foot, twelve-screen theater complex so close to gang territory. They said there would be shootings and stabbings and my theater would be ruined before the closing credits ran on the first movie.

Gangs have been a fact of life in Los Angeles for decades. Police officials say there are 250 gangs with an estimated 26,000 members. South Central was the scene of riots, killings, and lootings after the 1992 Rodney King trial.

Crenshaw Plaza was at the far edge of most of the violence. What outsiders did not grasp was that the surrounding Baldwin Hills has long been an upper-middle-class neighborhood for black professionals. It is a family-oriented neighborhood where screenwriters, actors, sound engineers, doctors, dentists, and lawyers raise their families and live honorable and productive lives.

I led Sony theater executives on a tour of Baldwin Hills to help them understand the community and its people. Our tour opened their eyes to the potential of the urban market. They had assumed, like anyone else who had never visited the neighborhood, that all of South Central was a combat zone. So many big-brand companies had the same misconception. In fact, there are black people in those neighborhoods with good jobs who can afford everything that suburban residents purchase for their families. They simply choose to live where they feel a sense of community.

Street gangs operate in most of the surrounding South Central. These are much bigger and more sophisticated gangs than those back in Lansing when I was young. On my way to school or work, I'd see old friends and teammates who I knew were getting into trouble. I'd grown up with them or with their brothers and sisters, so I didn't see them as gang members. A lot of the gang members were from poor and broken families. That's not an excuse for joining a gang and getting into drugs and violence, but I understood that some saw no other way out.

One of my goals is to provide young people in urban America

with more opportunities in their neighborhoods. The economic development we bring to minority communities also reduces crime and encourages civic pride. Gang members have welcomed the jobs created by our efforts. Many of them have left the streets and built better lives.

I am not surprised by that because I remember walking to school through gang turf in Lansing and hearing words of encouragement. They didn't try to recruit me or intimidate me. They supported me.

"Stay straight," they'd say. "Keep playin' and make us proud."

I don't claim to be an expert on street gangs in L.A. or anywhere else. I do know that gang members have mothers and sisters and wives and children they care about. My goal with the first Magic Johnson Theatre was to create a safe, comfortable place where all the people of South Central could relax and escape their worries for a few hours.

To accomplish that mission, I played brand defense. I took a meeting. The contact who set it up—who shall remain anonymous—told me that gang leaders demand respect. No problem there; I respect anyone who could easily shut down my businesses.

Ken Lombard, who was then CEO of my company, accompanied me to the meeting with the Crips and Bloods at the Boulevard Café, a landmark at the corner of Crenshaw and Martin Luther King Jr. Boulevard, across the street from the theater site. The gang leaders were friendly and polite as we introduced ourselves after putting a couple of tables together. I got to the point quickly.

"Look, I'm not here to tell you how to run your gangs, but we are building this movie theater in your neighborhood. We want to make it a neutral zone for the safety of everyone inside, including you and your family members."

I reminded them that several members of their gangs had

been hired to work construction on the project and others were applying to work in the theater.

"This will bring jobs to the community. It will be a great place to go and relax. Your families won't have to drive for thirty minutes just to see a movie anymore," I said. "But I need your help to make sure it stays safe so people will keep coming and I can keep it open."

Then I dropped the big one.

"So here's the deal: you and your family and friends are welcome, but you can't wear gang colors or otherwise represent in or around the theater," I said. "We want this to be neutral territory. I hope you understand that and see that it makes sense and that it is for the good of all concerned."

There was no negotiation. No request for concessions or favors. Nobody even asked for Lakers tickets—and I get that from Fortune 500 CEOs all the time. Instead, the gang leaders told me that they appreciated what I was doing for the community. We talked a little more about my plans for the theater. I promised that it would be as nice as any they'd ever seen in the suburbs.

Then, for the next hour we talked about the Lakers and basketball and enjoyed ourselves. At the end of the meeting, they said they would respect my rules. They thanked me for being "a positive brother." And they kept their word. There have been no major gang problems at that theater or any of my other Magic Johnson Theatres.

BRAND PLAYS

Gang members protect their turf. Those South Central Crips and Bloods understood that I was defending my brand when I established the theater as neutral ground. In recent years, we have become so zealous about guarding our brand that we have an entire department known as the "Brand Police." The staff members in this department are responsible for monitoring and managing the brand to make sure that we are always living up to our high standards by outperforming all expectations.

All of our employees are trained to be "brand ambassadors" as well. They are trained to see themselves as guardians and up-holders of the brand. We make certain that everyone is well versed on our mission and our activities so that they can commu-nicate to others who we are, what we stand for, and the high level of performance we strive for in all of our endeavors. We give our brand ambassadors statistics to back up their enthusiasm. Surveys that we have commissioned have found that the Magic Johnson brand:

- Is the number one brand in urban America
- Is perceived as having done more for inner cities than any other brand
- Makes a business more enticing to customers than those not affiliated with the Magic Johnson brand

So you see, we play offense when it comes to our brand too. When we do everything possible to make our branded businesses special, my staff calls it "Magicizing." This entails doing all we can to exceed expectations by catering to our customers' needs and desires.

For example, I wanted our South Central customers to feel at home in their Magic Johnson Theatre. So we did not build an im-personal or generic big-box movie theater. We created an envi-ronment in which our customers are the stars of the show. From the food we serve to the pictures on the wall, this theater was de-signed for their tastes and their culture. Our Wall of Fame fea-tures black actors and actresses as well as local political figures and community leaders.

Sweet drinks such as strawberry and tropical punch are popular among blacks because most of us grew up drinking Kool-Aid rather than soda pop. So we brought in a special selection of flavored drinks not found in most suburban theaters. We also expanded the menu because our customers were more inclined to have dinner with the show. Our theater chain was the first to offer hot sauces and spicy sausages popular with blacks and Hispanics.

Our customers appreciate those personal touches, and the best example was our brick Walk of Fame. While our first movie theater was being built, we discussed having regular patrons sign a wall inside, but then it hit me: "Let's do bricks. We can have our own Walk of Fame."

The sidewalks and entry patio hadn't been poured yet, so the timing was perfect. We sold bricks to benefit a local charity with the donor's name on each brick. They sold out so quickly that we had to order more. The great aspect of it was that whenever the brick donors come to the theater with family and friends, they see their names and truly feel like the theater belongs to them.

That feeling of belonging explains something that I can guarantee you won't find with any other theater chain. We have people who bring visitors to our theaters when they are closed, to give them tours and show them around. We've even had recording artists do their music videos at our theater because it has become a landmark in South Central.

Our theater has been a hit financially too. The *Los Angeles Times* called its success "phenomenal." Other movie-theater operators had tried putting big multiplexes in minority neighborhoods, but they had struggled to make a profit. In our first four weeks, the Magic Johnson Theatre in South Central was one of the top five highest-grossing theaters in the Sony chain. It has continued to be a success, consistently ranking among the top in gross revenues among theaters nationwide.

The theater's popularity helped spur renovations and improved business in the entire retail area around it. Stores in the mall adjacent to the theater reported increases of 25 to 50 percent after we opened because more and more people were attracted to the area.

DEFENDING YOUR BRAND

I don't want to give you the impression that this business lived happily ever after following my meeting with the gang leaders. It was a financial success from opening night, but every business has its day-to-day challenges. The fight to protect your brand never ends.

As opening night approached, I realized that even with the gang leaders buying in, we had to do more to keep the peace. We had to put in a "no hats" policy. Gang members were wearing baseball-type caps in gang colors to show their affiliations. I worried that displays of gang colors could cause conflicts in our theater, so I banned them. We enforced the rule for everyone, which offended some customers who did not understand our concerns for their safety.

Phone calls, e-mails, and letters poured in. In a typical complaint, an older gentleman said we had no right telling people what they could and could not wear. Then, a few weeks later, he wrote us again. He'd gone to a movie with his son, who had explained to him that sports caps were used to indicate gang affiliations. He told his father he was glad they couldn't wear the caps inside our theater because it made him feel safer. "Now I understand," the father said, "because my son showed me."

The sports-cap rule was quickly accepted, but the defense never rests when protecting a brand. Another controversy arose when the movie *Belly* was released. Some critics said the film glorified gang violence and fed into negative views of black people. There were concerns that it might trigger violence. We decided not to show *Belly* just to be on the safe side. I took the heat. Some said this defensive move showed that I wasn't supportive of black filmmakers. Others hinted that I'd sold out.

Most knew me better than that. My concern was for the safety of our customers. One fight or act of violence could have triggered a backlash that might have wiped out all the gains we'd made in creating a first-class, safe environment. I was determined to prove that the urban market was ready for the top brands. So I played strong defense, and I got some bruises for it. In the end, the rewards were worth it—for both our customers and our business brand.

Our success with the Magic Johnson Theatre in South Central L.A. got a lot of attention. We quickly built on that success with urban theaters in other major markets, including Harlem. In 1998, our first year, the first three theaters produced gross revenues of about $20 million! That's the payoff that comes when you play good offense *and* good defense with your brand.

The rewards have been incredible, but I never let my guard down, not even when I go to the movies myself. One night Cookie and I went to see a movie at a Magic Johnson Theatre. We slipped in after the houselights were turned off so we would not cause a distraction. Then, about a half hour into the movie, a cell phone rang. Someone five or six seats in front of us answered it and started a conversation as if he were alone in his living room.

Those seated around us couldn't believe it, and neither could we. It was really rude. The guy was ruining the movie for those around him who had paid to see it. Before someone else lashed out at him, I got up and eased into a seat directly behind the blockhead, who was still talking on his cell phone.

I tapped him on the shoulder and quietly told him that he had to turn his phone off. It was still very dark in the theater. I was scrunched down in the seat. He had no clue that it was me.

"Who are you to tell me that I have to turn my phone off?" he said.

I stood up then and said, "I'm the owner of the theater, and you are going to have to come with me."

He still didn't get it until he followed me out to the hallway. There he saw the light.

"Oh my God, Magic! I am so sorry," he said.

I told him that he was wasting his money and that of the other people in the theater who had paid to see and hear the movie.

"I'm so sorry," he said. "I'll just leave."

"No," I told him. "Go back in there and watch the movie, but turn your phone off so that we can all enjoy the show."

After the movie, Cookie suggested that I get fitted for an usher's uniform. If that's what it takes to protect my brand, I'll even wear the little hat and carry a flashlight.

Bank Financing

Make your bankers believe.

Ten banks turned me down when I went to them for business loans to finance my portion of the first Magic Johnson Theatre project.

At each bank, we'd gather in a big meeting room with everyone from vice presidents to loan officers, tellers, and janitors packed into the room. Every one of them wanted an autograph and a photo with me, and most wanted to talk about the Lakers.

Then we'd sit down to do business. I'd present my business plan, making my case with statistics, census figures, and economic data demonstrating the vitality of our market and how we intended to serve it with a first-class, state-of-the-art twelve-screen multiplex. I'd explain to them that they were missing out on the urban market because even though families there had lower incomes on average than suburban residents, there were far more of them packed into smaller areas and they had fewer entertainment options than suburbanites.

"They have discretionary income to spend, they just don't have any place to spend it in their own neighborhoods," I'd say. "Right now these people have to drive five to ten miles to see a movie. Imagine how loyal they will be to a theater in their own neighborhood."

The bank vice presidents and loan officers would smile and nod. After I finished my presentation, they would say it was nice to meet me and ask if I'd mind signing one more autograph before I left.

A week later, they would call me and politely tell me no.

Welcome to the real world of start-up financing. My experience is nothing new. Earl Graves, founder of *Black Enterprise,* has told me horror stories from his days of searching for financing for his magazine in the 1960s. Since he was a black man, most banks figured he was coming in for a handout. He'd find himself in the office of the bank's charity officer instead of the business loan officer. The bizarre thing was that banks were often willing to give money to minorities for charity but not to loan it to them to start businesses.

Things have gotten better over the years thanks to pioneers such as Earl Graves; J. Bruce Llewellyn; Robert L. Johnson, founder and CEO of Black Entertainment Television; and others of their generation who had to fight to open bank doors. Yet it is still very difficult to get a business loan from a bank, venture capital firm, or any other lender if you don't have a strong track record—and that holds especially true for minorities.

I know what you're thinking: *Magic, you made millions playing basketball, why would you need a business loan?*

Yes, I had a twenty-five-year $25 million contract, and yes, I socked away more money than many players of my era did. Still, I'd already dug deep into my savings to buy a 5 percent share of the Lakers. The $10 million represented roughly half of my entire savings. It proved to be a great investment that today is worth close to $50 million. Still, I was very nervous paying out such a big chunk of my savings.

Most business advisers recommend financing your start-up with "OPM"—other people's money—if you can get it for the right terms and conditions. Your goal should always be to try to minimize your personal financial risk in funding your start-up.

You should try to borrow at rates and conditions that will allow you to repay the loans and investments on time from your cash earnings from the business.

CATCH-32

Most minority entrepreneurs have similar challenges with banks. Being known as an athlete and not a businessman only added to my challenges when I went looking for financing. You will face your own unique challenges.

The coldhearted truth that hits nearly every entrepreneur is that lending institutions and venture capitalists make loans and investments based on the applicant's track record and assets. No track record means no loan. The catch, of course, is that you can't build a track record without getting start-up money.

Banks and bankers told us they liked our Magic Johnson Theatre business plan and the business model. Yet most said their boards of directors—the people who make the final decisions on big loans—were scared of the urban market. Since I didn't have a track record as a successful movie-theater owner, none of the bankers I talked to was willing to take the risk of lending me money to get started.

They aren't lying when they tell you that most banks lend money only to people who don't need it. Even though I was a well-known athlete with ample financial resources, bankers looked at me as a high risk, especially because I was going to invest their money in what they saw as an unproven market: urban America.

At every presentation, we pulled out the data showing that African Americans had more than $600 million in buying power. They lived in more concentrated areas. They had fewer entertainment options. And they were extremely brand-loyal when marketed to with respect.

Still, we could not turn the bankers into believers.

Most of the time, we found that there were no men and women of color in decision-making positions at those banks. The bank executives and their boards of directors seemed to regard all of urban America as a barren wasteland. We tried to educate them, but they weren't buying it.

I had one question that I'd pull out at every meeting with bankers who showed a lack of interest in the market we were targeting: "Have you ever been in urban America? Have you gone to Baldwin Hills to see that black professionals there live in well-kept homes with nice cars in the driveway and the grass mowed?"

There was always an uncomfortable silence when I asked that question. For most, their only knowledge of black neighborhoods came from television news clips of the Rodney King riots. Initially, I was shocked at the lack of understanding among bankers when it came to the urban market. I was naive.

In my years in the NBA, black and white players worked and socialized together. We visited one another's homes and families. The majority of our fans were whites who cheered us on as their team. I guess I just lost track of the real world outside sports. Talking to bankers gave me a reality check. They could not see the potential of the urban market because they had never gone into those underserved neighborhoods.

At the end of the day I was glad that I went through my experiences with the blind bankers. It grounded me and helped me understand that being *Magic*—the former NBA star—was not going to help. In fact, once I got in the door, it was often a hindrance.

To get banks to respect me as a businessperson, I had to prove myself in a whole new game. That realization drove me, and it still drives me today. After that experience, I told everyone at my company that we can't just deliver, we have to overdeliver. We had to do it right with the first Magic Johnson Theatre, because if we didn't, there would not be another opportunity—for me or for those coming behind me. I didn't want the banks to be able to say to the next urban investor, "If Magic couldn't do it, how can you?"

I finally gave up on bankers and tapped my own savings to pay my share of the start-up capital for the first Magic Johnson Theatre. Writing that check for $2.5 million caused me many sleepless nights. I grew up in a family that did not have a lot of extra cash, so I don't take anything for granted. Cookie jokes that I still call the bank every day to make sure my money is safe.

Every entrepreneur has sleepless nights during start-up. If you aren't worrying, you probably aren't paying enough attention. The number one worry is always money: getting it, keeping it, and making more of it. Like many people starting out in business, I had to tap my savings. Entrepreneurs who have had jobs might tap their 401(k) plan from their previous employers. Young people might have to go to their parents for help. I don't recommend it, but I've also heard of people financing start-ups on their credit cards.

First-time minority entrepreneurs often have to get creative because they don't have their own resources, and, as I discovered, banks don't exactly open the vault for them. Still, your neighborhood bank is worth a try. In fact, the one thing banks don't charge for—yet—is listening to business proposals from potential customers.

If you are going to ask a bank for money, you need to understand how they make their lending decisions and what they base them upon. Most of what they want to know is covered in your business plan. They will also be looking at your personal financial history and the all-important "Five Cs," which are:

1. **Character:** Banks, investors, and every other investor and potential partner will examine your personal finances, including your history of repaying college loans, car loans, and home loans. They'll also look to see if you've managed your checking

or money market accounts well or whether you've bounced checks and had overdrafts. They want to know how you performed with other businesses. If, like me, you have no track record in starting a business in the field or market of your proposed start-up, it could be a tough sell.

2. **Capacity:** Banks want to see that your start-up will bring in revenues and enough cash flow so that you can repay the money they lend you on the schedule they set. If you can't sell them on your revenue and profit projections, they won't lend you the money. In my case, with the first Magic Johnson Theatre, the bankers did not believe our projections. That was their mistake, because we exceeded our projections.

3. **Capital:** Banks will expect you to invest at least 20 percent of your own money in the business. They figure if you don't have anything to lose, they will. I was willing to put up my share for the first Magic Johnson Theatre, but the bankers did not buy in.

4. **Conditions:** This is the big picture, including the local and national economy, the competition, and trends in your business field. In my case, other efforts by major chains to locate multiscreen theater complexes in urban areas had not been profitable. So the bankers were skeptical when I said that our plan would work.

5. **Collateral:** When you get a car loan, the bank sees the value of the vehicle as collateral. If you don't make your car loan payment, the bank sends the repo man after its collateral. When you start a business, the bank wants to know the market value of the asset being pledged as collateral. It may include the property you are buying for your business location, plus equipment, vehicles, and other things the bank can take and

sell to get back its money if your business crashes and burns. We had the collateral, but again, the bankers we talked to did not believe in our business model.

Banks are tough on first-time entrepreneurs, and when the overall economy is struggling, they are even tougher. I encourage you to give banks a try, because sooner or later, you are going to need to have a working relationship with a bank. You may not get your start-up money from banks, but you need to learn how to deal with them.

It's their game, and you have to play by their rules. That means putting together a business plan that answers all their questions. It means getting your financial house in order, keeping good records, and showing the bank that you are a reliable person. It also means telling them the straight-up truth and making a strong case for the potential of your business to generate cash flow.

TRUE WEALTH

If this sounds like a lot of work and stress, it is. Yet starting and owning your own business put you on a path to pursue your passion while building true wealth. When I was growing up, I thought bringing home a regular paycheck was a sign of financial security. Being rich was having two cars parked out front and a color television in the family room.

When I was drafted into the NBA and signed my first contract for $400,000 a season, my vision of wealth expanded beyond the two cars and a color TV. Later, I got the $1-million-a-year contract over twenty-five years, and that changed things again. There is no arguing that at that point, I had more money than I had ever dreamed of having. I was blessed, and believe me, I did not take it for granted. For the longest time, I didn't even buy a house because I was so afraid of taking a mortgage. I may have been living in a nice L.A. apartment, but I was still the kid from a blue-collar family in Lansing.

Looking back, I see now that even then I was still drawing a paycheck. It was a big paycheck but a paycheck nonetheless. Even though it was enough to provide security for the rest of my life, my NBA salary was not "true wealth." When I was making $400,000 a year and then $1 million a year, I could buy anything I wanted. I had money, and people thought of me as rich. Still, I wasn't truly wealthy.

True wealth comes with ownership. It comes with a business or investments that generate income even when you are not on the job. There are only so many hours in the day, so if your income depends on the amount of work you can do personally, it is always limited by your capacity for that work.

You can certainly make a fine living and build up a strong financial base if you are paid enough for what you do. Yet true wealth lies in generating income regardless of what you are doing at any given time. After I was drafted by the Lakers, a friend urged me to buy a bar with my signing bonus. My Lansing business mentor Joel Ferguson intervened and offered great advice.

"Put your money into real estate and other investments that make money while you sleep," he said. "That is how you build true wealth."

I got my first close look at true wealth during the 1992 Olympics in Barcelona. As a member of the U.S. Olympic basketball "Dream Team" I was invited to a party on a 200-foot yacht owned by Micky Arison, who three years later became the controlling partner in the group that owned the Miami Heat.

I didn't know Mr. Arison prior to the party. We had just met when one of his crew members came up and said that the air-conditioning on the yacht was not working.

"Okay," he said, "let's just move everyone to the other boat."

He has two? I thought. *How much money does my host have?*

The answer to that is an estimated $6.1 billion, according to *Forbes* magazine. Micky Arison is the CEO and chairman of Carnival Corporation, operator of the world's largest cruise ship line. He is one of the world's richest people, and, it is safe to say, he has more than two big boats.

Meeting Micky was an eye-opening experience for me. It taught me the difference between being rich and having true wealth. I even thanked him for the lesson at the party, and he got a kick out of that.

I wasn't kidding. You have to know what is attainable before you can decide what it is that you want. Once I met Micky and learned how he had taken his family's cruise ship business and turned it into an empire, I saw how it was possible to build that sort of true wealth.

Is it possible for me and you to do that? I wouldn't count either of us out. I do know, however, that kids who grow up in neighborhoods where there are no merchants, no accountants, no nurses or doctors or lawyers, end up with a limited vision for their own lives. My goal is to restore their urban communities so that they will believe in themselves and those who control the money will believe in them too.

Private Investors

The big money lies with the big players in private funds.

J ust a few months after I had no luck with bankers while trying to raise $2.5 million for my movie theater, I found myself standing in front of ten strangers asking for $150 million for another project.

A hundred and fifty million dollars!

I was a wreck. This was a whole new financial realm for me. Going to the bankers for the theater money had been hard enough.

I had never heard of the California Public Employees' Retirement System (CalPERS) until a few months before I met with its ten-member Investment Committee and asked them to give me and my partner $150 million.

After we opened the first Magic Johnson Theatre, our success brought a lot of attention to the urban market. We wanted to keep the momentum going. This time, we had a bigger goal. We planned to build entire shopping centers. To finance that project my business advisers and my then CEO, Ken Lombard, felt we needed to move up to a higher level in the financial world.

BEYOND BANKS

Banks are just one of many sources of funds to tap when starting a business. If your start-up requires only a few thousand dollars, you may be able to borrow the money from your savings, from family members, or from friends. Again, I don't recommend maxing out your credit cards to start your business unless you are certain that it will begin generating enough cash to pay off that high-interest debt within a very short period.

Small start-up loans are available from a variety of public and private sources. The U.S. Small Business Administration (www .sba.gov) has a whole menu of loan programs for small businesses that are generally administered by banks and other institutions. The SBA's Basic 7(a) Loan Program is for small start-ups that may not be eligible for business loans from banks. It can be used to cover most start-up costs, including working capital, machinery and equipment, furniture and fixtures, land, and building expenses.

If you need "brick-and-mortar" financing for a small business, the SBA's CDC/504 Program offers long-term, fixed-rate financing to acquire real estate or machinery or equipment for expansion or modernization. Another popular program is the SBA's Microloan Program, which provides short-term loans of up to $35,000 to small businesses and not-for-profit child care centers for working capital or the purchase of inventory, supplies, furniture, fixtures, machinery, and/or equipment.

There are microloan centers around the country. Often they are administered by nonprofit intermediaries such as churches, credit unions, and neighborhood groups. Check with your local SBA office for those in your area.

The SBA also licenses one-stop funding shops called Small Business Investment Companies (SBICs) and Specialized Small

Business Investment Companies (SSBICs). These are for entrepreneurs who may be at a social or economic disadvantage. These investment companies have their own private funds, usually several million dollars, and they can borrow more from an SBA-sponsored trust at good rates. SBICs will usually take on more risk than banks or regular venture funds. Often, however, they want their borrowers to be capable of repaying a loan, which means they look for businesses that will have immediate cash flow and profitability. There are more than four hundred SBICs and SSBICs, and they have $21 billion in total funds, so keep this option in mind.

Remember, though, that they can be expensive. They charge interest and may want stock in your company as equity. Their loans are usually in the $150,000 to $5 million range.

The National Association of Investment Companies (NAIC) in Washington, D.C., represents SSBICs as well as other investment companies focusing on minority investments. The NAIC (www.naicvc.com) sells its membership directory for $35. The National Association of Small Business Investment Companies (NASBIC) is a trade group that consists of SBICs and SSBICs exclusively. You can check it out at www.nasbic.org.

Many communities now have Minority Business Development Centers and small-business entrepreneur programs. Many are connected to schools, junior colleges, and universities or to local business organizations. Your local chamber of commerce should have information on business loan programs in your area.

HIGH FINANCE

To finance our investment in urban retail centers, we needed the sort of money that wasn't handed out by small-business lenders.

So my team introduced me to the world of high finance and pension funds. They explained to me that a public pension fund contains the money put into a retirement plan for the employees of school systems or city, state, or federal government departments and agencies. That pool of money and assets is collected to pay the pension and health benefits of employees when they retire. The public pension fund's managers try to grow those assets by investing them.

Pension funds and the people who control them are power players in the world of finance and the stock market. Around the world, pension funds hold more than $20 trillion in assets, which makes them the globe's largest investment group—bigger than mutual funds, insurance companies, currency reserves, hedge funds, or private equity.

Once I had a feel for pension funds and how they work, my team introduced me to a San Francisco business leader who felt the same way we did about the untapped potential in urban neighborhoods. Victor MacFarlane and I both grew up in blue-collar midwestern families, and we both believe in creating economic opportunities in urban communities.

Victor is a self-made man who believes that every child should share in the American dream. He and his three siblings were raised by their single mother in Middleton, Ohio, where she worked at Wright-Patterson Air Force Base. He first worked as a real estate analyst for Aetna Life & Casualty's property division. Victor left the safety of Aetna to start his own San Francisco real estate investment firm in 1987 because he wanted to do business in places where many big corporations feared to tread.

Like me, he saw potential in the South Central neighborhood after the 1992 riots. Most other investment companies couldn't see beyond the burned-out buildings, the gangs, and the crime. They missed the fact that there were heavily populated neighborhoods where minority professionals and white-collar workers lived.

I asked this real estate pro to help us find a way to do business in those areas. Our plan wasn't complicated. We wanted to go in and buy up commercial areas that had been neglected or run down, fix them up, attract new big-brand businesses, and revitalize the area. The goal was to rebuild the community while also getting a good return on our investment.

We figured it would take $150 million to renew urban shopping centers and attract major tenants such as good grocery stores, and big-brand restaurants and shops. Victor had been a consultant with CalPERS since 1991, so we decided to go to it for the money to buy the Ladera Center to start.

Victor felt that "real estate should follow bodies": we should invest in properties surrounded by people with disposable income who are looking to dispose of that income nearby.

SWEATIN' IT

Once we had our proposal ready, we set up a meeting with the Investment Committee at CalPERS, and it was one of the scariest experiences of my life. Forget about meeting with gang members, those ten people from CalPERS had me terrified.

You'd think that all those years of running around at full speed against tough, fast, and intensely competitive professional athletes in front of thousands of screaming fans would have made it easy for me to stand in a suit and talk about money with just ten people quietly sitting at a conference table.

CalPERS was then the biggest public pension fund in the United States. Back in 1995, when we went to it seeking $150 million, the fund's Investment Committee controlled $96.9 *billion*.

I stood in front of that powerful group drenched to my socks. I really hadn't planned on talking basketball, but I was so nervous that when they asked me, "Why are you here?," I just said exactly what I was thinking:

"I've played against Larry Bird and Isiah Thomas in world championship games, but I've never been so nervous in my life!"

They laughed, thank the Lord. Then they got right down to business.

"We like your business plan, and we like what you want to do in urban America, but why should we give you the money? Nobody else has ever come to us with such a proposal. How do you know it will work when you have no track record?"

I froze up at that first bunch of questions. I could hear my own heart beating. Finally, all my preparation with Victor and Ken kicked in and I began making the case by talking about the population density and the high incomes of professionals in the underserved Ladera and Baldwin Hills neighborhoods.

It seemed as though I was not getting through to them. They kept coming back to the fact that "your company has no track record with this type of big project."

I countered by telling them about the Magic Johnson Theatre and the fact that its successful numbers had surprised everyone in the investment and banking communities. Our urban theater was even outperforming those in the suburbs.

There's more of that gold out there waiting to be mined, I told the CalPERS people. I also talked about social responsibility and the great need to rebuild communities in urban areas so that cities remain healthy.

"This community has annual purchasing power of $50 million per square mile, but the people have very few places nearby to shop, eat, or look for entertainment," I said. "Urban neighborhoods have been underserved and overlooked by retail developers and investors, so this area is ripe for retail products and services."

I told them that we could revitalize the area while providing hundreds of new jobs in the construction, retail, and service sectors. "Our project will have a lasting ripple effect, bringing more economic development and more entrepreneurs into the neighborhood," I said.

I could see some of the ten Investment Committee members nodding their heads in agreement with what I said. It might have been my imagination, but it seemed as if some were shaking their heads in disagreement too. This was unfamiliar turf for them. They had a lot of people to answer to for their investment decisions. Still, as the largest pension fund in the state and nation with many minority investors, they were also aware of their social responsibilities.

After my presentation and the questions and answers, they thanked me and told me they would be in touch with their decision. I didn't know if it was a good sign or not, but this time nobody asked for an autograph or a photo.

Later, Victor told me that the CalPERS people had seemed very nervous. The Investment Committee deliberated for several weeks, and then it took our proposal to the board of trustees for its consideration.

When the committee members called us back to discuss their decision, we braced ourselves for bad news. In their opening comments, they said they were impressed with the numbers we'd shown them. They praised our passion. Then they said they had "reservations" because there was really no precedent for this sort of undertaking in urban communities.

We aren't going to get the funding, I thought.

I was wrong.

"We're going to give you $50 million to start out, and then we'll see how you do," the committee chairman said. "If you do well with that, we'll look at giving you the other $100 million."

Fifty million was not a bad start. We took the money and ran with it. We purchased the run-down Ladera Center for well under $50 million and used the rest of the money to transform it into a vital community retail center. We added our branded T.G.I. Friday's restaurant and a Magic Johnson Starbucks. We also invited the L.A. grocery store magnate Ron Burkle to put a Super Ralphs grocery in our revitalized shopping center.

We were determined to show the CalPERS board members and all of those who had doubted us that a first-class retail center could succeed in an urban community. We knocked their socks off. We took the Ladera Center's occupancy rate from 40 percent to 100 percent and sold it for a substantial return. That deal was just the beginning of our strategy focusing on investments in urban communities.

Victor and I were among the first to see the benefits of using pension funds for profitable developments that help underserved urban neighborhoods. Since we pioneered the concept, pension funds have been used to revitalize urban areas such as the Hollywood neighborhood around the Kodak Theatre that you see on television during the Academy Awards. They were also used to give boosts to Times Square and Harlem's 125th Street in New York City as well as downtown Los Angeles and Boston's Chinatown. All those projects made money for the pension funds that invested in them, and the communities have benefited too.

Victor MacFarlane and I proved to institutional investors, who put money into pension funds, that investing in urban America makes economic sense. Harvard Business School professor Michael E. Porter noted in a 1995 report that our nation's inner cities were ripe for that kind of investment. Victor and I were glad to show them how to do it. We convinced the pension fund investors that our team knew those communities and the people in them. Thanks to our success, billions of dollars have flowed into urban neighborhoods. The biggest winners were the people living in the areas where we have spurred economic development. They now have wonderful and safe places nearby in which to work, shop, eat, and get together with friends.

Because of our success with the Ladera Center, CalPERS too has reaped rewards. The CalPERS Investment Committee bought in to our faith in urban America too. We received another $100 million from it to invest in minority communities. Other entrepreneurs and pension funds saw what we were doing and

have poured billions of dollars in retail development into underserved areas. CalPERS alone has put out more than $3 billion for
economic development in urban communities!

The lesson here is not to be intimidated by the numbers or by
the folks who control the money. I was turned down by one
banker after another in my early business ventures. Yet a few
months later, another group of financiers handed us $50 million!
The right deal at the right time and right place will sell itself. If
you've got a big deal, go to the big moneylenders, and let them
know why you belong on their team.

Partnerships

**A good partner can help you build
your business faster and farther.**

My friend and business adviser Warren Grant introduced me to Bobby Turner at a Lakers game in 1998, but our relationship got off to a funny start.

Let me offer my first lesson on partnerships: *Clear communication is critical!*

I knew that Bobby was a serious player in commercial real estate and high finance, so, during a lull in that game, I asked him what sort of projects he had going.

Bobby answered just as something exciting happened on the court and the crowd cheered. I couldn't hear him very well. It sounded as if he made a joke about my first name. I thought I heard him say he was working on "an Earvin fund."

"That's great," I said, trying to humor him.

About three quarters later in the game, I decided to play along: "So, Bobby, what exactly is an 'Earvin fund'?"

Bobby laughed. "No, Magic, I said *urban* fund."

Several hundred million dollars in profits later, we still laugh about that first miscommunication.

When it comes to partnerships, Bobby and I might be described as an odd couple. He came from the world of real estate and high finance. I came from the world of sports and entertainment. Still, we share the entrepreneurial instinct, and at that Lakers game in 1998, I learned that Bobby and I share something else critical to any successful partnership: a vision.

We believe that it makes financial *and* social sense to invest in urban America.

Bobby likes to say that Canyon-Johnson Urban Funds looks for a "double-bottom-line" return: we do well financially while doing good things for society. Our ability to work together as the double team for that double bottom line has made for a great partnership.

We have invested about $1.5 billion in projects designed to provide strong financial returns for investors while raising the quality of life in urban communities. We have invested in and helped transform neighborhoods in Atlanta, Baltimore, Brooklyn, Chicago, Cleveland, Las Vegas, Los Angeles, Baltimore, Miami, Milwaukee, San Diego, Tennessee, and Washington, D.C.—and we are just getting started.

Our fund targets investments in communities characterized by the "Six Ds" of urban revitalization:

- Density: 250,000 residents within five miles
- Diversity: at least 40 percent diverse
- Demand: strong market fundamentals for retail and housing
- Developer: committed local development sponsor
- D-leadership: committed to and supportive of urban revitalization
- Do good: financial mandate with a social and environmental responsibility

Before we started our partnership fund, I was using my brand as currency to transact business and bring change to urban neighborhoods. With the Canyon-Johnson funds, we are using much larger sums of money to transform communities in an even bigger way.

We have gone where developers were afraid to go. Together, Bobby and I have worked to create more than 11,000 construction jobs and 5,000 permanent jobs in urban communities. We have built more than 6,000 affordable housing units and more than 2.5 million square feet of retail space in neighborhoods that had been underserved.

Our revitalization efforts have helped reduce crime in those communities. Lives have been uplifted and opportunities created. We are bringing social change along with economic growth, and that is why governors, mayors, and community leaders are inviting us into their cities to do business.

In the spring of 2008, Bobby and I brought in another great team member, former California state treasurer Phil Angelides, a veteran commercial real estate investor. Phil is helping us respond to the need for rental housing in urban areas where residents have been particularly hard hit by the mortgage and banking crises and the crash in the housing market. He leads the Canyon-Johnson Urban Communities Fund.

We created the fund after seeing that the next five years or so would bring a growing need for affordable rental housing for immigrants, minorities, and "echo boomer" residents in urban communities. The UCF will focus on acquiring, improving, and greening urban rental housing across the nation.

Our goal was to raise $2 billion with institutional partners to create more and better rental housing for working-class professionals such as teachers, nurses, firefighters, and construction workers. Bobby and I saw a gap in many urban markets between home ownership and low-income and subsidized rental housing. So we are moving to fill that gap while getting strong returns for our investors.

PARTNER UP

Bobby has helped me take my business to levels I never could have reached on my own. He will tell you that I've done the same for him and his business. That's what makes our partnership work. We each understand our roles. We appreciate what the other partner brings to the table.

Minority entrepreneurs often start at a disadvantage. It can be more difficult for us to break into a field or a market because traditionally we have not had equal access to higher education, financing, and social networks. Finding an established partner can help move things forward for a minority entrepreneur—and any other businessperson looking to grow.

Yet a partnership, like a marriage, should be made only after you are certain of a good and lasting match.

Researchers from the Kohler Center for Entrepreneurship at Marquette University examined nearly two thousand companies and found that among the very top performers only 6 percent were owned by one individual while 94 percent had three or more partners. In fact, partnerships are four times more likely to succeed than sole proprietorships, according to the National Federation of Independent Business.

Yet BizStats (www.bizstats.com) says that only 6 percent of small businesses are partnerships. Why is that? Well, entrepreneurs, especially minority entrepreneurs, tend to think of themselves as independent, self-reliant types. After all, many entrepreneurs start their businesses so they can be their own bosses and reap the full benefits of their own hard work.

And that's perfectly fine. Going it alone can be a wonderful and rewarding route. I've done ventures on my own, and I expect to do even more of them with the help of those who work on my team.

Still, I could not have raised $2 billion to invest in urban

America if it wasn't for my partnership with Bobby Turner, who needed to be convinced that I would be a good partner. I understood his skepticism. High finance and real estate are his domains. He was the big man on that campus. He had been very successful, and his investors trust him with nearly $20 billion to invest.

However, when Bobby tried to take his suburban strategies into the urban neighborhood of Harlem, he hit a few snags. It was then that he realized his *urban* projects might really work better as *Earvin* projects.

PIONEERING PARTNERSHIPS

Bobby and I met just as my team was breaking new ground in the urban market, thanks to my movie theaters and my first Starbucks stores. I had established credibility with the people who live, work, and make their purchases in that market. Yet I didn't have the infrastructure to move as quickly as I wanted to.

Bobby had that infrastructure as well as the expertise and the financial resources. He'd been a major player in the world of commercial real estate for about seventeen years. He'd done more than $7 billion in transactions all over the country.

So what brought us together? Bobby has a story to explain that. Like most in his business, Bobby focused his real estate dealings on suburban areas for most of his career. That's where the growth was. Up until 1996, his Canyon Capital fund had invested $3 billion in 210 deals with a total value of $7 billion—all in suburban properties. Then, that year, his fund paid $3 million for a three-block parcel—six and a half acres of land—between 116th and 119th Streets on the upper east side of Manhattan.

Now, if you don't know New York City, you might be inclined to think that $3 million is a bargain price for three full blocks in one of the greatest cities—and most expensive real estate markets—in the world. But this piece of property was an old abandoned wire factory, closed for sixty years, and it was in Harlem.

Back in 1996, most of Harlem was still viewed as undesirable by big real estate developers and major-brand retailers. When other real estate investors heard that Bobby had purchased the industrial tract in Harlem, they told him he had overpaid.

"By how much?" Bobby asked.

"Three million dollars," they said.

To his credit, Bobby understood the conventional wisdom, but he had done the numbers too. He realized that there were a million people living within a mile of the old Washburn Wire Company site. My future partner grasped that even though Harlem residents did not have as much income per capita as suburban residents, there were *many* more people packed into the neighborhood. The density of the population more than made up for the income difference!

Those Harlem residents had $1 billion in disposable income, yet they were forced to spend 60 percent of it outside their neighborhood because there were so few Harlem stores serving coffee, selling groceries, or stocking household goods.

Bobby saw the same thing that I had seen: commercial and residential developers were missing the boat by neglecting urban America. The greater population densities of city neighborhoods translates to greater spending power for their residents—as much as six times that of suburbanites spread out across a wider area.

Developing new properties in the suburbs had also become more difficult because of no-growth and slow-growth policies. At the same time, leaders in urban areas were welcoming commercial development to increase jobs and strengthen the tax base. Inner-city leaders were offering financial incentives to developers in the form of tax abatements or tax increment financing.

Bobby was on to something with that first Harlem property.

He decided that Canyon Capital would build a Home Depot and a PriceCostco on the neighborhood's old wire factory property.

What could be better for the residents of Harlem? Bobby thought.

To build his retail center in Harlem, he needed to get a zoning change, and for that he needed public approval. He held a meeting with elected leaders, neighborhood activists, and Harlem residents to talk about the plan.

At that meeting, he got an education in the difference between suburban and urban development.

"One of the council people said that I was there trying to make money off the community. I said that was true but my project would also bring money into the community in the form of jobs and tax revenues, as well as providing goods and services that weren't easily available," Bobby told me.

"Then another person at the meeting said, 'The problem is that you are telling me what I want instead of asking me what I need,' " Bobby recalled.

One woman stood up and said, "Mr. Turner, I want you to stop talking and to start listening."

She told him that she was worried about the hours of operation of the Home Depot.

Uh-oh, Bobby thought.

"With all due respect, Home Depot is investing fifty million dollars and hiring three hundred people. I don't think they will accept a cut in their standard operating hours," Bobby said.

"Once again, you aren't listening," the woman said. "And you are showing that you don't understand Harlem. I don't want shorter hours; I want that place open *twenty-four hours a day, seven days a week,* because as long as it is open and there is a lot of traffic, the drug dealers and the prostitutes will stay away!"

At that point, Bobby realized that he was dealing with a whole new set of rules and a community he did not fully understand.

"That was a wake-up call for me," he told me. "I thought I was a pretty smart developer, but I saw that the skill sets are different when dealing with a minority community. I saw that developers and retailers had been arrogant in assuming that the urban consumer is the same as the suburban consumer.

"I realized that to deploy capital in urban neighborhoods successfully, I needed someone who was trusted there, someone who had earned not just goodwill but great will in those communities, and someone who understood that our projects could benefit the residents while also turning a profit for our investors."

Bobby understood that the urban consumer was very savvy and wary too. If he took on a partner, it had to be someone with a great deal of credibility as well as a businessman who would carry his own weight.

The more Bobby and I talked, the more we realized that we'd make a great team. He came in with incredible financial and real estate expertise, the huge buying power of his funds, and a great track record in developing profitable projects in suburban areas.

My theaters and Starbucks stores were exceeding all expectations and sending a message that the urban community was ripe for investment—if the developer had the respect and trust of its residents.

DEEP POCKETS

Once we decided that we were a good match to lead economic development in underserved communities, all we needed was the money to do it. When Bobby told me how much he could raise with his investors, I was in awe.

I am *still* in awe. He is an All-World player when it comes to raising investment funds. Yet Bobby appreciated what I brought to the game too. His first experience with the Harlem site taught him that successful urban investing required a new approach.

"Past performance in suburban markets is no indication of future success in urban markets," he said.

To be as successful in inner-city neighborhoods such as Harlem and South Central, Bobby needed a better grasp of the dynamics: the needs and goals of their residents, safety issues, and the political environments. He saw that I had success in those markets and that my brand was welcomed in them.

By the time we sat down to discuss working together, I was in the early stages of my great joint venture with Starbucks. We had opened our first Starbucks in Ladera not far from the first Magic Johnson Theatre and then another at 125th Street and Lenox Avenue in Harlem.

Starbucks executives explained to Bobby that they had been considering urban areas for future development but I had convinced them to accelerate their plans. My knowledge of the community and its needs was a major contribution to the partnership.

Bobby also saw that I could bring our projects to the forefront in the media and in the public consciousness. It's a bonus of great value for my partners when I go on television with Jimmy Kimmel, Jay Leno, or David Letterman and talk about our business ventures. It's also a benefit that I can bring together mayors, ministers, and other major political, social, and financial figures to get them excited and involved in our projects in urban America.

Bobby sometimes gripes that the biggest challenge of our partnership is staying on schedule because so many people want autographs or to have photos taken with me. Yet he knows that I bring more than a good pen and a big smile to the table. The partnerships that I had already established meant that I could bring those respected brands into our projects too.

PARTNERING

When we first talked about becoming partners, I assured Bobby that I would be fully engaged. I had learned a lesson in my earlier partnership with Earl Graves and our Pepsi-Cola distributorship. I had been committed to that partnership too, but my "day job" with the Lakers had kept me from doing all that I needed to do.

I told Bobby that I would be at every meeting and would play an active role by pitching the projects to residents and local organizations as well as local government. I would find out what people wanted, what they were worried about, and what we could do to make their lives better, I promised him.

Once Bobby and I were sold on each other, we put together our strategy to sell to other investors. We focused on retail, residential, and mixed-use projects in neighborhoods that were 40 percent minorities with 250,000 or more people living in a five-mile radius.

We teamed with midsize to small developers with roots in those communities, rather than bringing in major developers from the outside. Unlike typical developers in suburbia, we didn't set out to build what we wanted and then expect people to like it. We talked to residents and listened to their needs and desires for their communities.

Once we developed that strategy, the next step was to convince investors that our vision for an urban fund made financial sense. Based on Bobby's experiences raising money for suburban developments, he figured it would take about six months to raise the $300 million that we'd set as our goal.

I am usually Mr. Optimist, but I remembered all those bankers who had taken my autograph but held on to their money.

"I think it'll take us at least two years to raise that kind of money," I told Bobby.

We were both right.

It took two years *and* six months.

As I'd feared, in 1999 people were still very leery of investing in urban America. It was tough. We had a great plan and a great strategy for carrying it out. We understood the marketplace. We had deals in the pipeline ready to roll. Still, it took a while to convince investors that urban markets could be as rewarding as the suburbs.

After we put together our $300 million fund, we invested in thirteen projects in ten states. We earned a 20 percent rate of return internally when we sold them. That success meant that by the time we launched our second Canyon-Johnson fund in 2005, eager investors were lined up. This time, we received commitments totaling $1 billion in one month, even though we were seeking $600 million!

With nearly $2 billion in committed capital from our investors in 2008, Canyon-Johnson Urban Funds is the nation's largest private equity fund focused solely on revitalizing ethnically diverse communities in urban areas. I am proud of that, and I am proud to be a good partner to Bobby Turner.

TEAM PLAY

Oddly enough, my relationship with Bobby often reminds me of another one from my NBA days. Bobby and Kareem Abdul-Jabbar don't look alike at all, but the things I learned while playing with Kareem have helped me in my partnership with Bobby.

When I came into the NBA as a rookie, the Lakers were Kareem's team. I was the boisterous, enthusiastic, jumping-up-and-down kid fresh out of college. I got a lot of media attention as the flashy rookie. Still, I focused on finding ways to use my strengths to complement those of Kareem, who was a force of nature on the court.

My role, I decided, was to get the ball to Kareem. I've tried to do the same with Bobby. I open doors for him in urban neighborhoods so he can fully deploy his talents and resources. Being a good partner means understanding your own strengths and weaknesses as well as those of the other party. I understand what

I can contribute and what Bobby can contribute—and what each of us needs to do to make it all work.

It's crucial that neither of us let our egos get in the way of our ultimate mission. I never minded staying in the shadows so that Kareem could be the star, and I don't mind doing the same with Bobby. I may be better known as a celebrity athlete, but make no bones about it: in the world of real estate financing, Bobby Turner is the All-Star. I am very grateful to have him as a partner.

IN GOOD TIMES AND BAD

The most important thing in any partnership is to make sure you share the same philosophy and vision and that you agree on how to implement them. As Bobby describes it, "It's like a marriage. It is easy to get along in the good times, but the question is whether your partner will be there for you in the bad times. You want a partner with integrity and morality, someone who is willing to listen and be flexible. And, like marriage, a successful business partnership is a never-ending set of compromises."

A good partner shares your goals and works just as hard as you do to accomplish them. Now that I have had success in business partnerships, I get many requests to form them. I have learned to be just as cautious in choosing my partners as Bobby and others were with me.

Minority entrepreneurs, in particular, need to be wary of potential partners who see us only as figureheads to help secure minority contracts. There is nothing wrong with that being one of the goals, but we need to make certain that we are full and active partners who participate in business decisions and share fully in both the work and the rewards.

As my own business dealings have become more complex, I make certain that new partnerships do not create conflicts with existing partnerships. That means looking behind and looking ahead with due diligence before partnering. Your good name and your company's brand should always be protected.

Partnerships should always add value to your brand. I look for partners who buy in to my brand and my vision for economic development in urban America. Ken Smikle, the president of Target Market News, the Chicago-based marketing research firm that monitors black consumer trends, told *Black Enterprise* that my success with Starbucks would help other African-American entrepreneurs break into the urban market.

"He's opened the door for creating partnerships with major retailers interested in black consumers," Smikle told *B.E.* "Many are interested, but they don't understand [the market] and frankly are a little frightened by it. So there's a possibility that because of his success, corporations will look for a Magic to help them do their deals in the urban community."

That's great to hear. I encourage all entrepreneurs to build and grow their business by doing the double team with like-minded partners who will help them build collectively on their individual successes, creating new market opportunities for both parties—and building stronger communities in the process.

Finding the Right Employees

The quality of the people you hire determines how successful you become.

Lakers owner Jerry Buss introduced me to Eric Holoman in 1987 at a party celebrating our championship season. Eric and I talked basketball for about five minutes, and then we talked business.

It's been that way with us ever since.

Back then Eric was running his family's food franchise operation, and later he worked in the financial industry. I never gave him the chance to talk about basketball because I kept peppering him with questions about running franchises and the workings of the financial world.

More than twenty years after our first meeting, Eric and I are still talking business. Now we talk about *our* business. In 2007 I hired Eric to be president of Johnson Development Corporation, which we later fully incorporated into Magic Johnson Enterprises. He directs the day-to-day operations and oversees strategy, finance, and business development, as well as all of our partnerships.

TEAM BUILDING 101

It seems a little crazy now, but we spent more than two years searching for the right person for the president's job at my company after Starbucks hired away Ken Lombard and made him president of Starbucks Entertainment in the spring of 2004. I interviewed a dozen or so highly qualified people, but there always seemed to be something missing.

I don't hire people to work for my company. I hire them to *be* my company. My business—any business—goes only where its employees take it. If you have trustworthy, honest, hardworking, entrepreneurial-minded people working for you, your business will have those same characteristics. That's why I make sure that every person we hire understands and shares my vision, my mission, and my passion. Those elements make up our corporate culture and define our brand, driving everything we do.

The quality of the people you hire determines how successful your business will be. This is especially true for your top executives, but it applies to everyone you bring in. The Lakers always had talent, but we won championships in the seasons when we melded together and created a single identity focused on sharing both the work and the glory. From those championship teams, I learned that once you create a culture with a strong single focus, it empowers everyone on the team.

The success of your business will depend to a great extent on how well you and your executive team attract, hire, and develop talented, creative, and enthusiastic people. It is your job to define their positions and then to give them room to expand beyond those definitions and grow individually—so that you can all grow collectively.

I look for and hire entrepreneurial people, and then I encourage them to use their talents to achieve their goals within our organizations. I don't want to control them; I want my business to ride on the jet stream created by their energy and creativity.

Hiring people is part art, part science, and, honestly, a roll of the dice. By getting to know each person you hire, you save yourself and your other employees a lot of grief, and your company will reap the rewards. This is especially crucial in the early going. When you are starting a company and you have only a few employees, it's very important to find people who can grow and adapt with the business. Some of them may even take your business in directions that you never dreamed of.

DEFINING THE POSITION

As an NBA player, I defined my role before each game. I studied our opponents to see how we matched up. Then I decided what I needed to do in each game to be the best teammate I could be.

Sometimes that meant I needed to be a scorer. Other times, I had to focus on defense or on getting the ball to the teammates with the best opportunities to score. It was important to define each player's role and then to adjust those roles as the game unfolded.

As your company grows, you must redefine each hired position. We began interviewing candidates for the president's position only after we determined the qualities required. We wanted someone with a background in finance, someone who had run a business, someone who could operate in the political arena—a detail-oriented person with strong self-discipline. Most of all, we wanted someone passionate about economic development in urban markets.

I liked all of the people we talked to about the job, but none of them struck me as a perfect match and I didn't want to settle for less. I had started to worry that maybe I had set the bar too high. Then a mutual friend said at lunch one day, "What about Eric?"

Most experts will tell you that hiring one of your best friends to run your business will likely produce one of three results—all of them bad:

1. You will lose your friend.
2. You will lose your company.
3. You will lose your friend *and* your company.

I've heard other entrepreneurs say—only half in jest—that they would gladly pay most friends and family members *not* to work for them. It can be tempting to hire those close to you because you are comfortable with them, but the dynamics of working together can put tremendous strain on your relationship. Could you fire your sister if her position became obsolete or if she did something that endangered the finances of your business?

Things can go sour quickly if you hire a friend or family member simply because of the relationship and your comfort level with the person. That was not the case with Eric Holoman. I was intrigued but wary when a mutual friend suggested him. I scrutinized Eric's qualifications more carefully than those of any other applicant.

Yet the more I looked at Eric's business background, the more I wondered why I hadn't thought of him in the first place. It was as if we'd drawn up the qualifications with him in mind. Eric grew up in Baldwin Hills, a great neighborhood of black professionals near South Central L.A. His father, a pioneering banker, nourished his entrepreneurial spirit. Eric has a degree in finance from the University of Southern California, but he has also had invaluable real-world experience as both an entrepreneur and as a corporate executive in the financial world.

He had served as president of his own business, Holoman Food Services, overseeing the operation of seventeen Church's Fried Chicken franchises in minority neighborhoods around L.A. He'd been a senior investment specialist and vice president of high-net-worth sales for the Bank of America before joining Wells Fargo, where he was head of the private mortgage bank in Los Angeles.

Eric also had intimate knowledge of the workings of government because he served on the board of the Los Angeles city employees' retirement system and had long been active in local politics. Eric knew all the players, and he knew how to get things done when dealing with politicians and government bureaucracies.

As I reviewed Eric's qualifications, it struck me that I shouldn't rule out a highly qualified person just because he was my friend. Eric and I became close because we shared a lifelong interest in business and we wanted to revitalize urban communities.

Every one of the people I interviewed for the president's position at Johnson Development Corporation had impressive qualifications and experience. Eric had those credentials and more. He had my three biggest requirements:

1. A shared vision and sense of mission
2. Total trustworthiness
3. An entrepreneurial spirit

When you hire entrepreneurial people, you don't have to worry about motivating them. It's in their blood. Now, it's true that natural-born entrepreneurs dream of having their own business one day, but that's okay too because you can always partner with them down the road. I try to keep them around as long as possible, though, by giving them the power to develop new businesses within the company.

It works for me and it also works for Starbucks, where CEO

Howard Schultz and other top executives have always encouraged their teams to keep reinventing the Starbucks experience.
The company began selling special jazz and blues CDs after a
music-savvy store manager who had been in the recording industry began putting together a "tape of the month" for customers at
his store. He told Starbucks executives about the popularity of his
tapes. They researched the idea and found that customer comment cards had often suggested that Starbucks sell music too.
Based on that, a new line of music was launched, creating a whole
new revenue stream for the business and giving people another
reason to come into Starbucks.

GOOD MATCH

Recently, Eric called my cell phone while he and his wife were
looking at the video from their 1990 wedding. They were laughing because there is a scene on that video of Eric and me talking
about our plans to do business together someday. Long before
we teamed up, we shared our big dreams and encouraged each
other, talking for hours about business ideas.

Eric was an athlete too, so he has the same sort of competitive
drive. There's another danger in hiring a good friend to run
your business: he might get too busy to hang out anymore. One
day Cookie asked me how Eric was doing, and I had to tell her
that he was so busy I hadn't had a chance to talk to him! I hired
him because I know I can give him the keys to the front door and
turn him loose and he will only make my company better and
stronger.

Eric is very detail-oriented, and that suits his role perfectly. It
frees me to keep my eyes focused on the overall mission while exploring new opportunities. Once I latch on to something, I know
I can turn it over to Eric and he will break it down from every
angle before making a recommendation. That brings me to

another point to consider when you are building your own team. We have such a high level of trust and so many shared values that Eric has no problem telling me things that I may not want to hear. He is not afraid to step up and intervene when he thinks someone is wasting our time or if a partnership is not a good fit. He listens to my opinions, but he is not a yes-man. He gives me a deeper and wider perspective on things, which is what you want in your top executives.

FEEDBACK

Everyone on our team knows that I will listen when they have suggestions or concerns. This open-door policy works for us because we're not just a company out to make money; we all share a strong sense of mission about bringing economic development and jobs to urban America.

No one is more focused on that mission day to day than Kawanna Brown, a native of South Central L.A., who came to us shortly after graduating from UCLA. I hired Kawanna on the recommendation of her mentor, Taylor Michaels, the first chief operating officer of Magic Johnson Enterprises. I did not have to sell Kawanna on our mission. She was still living in South Central when we opened the first Magic Johnson Theatre a few blocks from her home. She saw firsthand what it did for her community, and it excited her.

Well, "excited" may be too tame a word. Kawanna came to us with a fire in her belly. She mounted a one-woman siege to join our team, and in 1996 she became our fourth member.

Kawanna claims she took a lunch break on her first day and hasn't had one since. I doubt that she ate lunch even on the first day. I quickly learned—we all learned—that Kawanna is a force of nature.

Kawanna did public relations and marketing and joined our strategy sessions. That was just in her first week on the job—as our receptionist! Later, I promoted her to the post of my executive assistant just to make sure she didn't stage a coup and take over the company! Kawanna eventually rose to vice president of programs for the Magic Johnson Foundation, and at that point, we realized there was no stopping her.

Sadly, we lost Kawanna's mentor and friend, Taylor Michaels, who died of cancer in 1997, but Kawanna turned even that great loss for all of us into a force for good by helping me create a college scholarship program named in Taylor's honor. Today, hundreds of young people have benefited from those scholarships.

Kawanna, who now has a family as well as a job, continues to take me and our company places I never dreamed we would go.

So it was no surprise when Kawanna came into my office several years ago, closed the door, and said, "Earvin, we need to talk."

At that point, Kawanna was president of our charitable foundation. Still in her twenties, she had created the Taylor Michaels Scholarship Program and led the development of our first Community Empowerment Centers to help bring technology training to urban neighborhoods.

Kawanna lived and breathed the values of our company. Still, I got my first look at just how deeply passionate she was about our shared mission at this meeting.

"We have a brand problem," she said.

That shook me up. I thought we had a great brand, and it seemed as though everyone else felt the same way. Magic Johnson Enterprises had just one movie theater open when Kawanna joined us as a receptionist and our fourth employee. We had grown rapidly to several thousand employees. Executives from Fortune 500 companies were lining up to join forces with us. Mayors and even governors were calling to invite us into their communities and states.

"Where's the problem?" I asked. "We're doing great because of our strong brand!"

Then she explained, and again I listened.

"You're right. The Magic Johnson brand is doing great around the country," she said. "To everyone we deal with, our brand stands for community, trust, and loyalty. It's that way in every market that we've entered. So it's a great brand—externally. Still, we've grown so fast with our businesses and our nonprofit foundation that we have lost our brand focus internally. Outsiders don't understand the difference between all of our divisions because we haven't taken the time to bring everything together on the inside.

"We need to have one vision and one voice throughout the organization, and we need to create a strategic plan to carry that out. The stronger we are internally with the brand, the stronger we will be externally."

I have always made it clear to my employees that they can talk to me about anything. I tell them that they should be careful about making suggestions, because if they come to me with a good idea, I consider it theirs to carry through.

On the day Kawanna shared her concerns with me, I decided to give her yet another title: chief operating officer of Magic Johnson Enterprises. She is responsible for operational and strategic leadership of the organization, business development, negotiations, licensing, endorsements, and asset acquisitions.

Then I told Kawanna to get busy on her brand strategy. You better believe that she did!

Handling Lawyers and Accountants

Top-of-the-line role players will put your business on top.

I was still playing for the Lakers and just getting into my business career when I hired one of L.A.'s top lawyers to look at some contracts. I was shocked at the fees charged by his law firm, and when I griped about the high cost to my business adviser, Michael Ovitz, he responded with a strange question.

"Do you consider yourself among the best players in the NBA?" he asked.

"Sure," I said.

"Don't you always want to have the best players on your basketball team?"

"Sure I do," I responded.

"Well, if you want to be the best in business, you have to have the best on your team there too," he said.

When it comes to hiring essential role players in business—such as lawyers, accountants, information technology experts, Web site designers, and public relations pros—the smart move is to hire the best you can afford. If you don't pay for the best up front, you will end up paying them later to fix whatever goes wrong.

There is yet another reason to hire the best role players to boost your business. When you hire the best, it sends a message that you are a serious player too. Your clients and potential partners take notice when you come to the table with the top guns. Top guns in one field always know the best of the best in other areas, so you get the benefit of their networks too.

A STRONG BENCH

God has blessed me by putting the right people in my path at critical moments. Time and again, these key players just seem to step into my life at the right time. Many of them have been mentors, such as Lakers owner Dr. Jerry Buss, Earl Graves of *Black Enterprise,* the entrepreneur Bruce Llewellyn, and Michael Ovitz. Others, such as Ken Lombard, Kawanna Brown, and Eric Holoman, have moved my businesses forward as members of my corporate team.

Role players are also critical to my business success. Their specialized skills are vital at key moments. Your business may grow big enough to sustain a full-time accountant, lawyer, and other key professionals on your payroll. Yet in the initial phases you will likely have to pay for their services as you go.

I have two critical role players who are hybrids because they are not on the company payroll, but they are absolutely essential and involved in nearly everything I do. As I noted earlier, Corey Barash and Warren Grant are business managers in Los Angeles. Warren is a CPA out of the Wharton School at the University of Pennsylvania. Corey has an accounting degree and a master's degree in taxation from the University of Southern California.

They have many clients among the rich and famous, including Brad Pitt and Patrick Dempsey. I guess you could call me a client too, but I'm more like Corey and Warren's adopted brother. In fact, early in my career, I had a desk in their office so

I could soak up the basics of business from them. I still keep them close. Their offices are in the same building as mine on Wilshire Boulevard in Beverly Hills.

Another one of the key people in my business career, Lon Rosen, introduced me to the business adviser Warren Grant. Lon worked for the Lakers in marketing and public relations before he became my agent for a while. Today, he is one of the biggest in the country. Lon saw that I had a deep interest in building a business career but needed guidance. He introduced me to Warren because his firm does it all. It will keep your checkbook, manage your business's financial records, do your taxes, and even handle the contracts if you are buying or renovating a home.

Its trained professionals served as the infrastructure of my business dealings while I was building my own team. I still call upon their services in most of my deals because I trust their judgment. They have been major role players for me, as well as trusted advisers and friends. They served as my financial guardians in the early days. Any deals that were offered to me had to go through them, and they weren't the least bit afraid to tell someone if they were trying to take advantage of me. Even if it was a friend or family member who thought they were doing me a favor, Warren has been vigilant in guarding my brand.

Of course, these role players will tell you that one of their biggest challenges is protecting me from myself. There were times when I'd get bullheaded about getting into a business or investing in something that they weren't so enthused about, and I'd drive them a little crazy trying to convince them to let me do it.

A few years ago, I was intrigued by the prospect of getting into the Las Vegas hotel and casino business. Big numbers were being tossed at me by a potential partner. I don't gamble or drink, but the potential profits and the opportunity to create jobs in one of the less developed parts of Vegas appealed to me. My advisers and in-house team took a good, hard look at it. We brought in a team of experienced accountants and lawyers from the gaming world. They convinced us that we did not want to roll the dice on this deal.

Shortly after that, several major development projects in Las Vegas experienced serious problems. That doesn't mean I don't keep trying, but at the end of the day, if they tell me something isn't right, I respect and trust their judgment. Our system of checks and balances gives me peace of mind. I know that they are on guard, with my best interests at heart.

GO TO YOUR BENCH

Strong role players allow you to focus on doing what you do best and what you most enjoy about your business. They can be crucial to the success of a start-up, and once you have established your business, you can find role players to handle those things that you would rather not do or don't have the time or expertise to do yourself.

Many businesses begin with just one or two people, so you may find yourself answering the phones, doing the books, paying the bills, handling contracts, setting up your own Web site, and multitasking like crazy. That's not a bad thing because it forces you to learn every aspect of your business. There will come a time, hopefully, when you can afford to hire more employees or to outsource some of the work so that you can focus on growing the business.

I would advise you to leave the serious technical matters to the pros—role players who are "professional service providers"— even if it cuts into your profits. Complex contracts and lawsuits are best left to attorneys you trust. The same goes for the heavy accounting work, especially taxes, unless you have a strong background in financial matters. You may be able to master some bookkeeping and payroll tasks, but the time you put into them can take you away from building your business. The money you save by doing them yourself may cost you in the long run. Fixing mistakes costs more than doing things right the first time.

I would especially recommend that you find a good business lawyer and establish a long-term relationship. You'll want a lawyer with expertise in business law and contracts. Don't assume that one lawyer can handle it all. You may need different lawyers to handle negotiations, lawsuits and courtroom litigation, and estate planning. Often law firms have members who specialize in these areas so that you can at least stay with one firm. Remember, however, that big law firms have high overhead costs paid for by their clients. If yours is a small business, you are likely better off with a smaller firm.

Some entrepreneurs view lawyers as a necessary evil, but most of us just don't have the training to handle complex issues such as setting up partnerships or corporations and dealing with government regulations, trademarks and patents, major contracts, export and import deals, and debt collection.

The same holds true for accountants, who can help guide your business decisions with an eye to how they will impact your taxes, your retirement funds, and your ability to keep growing the business. Their expertise can save you from making costly mistakes, protect your financial health, and keep you in good standing with the Internal Revenue Service.

Still, a paralegal can do the more basic legal services for less than a lawyer, and an experienced bookkeeper can provide the basic accounting work too. If you don't need more than the basic services, don't pay for them.

Legal and financial experts are the most crucial because they can protect you from serious problems. You may find yourself in need of other key role players during start-up and as your business grows. Most businesses today have a Web site, and many do transactions over the Internet. Web site designers and information technology experts are role players of increasing importance to entrepreneurs. At some point, you may also want to hire management and marketing consultants and public relations professionals to take your business to the next level.

As your business grows and changes, you may need higher levels of expertise or more specialized help, so make it a policy to look at the role players on your bench every year to make certain they are providing the level of professional service you need at each stage.

THE BEST AND BRIGHTEST

How can you find the best and the brightest role players for your business? One of the benefits of belonging to local, state, and national professional networking organizations is that you can find and share information about professional service providers. Your local chamber of commerce, minority business organizations, and service organizations such as the Rotary Club and entrepreneur groups are also good sources for gathering references on role players.

Your lawyer and your accountant should have a good working relationship. I would never hire a lawyer, accountant, or IT, management, or marketing consultant without asking for references or talking to at least a couple other businesspeople who have used their services and recommend them.

Professional services are expensive, so you should make sure you are getting exactly what you need, when you need it, from your role players. Look for those with experience in your type of business, but be wary of hiring a role player who works for your competition.

If you are paying for a top-of-the-line lawyer, make sure that your work isn't being handed down to an inexperienced member of the law firm. Ideally, you will build a long-term relationship with your key role players, so it is important that you like each other and that you can communicate easily. If your lawyer makes you feel stupid, find another lawyer. If your accountant can't explain a problem to you, get another accountant. Mutual respect is crucial.

Make sure your contracts with them clearly state what they will provide and how they will be compensated, as well as how your agreement will be terminated if they fail to live up to it.

Set the ground rules early on, and negotiate fees according to the type of agreement. If you are paying a retainer fee, you should get a discounted rate and a refund if services are not used. Professional service providers will also offer discounts for prompt payment. Be sure to check their bills and invoices to make certain you are getting your money's worth.

Professional service providers set minimum fees for consultation. They will bill you at those rates for phone calls and "quick questions." Use their time and expertise wisely, because you are paying for it.

PART III

BUSINESS OPTIONS

Considering a Franchise

Franchises can launch your business career.

I was working out in a Laguna Beach hotel's fitness room during a family vacation and business retreat in late 2007 when another guest on the treadmill next to me struck up a conversation. He said he'd heard that I had become a successful businessman. After congratulating me on making the transition from basketball to business, he said, "I own ten Burger Kings. It's a great brand. Maybe we should talk to you about getting some of our restaurants."

Lisa Meyers, who is senior vice president of communications and branding at Magic Johnson Enterprises, was with us in the workout room, and she gave me a little smile as our new workout partner rolled into an informal pitch about the benefits of owning a Burger King franchise and how he could help me get started.

I didn't say anything. I just smiled and nodded as he kept talking. It wasn't that his pitch had no appeal to me. I was just trying to think of a polite way to tell him that he was preaching to the choir.

Finally, I just came out with it.

"I really agree with you. It's a great company. In fact, I'm already part of the Burger King system," I said.

I thought he was going to fall off his treadmill in midstride.

"You are?" he said.

"Yes, I've got thirty-one franchise stores," I said.

"Oh, man, I'm talking to the wrong guy," he said.

Well, no, he was talking to the *right* guy; he was just coming to the party a little late!

I don't have to be sold on Burger King or on the benefits of franchise ownership. I am a big fan of both. Like many entrepreneurs, I've learned a great deal and made a very good income from owning franchises.

You learn to keep a close eye on your ketchup, your mustard, your pickles, and all of your other condiments when you own a fast-food restaurant franchise, because they have an impact on your bottom line.

That's just good business, and that is why franchises can be a great place to start building your entrepreneurial career. Franchises are excellent training grounds because of the strong support network you get from the corporate headquarters and from your fellow franchise owners.

A GOOD OPTION

The franchise option is an excellent one in particular for minorities who may not have had educational opportunities or financial resources. I am certainly not the first minority entrepreneur to recognize that buying in to well-known franchise brands is a great opportunity. One of the nation's largest restaurant franchise companies was launched in 1982 when Valerie Daniels-Carter and John Daniels, Jr., started V & J Foods in Milwaukee with just one Burger King. By 2008, they were doing more than $97 million in sales with thirty-eight Burger Kings and more than sixty Pizza Huts.

Franchises offer established products or services, systems,

trademarks, and brands that you can buy in to at rates that are usually much less than you would pay to start a comparable business on your own. Franchising is considered less risky than starting your own business because the model has already been tested and refined by the franchisor. You also get the benefit of training programs, marketing support, and other expertise from the home office of the franchise parent company.

There are more than 900,000 franchised businesses in the United States, offering every sort of service and product you can imagine—from burgers and pizzas to closet organizers, dating services, lawn care, hotels, car rentals, and tax preparation. Franchises account for more than 18 million jobs and $1.5 trillion in economic impact, according to a recent PricewaterhouseCoopers report.

It's also true that, traditionally, minorities have had a tough time getting into franchises. Less than 10 percent of U.S. franchise businesses are minority-owned. Yet I believe franchise opportunities will grow as we open up urban markets for business development and as minority owners who have had success with franchise businesses push for greater inclusion for women, blacks, Hispanics, Asians, and others.

If you are looking for a way to get started in business but don't have a business degree or much training, or if you don't have access to enough cash to do it on your own, buying a franchise can be a great way to get in the door.

Franchisors—companies such as Burger King that sell franchises to people like you and me—usually provide managerial training and ongoing support. They often also provide property leases, product research and development, equipment financing, advertising and marketing support, leaseback programs, and help in getting financing for the business. That is why there are huge opportunities in and many benefits of franchise ownership. It can be a challenge also, especially if you are one of those entrepreneurs who wants to "have it your way" all the time.

Franchise companies generally have set ways of doing things that they believe guarantee uniform standards so that their customers and clients get what they pay for no matter where the franchise is located. These set ways—which are usually part of the franchise contract agreement—can make franchise ownership a challenge for entrepreneurs who want to be creative and do things differently.

Still, I've found ways to get creative with my franchise businesses while keeping the home office happy, and I think buying a franchise is a great move. That should be obvious since I've had long-term relationships with major franchise brands such as Pepsi-Cola, Burger King, 24 Hour Fitness, T.G.I. Friday's, and others.

BUYING IN

We have quite a few former franchise players on our team at Magic Johnson Enterprises, including the president, Eric Holoman. Like thousands of today's—and tomorrow's—business leaders, Eric gained valuable early experience working in a fast-food franchise. He was a shift supervisor for a McDonald's in L.A.'s Crenshaw neighborhood in high school, and he continued to work in another McDonald's during college to pay for his books and other expenses.

People sometimes joke about working at McDonald's and other fast-food franchises and put those jobs down as low-level work, but in truth, there have been surveys showing many Fortune 500 executives have noted that their first jobs were in the fast-food industry. Eric is among the current generation of business leaders who credit their fast-food franchise jobs with teaching them the basics of business long before they got their college degrees and MBAs.

"I learned a work ethic for sure, and because I was always interested in how things were done, I learned a lot about inventory, cash flow, and customer service," he told me.

After he got his degree in finance at USC, Eric and his banker father teamed up and became the owners of seventeen Church's Fried Chicken franchises. "It was definitely risk capital, but it wasn't like starting a whole new business like 'Eric's Fried Chicken' because we were buying in to an established brand," he said.

If you want to be in the restaurant business, one of the big advantages of buying in to an existing franchise is that the franchisor develops and tests products. "If you had to test your new menu items on your customers, they might not like something and never come back," Eric said. "They do test marketing to ascertain how an item or preparation process is received before rolling it out for all of their franchises. From a cost perspective, that is a huge deal for the franchise owners because it eliminates so much of their risk."

FIT FOR FRANCHISES

Franchising is one of the first opportunities I mention when other athletes come to me to talk about getting into business. It is a way to transfer brand equity to the consumer—through a familiar face. I've helped Shaquille O'Neal and several others get into the 24 Hour Fitness business. I brought Queen Latifah into the Fatburgers franchises, and I helped Keyshawn Johnson get into Panera Bread.

So I'm a believer, but what about you? Can you see yourself as a franchise owner? I'm going to lay out both the strong side and weak side of franchises for you in the next two chapters. For now, let's look at you and whether you are suited for this type of business opportunity. This is going to involve a bit of a reality check, which is always a good thing for business matters, even if the news isn't always good. It's better to decide now that you aren't fit for franchises, before you invest your money and your time.

You should start with an honest self-evaluation. If you owned Burger King or U-Haul, would you sell a franchise to someone with your qualifications, temperament, education, experience, and financial resources?

Then ask yourself what sort of franchise business appeals to you. There are more than seventy-five categories of franchises available. You can figure that just about every profitable type of business—and some unprofitable types too—has been franchised at one time or another.

It's important to include the fun factor as a consideration, because you will be spending a lot of time in the business. So what do you enjoy doing? Are you mechanically inclined (Jiffy Lube)? Do you like housecleaning (Merry Maids)? Are you good with hairstyling (Great Clips)? There are even franchise opportunities for people who like the smell of ink (Cartridge Depot) and for those who like putting up blinds and shutters (V2K).

Entrepreneur.com is just one of the online sources of lists of the top-ranking franchise opportunities. Take a look at the companies on such lists and decide what type of business suits you best. Check out those that appeal to you and decide whether you believe in their product or service. There is no sense in getting involved with a brand that you don't buy in to as a customer.

In many ways, buying a franchise isn't all that different from starting your own business. Franchise owners work every bit as hard as—and often harder than—people who start their own businesses from scratch. So don't buy a franchise because it looks easy. It's true that franchisors provide infrastructure and give you support in many areas, but there are franchises in which the corporate office and all the rules and regulations may result in even more work and anguish than you'd experience on your own.

Once you've looked at the upside and downside of franchise

ownership, do a thorough study of the different types of franchises out there and figure out which is the best match for your interests, talents, abilities, and financial capabilities. Remember that the most successful and most established franchise brands are likely to be the most expensive to get into, and the competition for them is tougher. So take a realistic look at how much money you have to invest and how much you can afford to lose if it doesn't work out. There are no guarantees that your franchise will be successful, even if others with the same brand are money-making machines.

I would advise you to look at the franchised businesses that have the most opportunity for growth. McDonald's, Burger King, and Subway franchises have made millions of dollars for those who invested in them early, worked hard, and played their cards right.

Experts in franchising will tell you that the growth areas for franchises are now in service businesses such as home remodeling and repair and cleaning. Business support services are another growth area. These include bookkeeping and accounting services, packaging and shipping, personnel and temporary worker agencies, and printing and copying shops. Other growth areas identified by franchising experts include automotive repair services such as oil change and tune-up shops, hair salons and health aids, computer services, educational products, and telecommunications services.

When you identify the franchise business that appeals to you, take the time to look carefully at the performance history of each company in that field that offers franchise opportunities. You don't necessarily want to buy in to the fastest-growing operation, because many franchise companies have grown so fast that they couldn't give their franchise owners enough support, causing the whole company to crash and burn. I'd advise you to look for a franchise operation with experienced management that is interested in controlled growth at a steady pace.

You will also want to consider the operating hours of a franchise and whether you will need to work weekends and holidays, how many employees you will need to hire, start-up and operating costs, the products and services that you are required to buy from the franchisor, and the procedures and costs for getting out of a franchise agreement.

It always helps to know someone who already has a franchise or several of them, so you can get honest information from them about the parent company and its products and services. You should visit several franchises to see how each operates. If possible, get an assessment of their overhead costs, their capital needs, and the number of employees they are required to have. The parent company should be willing to provide you with information on how its franchisees are doing. You should also try to find out how many franchisees have failed or quit.

As with any business, you will have to find a way to finance your franchise operation. Often, the franchisor will have programs to help those who meet their qualifications find financing. Every legitimate franchisor will provide you with its Uniform Franchise Offering Circular. This is a legal document that gives you the information you need to evaluate the opportunity. If a company refuses to provide it, I'd suggest you be very careful. Once you decide to get serious about purchasing a franchise, you may want to hire an attorney with experience in this area. The Federal Trade Commission offers good advice on this and other aspects of the franchise world in a consumer guide that is available online at www.ftc.gov/bcp/edu/pubs/consumer/invest/inv05.pdf. Another good source of franchising information is the International Franchise Association (www.franchise.org). For minorities, one of the top sources on franchising is *Black Enterprise* magazine (www.blackenterprise.com), which offers lists of the best opportunities.

FRANCHISE MAGIC

One of the warnings you hear about franchises is that often the franchisor discourages the franchisee from breaking away and doing things that aren't part of the standard operating model. That can be true, but I've found that if you have a good idea that increases profits and boosts the brand, your efforts will be respected, rewarded, and maybe even adopted by the franchisor.

Still, I've found that those in the corporate office sometimes need to be convinced before they buy in. That's okay too. I can be *very* convincing when I think I've got a good idea for my franchise properties. As I've noted earlier, I like to "Magicize" my businesses by adding personal touches. So when customers went to the drive-through at my Burger Kings, they didn't hear just any old automated voice welcoming them, they heard mine. There are also murals and pictures from my NBA days on the walls of my Burger Kings, which usually have a little livelier decorating scheme and better music than most.

Executives at Burger King encouraged me to be creative because they understood that I knew the urban market. Still, I could not convince them to join me in a marketing plan I created in 2007 when the Indianapolis Colts were set to play the Chicago Bears in Super Bowl XLI.

The game was to be held at Dolphin Stadium in Miami. I had several Burger Kings in south Florida, so I wanted to do something special and fun for our customers. I proposed to Burger King that we have our customers sign up for a big drawing with Super Bowl tickets as the prize. Tickets to the game were scarce, so I figured it would be a popular promotion, but marketing executives in the corporate office said they had other Super Bowl promotions going on. I decided to have it my way.

I contacted my friends at NFL headquarters and they scratched up some tickets, which I purchased for our promotion.

We then did a lot of grassroots marketing with south Florida radio stations to promote the Super Bowl ticket giveaway at Magic's Burger Kings. Let me tell you, I was *shocked* at the response. Apparently it was an especially tough year to find tickets, because people were lining up to get into my stores so they could get a shot at the drawing. Our sales increased as much as 15 percent in the weeks before the drawing!

Even better, we held the drawing with great media coverage and the winner started crying for joy because he was going to get to take his son to the Super Bowl. It was a great moment that really touched a lot of people. I watched that Super Bowl game in the Burger King skybox at Dolphin Stadium, and there were a fair number of executives from the corporate headquarters telling me, "We should have listened to you and gotten on board with that drawing."

Franchise Benefits

Know the upside of franchises.

O bviously, I believe that there are more positive than negative aspects to owning franchise businesses. I am especially fond of them as an entry point into business for people who can benefit from a strong support system. At minimum, owning a successful franchise is great training for starting your very own business someday. So with that in mind, let's look at:

THE STRONG SIDE OF FRANCHISE OWNERSHIP

1. Your risk is reduced. The annual failure rate of franchise systems in the United States is only about 5 percent, while 30 to 35 percent of independent businesses fail within the first year. When you buy an established and successful franchise, you are buying in to a proven system for operating the business and generating profits, so your level of risk is less than it would be if you were starting a business from scratch.

2. Though there are substantial fees for buying in to an established major brand franchise such as McDonald's or Subway,

a newer and smaller franchise operation might cost you less initially than doing your own independent start-up.

3. The business support system is built in. Franchisors create procedures and systems designed to work for all of their franchise owners. They set up training, financing, money management, health care, and other programs, and they generally provide guidance and expertise when you need it.

4. The psychological support system is in place. First-time entrepreneurs and small-business owners often feel that the world sits on their shoulders and they have no one to turn to. When you buy in to a franchise, you plug in to a network of business owners facing the same daily challenges and problems. Ideally, they work together with the franchisor to come up with answers.

5. The marketing support system is established. Most franchise operations create and share the cost of national and local marketing and advertising for franchisees.

6. The brand is already built. When you buy an established franchise with an established brand, you plug in to its customer base. The brand's loyal customers will likely become your loyal customers from the day you open the door—as long as you live up to and, hopefully, *exceed* their expectations.

7. You get a group rate. One of the big benefits of owning a franchise business is increased purchasing power. Your fellow franchisees are part of a collective group that can leverage your buying power to reduce the costs of supplies, inventory, equipment, and even medical, dental, and eye care. Starbucks isn't really a franchise operation since I am the only partner the company has ever had, but I learned about the buying power of a big brand from them. When its average store-opening costs reportedly* reached $350,000 in 1995, Star-

* Thompson, Arthur A. and John E. Gamble, 1999. Starbucks Corporation, Online Case Study, *www.mhhe.com.*

bucks centralized buying, developed standard contracts and fixed fees for certain items, and consolidated work under the contractors who proved they could control costs. Its retail operations group created guidelines for exactly the minimum amount of equipment each core store needed, and after that standard items were ordered in volume from vendors at 20 to 30 percent discounts. They were then delivered to the store sites just in time. In addition, modular designs for display cases were developed. Store layouts were developed on a computer, using software that allowed costs to be estimated as the design evolved. As a result, store-opening costs dropped to a reported $315,000 and store development time was cut from twenty-four to eighteen weeks.

8. It's easier to recruit good help. A recognized brand makes it easier to hire good employees because they know that certain standards will be met. It can be considerably more difficult to hire good, experienced employees for a start-up with no track record than for a franchise with a proven brand.

9. Your opportunities for growth are better. Successful brand franchises generate steady cash flow. Bankers are more willing to provide loans to a successful franchise owner who wants to buy more because they know there is a strong support network and a proven system with a good track record in place. Franchisors also often have in-house financing programs for successful franchisees who want to grow within the company.

Franchise Drawbacks

Know the downside of franchises.

I have owned and worked with many of the best franchise brands in the country, but I know that franchise ownership may not be for everyone. Here is a quick list of the "weak side," or potential pitfalls, of franchise ownership that you might want to consider before you decide to put your money and hard work into this type of business.

Every business has its pros and cons, and franchises are no different. I am a big fan of franchises and I don't think any of these "weak-side" listings should scare you away, but these are things you need to be aware of in making your decision on whether to become a franchise owner.

THE WEAK SIDE OF FRANCHISE OWNERSHIP

1. It's *their* company. Your name won't go on the door or on the signs—and you will have to share your financial records and the financial rewards of your hard work with the franchisor or parent company.
2. It's *their* product or service. In most cases, you are selling a product or service that is created and controlled by the fran-

chisor. If the corporate office comes up with mint-flavored French fries, you have to put them on the menu.

3. It's *their* system. You will have to do things the way the franchisor wants them done, often down to the smallest detail.

4. It's not always cheaper. Your start-up costs might be considerably higher for a franchise than for your own business if the franchise is a well-established and successful brand.

5. If you have a low credit rating, it can be tough to get financing for even a small home-based franchise. Though it's usually easier to get a bank loan to buy a franchise than to undertake your own start-up, a bad credit rating can knock you out of the game. If your credit rating is below 660, you might try to get a microloan of $35,000 to $50,000 designed for borrowers turned down by bankers. Usually these are easier to get and more flexible than bank or even SBA loans. Watch out, though, because interest rates are higher on these loans because of the higher risk. You can learn more about these loans at www.sba.gov.

6. You may have to pay up front and annually too. Seventy percent of franchisors charge an up-front franchise fee of $40,000 or less. Annual royalty fees are another expense. You will be required to make royalty payments every year in return for the operations and advertising support your franchise receives from the corporate office.

7. You may not get all you want from the corporate office. Franchisors have established systems and may be reluctant to make exceptions or fulfill requests based on your special needs.

8. You will have to learn to go along to get along. There may be times when you feel more like the employee of the franchisor than a co-owner. Some experts advise that you think of yourself more as an investor than a business owner because you are essentially buying the rights to run someone else's business for a specific period of time. Most franchisors recognize

an independent franchisee association made up of franchise owners who share information and resources.

9. Cannibalization—not people eaters but profit eaters—is a major concern for franchise owners. Franchisors sometimes get so eager to keep growing that they allow franchisees to locate so close to one another that they cut into one another's profits. You should talk to existing franchisees before buying in to any franchise to see if this is a concern for them.

10. Success is not guaranteed in a franchise or any other business, particularly in tough economic times with high fuel prices and tight credit. Some franchise businesses—such as restaurants, hotels, and motels—have higher costs and failure rates than those in technology or equipment.

11. You will still need a lawyer and an accountant. Franchise contracts aren't light reading, and you will want a lawyer who has seen a lot of them so he can protect your interests and translate the legalese for you. If your spouse is a co-owner, make sure that you are both adequately protected. It's also not a bad idea to line up an accountant who can help you project your financing needs and profit potential before you sign on the dotted line.

12. If things go bad for one franchisee in your group, it can hurt all the others. You are sharing a brand name. If customers at one restaurant in the franchise get sick from food there, it could impact your business even if it is hundreds of miles away.

Joint Ventures

Joining forces with other businesses can bring big rewards.

Despite our shared last name, I am no relation to a certain Charles Johnson who grew up on Chicago's South Side. I probably never would have met this South Side Charles Johnson except for something else we have in common: Charles and I both dream big, and we don't give up easily on our dreams.

A Tuskegee University graduate, Charles was twenty-nine years old and working as a senior business development manager at Sodexo, when he came up with a really, really big dream in 2005.

Sodexo had not received a lot of media attention up to that point, though it is one of the leading providers of food service and facilities management in the world. It operates cafeterias and janitorial and grounds-keeping services for corporations, schools, colleges and universities, hospitals, nursing homes, and military bases. Sodexo was mostly a behind-the-scenes outsourcing company, not a glamorous business but highly profitable.

Charles worked in Sodexo's Emerging Markets division, which provided services to thirty historically black colleges and Hispanic institutions. Sodexo serves more than six thousand health care centers, schools, and military sites, so it is a huge, complex corporation. Yet Charles was not intimidated. He was young and ambitious, and as I said, he was not one to give up easily on his dreams.

He saw that Sodexo was involved in a highly competitive industry that, overall, was not considered a hotbed for ambitious minorities. There were very few black owners or managers involved in the entire field of food service and facilities maintenance, he noted.

That situation might have discouraged a lot of people. To Charles, it looked like an opportunity.

Many of Sodexo's clients are government agencies and private companies that require a certain percentage of their vendor and outsourcing contracts to go to minority contractors. There just wasn't a strong minority presence in the industry.

A second component of his vision emerged, and that is where I came into the picture. Charles said that he had followed my transition from basketball to the business world. He had been excited when I joined Starbucks in a joint venture to open our co-branded cafés in underserved urban neighborhoods.

Charles thought a similar arrangement—but one that made me the majority owner of a joint venture—might help Sodexo develop its own business in new areas while qualifying it for contracts set aside for minority business owners. Charles also felt Sodexo might benefit from my network of other partners and business allies.

"The idea was to expand Sodexo's presence in the marketplace while transferring some of Earvin Johnson's brand equity and credibility to Sodexo in markets where its own brand image was soft," Charles said.

TEAMING UP

Like partnerships and strategic alliances, joint ventures are a method of growing your business by combining your strengths and resources with those of another company. I compare joint ventures to the pick-and-roll play in basketball, when two teammates work together to create scoring opportunities that they couldn't produce individually. In this case, our partner Sodexo picked us, and we have been rolling ever since!

In joint ventures, two separate businesses sign a legal agreement, usually for a specific period of time and with a clear exit strategy, to share information, expertise, markets, and profits. Small companies can come together in joint ventures to take on bigger competitors by bulking up and lowering costs. Big companies such as Sodexo and Starbucks form joint ventures with smaller companies such as Magic Johnson Enterprises to reach new markets, access new technologies, or build strength in an area where they want to grow.

A smaller company can benefit from a larger partner's brand recognition, resources, and market reach. If a small company suddenly finds itself with a hot product or service, it might benefit from a joint venture with a company that has a larger sales force and stronger distribution channels. It's also common for a company in one country to form a joint venture with one in another country so they can access each other's markets.

In some cases, joint ventures are formed by two big brands to create a new product line. Starbucks and PepsiCo entered into a joint venture in 1994 to introduce a new line of cold coffee products. Starbucks provided the coffee expertise, and PepsiCo contributed the mass distribution network. Starbucks CEO Howard Schultz saw the joint venture as a way to create all sorts of new opportunities while also taking the company into more mainstream markets in the United States and in foreign markets such as Japan, where there was an $8 billion market for ready-to-drink coffee-based beverages.

The first product in the Starbucks-PepsiCo joint venture was a flop. Mazagran, a carbonated coffee drink, didn't do well in initial tests. Howard Schultz and Pepsi's leaders kept trying, and, in the summer of 1995, they came up with a huge winner—a new cold coffee drink called Frappuccino. In the 1996 launch, sales were ten times initial projections. Frappuccino helped Starbucks, and PepsiCo created a new premium ready-to-drink global coffee market that was estimated to have $1 billion in sales in 2007.

MAKING IT WORK

It is not difficult to form a legal joint venture, but to make sure it will be successful both companies need to be certain that their reasons for forming the joint venture are in sync and that they share the same values and principles. Magic Johnson Enterprises would never form a joint venture with a company that did not put a high priority on diversity and on investing in underserved minority communities. We care deeply about that, and we need to see a similar commitment from anyone we do business with. I look for joint venture partners who share our belief in doing well by doing good. It is also important that both companies contribute equally to the venture and both share in the rewards of it. Our process for that is spelled out clearly in our legal agreements. Once the agreement is in place, we put a high priority on monitoring the joint venture and our relationship with our partners. Keeping the lines of communication open and staying on top of the new business have to be priorities for both parties.

A true joint venture is different from a strategic alliance because in a joint venture both companies contribute equity to the new business and then share in the revenues, expenses, and control of it. Strategic alliance partners do not put in equity, and it is a less formal arrangement. My first joint venture was with Earl Graves in our Pepsi-Cola distributorship. Earl had a couple of extra percentage points as a controlling interest of our joint venture, and I learned that a controlling interest is very important. It gave Earl control over every aspect of the business. It made him the dominant partner in the joint venture, which was fine given that I was still playing in the NBA and did not have nearly as much business experience.

Now that I am a proven businessman, my goal is to be the controlling partner in my joint ventures. That is not only my desire, it is necessary if my joint venture partner's goal is access to public and private minority contracts through our deal by qualifying as a certified Minority Business Enterprise (MBE).

SELLING THE DEAL

Charles Johnson felt that a joint venture would be a win-win deal for both Sodexo and Magic Johnson Enterprises. He had a good idea but not much else. He was a young black executive in a huge corporation where there was not a strong minority presence. Most people in his position might be tempted to file even such a good idea in the "Beyond My Power" drawer.

Not Charles.

"I was nervous about overstepping my bounds in the company hierarchy and maybe being fired, but I just thought it was the right thing to do, the next logical step for Sodexo, and a great opportunity for Magic Johnson Enterprises too," he said.

Still, he worried that he might be risking his career by making such a major proposal to his supervisors. He feared they might think he was a dreamer or too ambitious. "But finally, I came to grips with that risk by deciding that if this organization didn't see that this was a great opportunity, then I should leave anyway," Charles said. "That is how I made peace with my decision to go ahead. I had faith that it was a great idea and that if my supervisors didn't like it, I would have to figure out something else to do with my career."

And so Charles stepped up his game. He went to a number of his supervisors and told them his idea for the joint venture with MJE as the majority owner.

It didn't go well.

"They pretty much told me I was crazy and that it would never happen in our industry," Charles said.

At this point, Charles was committed to making his vision a reality at Sodexo or somewhere else. So he kept pushing. He got permission to take his proposal up the ladder but received the same reaction from several managers.

Still he did not give up.

Wisely, he did some networking instead. He contacted a young lady working in Sodexo's public relations office and told her about his joint-venture proposal. She got it, and she agreed to set up a meeting between Charles and a Sodexo vice president who served as the assistant to the CEO for Sodexo's U.S. division at its headquarters in Maryland.

The vice president didn't throw Charles out the door, which he took as a good sign. He had his reservations, but he agreed that it was a proposal that the CEO should hear for himself. He gave Charles a week to prepare for his meeting with the top executive at Sodexo.

TESTING THE WATERS

While Charles was pushing his proposal up the ladder at Sodexo, he was also knocking on the door at Magic Johnson Enterprises to see whether it would appeal to us. He first proposed the joint

venture informally at a social event where he met up with an ac-
quaintance, a marketing consultant who had worked with us in
the past.

"I told him that I had a business proposal for Earvin Johnson
but I didn't know how to reach out to him," Charles said. "I asked
him to connect me to someone at Magic Johnson Enterprises."

The marketing consultant was not familiar with Sodexo and
its services, so Charles had to convince him that this was a worthwhile and potentially lucrative proposition. After hearing him
out, he set up a meeting to introduce Charles to my chief operating officer, Kawanna Brown.

Charles took a vacation day from Sodexo and flew out to L.A.
at his own expense to make his introductory pitch, because he
didn't want his supervisors to think he was trying to broker a deal
on his own. He was just testing the waters to see if we had any interest in his proposal and whether we had a structure in place to
make it work.

Kawanna surprised Charles with her knowledge of Sodexo
and his industry. That was the good news. The not-so-good news
came when Kawanna told him that Magic Johnson Enterprises
was already in negotiations with a Sodexo competitor to do a similar deal!

Charles asked Kawanna if she would give Sodexo a shot before signing with the competitor. She agreed to do that because
she liked Charles and his passion for the project.

With that assurance, Charles returned to Sodexo and prepared for his meeting with the CEO. He spent a week putting together his presentation. It was nerve-wracking but exhilarating
too, because he believed so strongly in what he was doing.

Yet he probably didn't need to prepare so hard for this big
meeting.

"Five minutes into it, our CEO said he thought it was a great
idea and that it would create a competitive advantage for
Sodexo," Charles said.

The CEO was sold on the fact that my business brand had become not only credible but trusted. He agreed with Charles that Sodexo would reach new markets through this joint venture and that Sodexo would benefit from my "web of influence" in urban and corporate America as well as in politics, entertainment, and sports.

"Our industry is not very exciting, but once we bring Earvin Johnson into the process, we will be viewed in an entirely different way," Charles told his CEO. "We will be able to sell from the top down. After all, who is not going to take a phone call from him?"

And so Charles didn't get fired for overstepping his bounds. Instead, he got the green light from top management at Sodexo, who also gave him the resources he needed to put together a formal presentation to us.

The fact that Sodexo's management put their trust in Charles said something to both Kawanna Brown and me. The Sodexo executives could have thanked Charles for his good idea, given him a pat on the back, and then put someone else in charge of selling it to us. They did not do that. They let him carry the ball. That decision would be a critical factor when I sat down to look at whether to go with Sodexo or its competitor.

DUE DILIGENCE

With any partnership, strategic alliance, or joint venture, we do our homework. We check out the other party thoroughly to see what resources it will bring to the deal, whether there are any conflicts with current business associates or clients, and how our organizations will work together. We have lawyers and accountants and both in-house and outside business and management experts look at every aspect of the other company and the field that we'll be playing on.

We want to make sure that we do business only with companies that enhance our brand and contribute to our success. So we look at the usual things. We make sure the other company is profitable and respected and that it doesn't have any messy legal problems that might impact either them or us.

But the most important thing we look at is whether the other company buys in to our guiding vision and our mission for serving underserved minorities and their communities. That's why I called Charles Johnson early one morning at his home.

We'd met earlier, after Kawanna heard Sodexo's formal presentation and decided it had merit. Charles admitted he was a little nervous, but he did fine in that initial meeting, which was also attended by several top Sodexo executives. I liked Charles and his suggestions. Sodexo's faith in this young African American impressed me too. Still, I wanted to make certain that the company executives were committed to diversity and to doing the right things in urban America.

So I called Charles at home in Chicago one morning, catching him by surprise, he later told me.

"When I picked up the phone and heard an assistant say Mr. Johnson wanted to talk to me, I thought, 'Oh no, the deal is tanking and he's going to ask me something I can't answer or do,'" Charles said.

I wanted to have a frank discussion with Charles about Sodexo and the people who ran it. My goal was to learn if they were committed to serving the minority community and building a diverse workforce. I told Charles that I did not want to do business with Sodexo unless it shared my values and lived them.

Charles answered my questions to my satisfaction.

Then I cut to the chase.

"Why should I take Sodexo's offer instead of the deal with your competitor that we have already negotiated?" I asked.

There was a pause on the line for just a few seconds; then Charles stepped up and delivered.

"With all due respect, Mr. Johnson, you have been on championship teams all your life, in high school, in college, and in the NBA," Charles said. "If you signed the deal with our competitor, it would be the first time in your life that you joined a second-class team."

Now it was my turn to pause. Charles had just blown me away.

"Okay," I said. "I see what you're saying. I'll be talking to you soon, Charles."

SodexoMagic was formed in 2006 as a joint venture with Magic Johnson Enterprises holding an equity share of 51 percent and Sodexo 49 percent. We have worked together to secure major contracts with some of the biggest brands and top companies in the nation.

We provide dining and catering services, grounds keeping, plant operations and maintenance, asset management, environmental services, and laundry services to college campuses, hospitals, health care facilities, and corporate offices around the country.

Within two years of its creation, SodexoMagic was doing more than $45 million in annual sales and growing fast thanks to my pick-and-roll partner, Charles Johnson, who is still dreaming big. His innovation, determination, and fearlessness have reaped benefits for both our companies, and I am happy to say that Charles has been rewarded too. He is now a Sodexo vice president in charge of managing its end of our joint venture, and I look forward to many more ventures—and adventures—with him.

Buying an Existing Business

Buy a good business and make it better.

I n college I lived on hamburgers and sausage pizza. My motto was "I'm from Michigan, we eat beef!"

As a rookie, I nearly passed on playing for the Los Angeles Lakers because they wouldn't give me a burger during my contract negotiations. The Lakers selected me in the NBA draft after my Michigan State team won the NCAA title in my sophomore year. The Lakers' owner, Jack Kent Cooke, invited me to discuss my contract over lunch in the Trophy Room at the Forum. The meeting got off to a bad start when he insisted on ordering me some California fish dish that I'd never heard of.

Sand dabs?

"You're going to love them," Mr. Cooke said.

I didn't.

"Well, Earvin, how do you like your sand dabs?" he asked several minutes into the meal.

"They're all right," I said.

It was obvious I was just trying to be polite.

Things got quiet in the room. Mr. Cooke seemed to be hurt that I wasn't a seafood lover.

"All right?" he said. "These are delicious."

I was nineteen years old and still growing. I needed more protein on my plate.

"Would you mind if I ordered something else?" I asked.

"Like what?"

"A hamburger? Or maybe a roast beef sandwich?"

Mr. Cooke acted as if I'd just kicked in his car door, but he told the waiter to bring me a couple of burgers. I think he felt as if he'd lost the first round of negotiations. He came on strong after that, insisting that they were going to pay me only $400,000. I told him I wanted $500,000.

I won that round too.

WHOPPER OF A DEAL

I'm still a meat lover. Now, however, I love burgers as a business. One of my most successful early investments was my purchase of more than thirty Burger Kings in Dallas, Miami, Atlanta, and Birmingham. I have had a great relationship with Burger King's management. As one of its major owners, I have learned a lot about the fast-food business and how it works. I have come to understand the food chain of the food industry, and just recently, I moved up several links.

In the summer of 2008, our Yucaipa-Johnson Corporate Initiatives Growth Fund stepped up and made a multimillion-dollar acquisition that put us in position to become the major supplier of hamburger patties—for Burger King and other major-brand restaurants and supermarket chains. My company partners with Los Angeles supermarket king Ron Burkle in the Yucaipa-Johnson fund. Our goal is to invest in businesses that meet at least one of the following criteria, if not all of them:

1. They are located in urban America.
2. They employ mostly minorities.

3. They have some tie-in with our existing corporate partners.
4. The companies are owned by women and minorities.

This deal matched up perfectly with our criteria. The companies we purchased are in urban areas and employ mostly minorities, and the deal will grow our ties with Burger King and other partners in the food and restaurant industries, including Ron Burkle's supermarket connections and our joint venture with Sodexo and its food service businesses. The companies we purchased have been around a long time. They are already profitable. Their employees know what they are doing. Now we can take them to the next level while growing our own business.

Because we will now become suppliers to Burger King, I will have to sell my franchises, but that is okay because this will take my business relationship with Burger King to a whole new level. This deal also fits into our long-term effort to build a multifaceted company that will continue to thrive and create jobs long after I step aside as the day-to-day leader.

BUYING IN

In earlier chapters, I've offered advice about the ins and outs of creating your own business and buying a franchise. There's a third option that many veteran entrepreneurs prefer: buying an existing business. This is usually a viable option only for veteran entrepreneurs because of the cost of purchasing an established, profitable business.

Bankers and private investors are often more willing to make loans for the purchase of a proven business. The amount they will lend depends on the business, its assets, and your level of experience in the industry. A proven veteran buyer might be able to get half of the acquisition money from a bank and the rest from private equity groups, which make their determination of how much they will loan you based on your assets and the value of the business you are buying. They often demand that you put up a stake in the new business so that you are invested too.

Sometimes, a seller will help finance the sale of the business. Often, the buyer can use seller financing to cover as much as 75 percent of the purchase price. There are many other benefits of this option for those who have access to the capital.

There is usually much less risk and less expense involved in buying an existing business than starting your own because the established company already has a location, employees, suppliers, distribution, training and education, and a track record. You can walk around it and kick the tires, checking out its cash flow, revenues, expenses, employees, customers, and suppliers. With a start-up business, you normally can make only predictions and estimates of all those factors; with an existing business, the vital information is all there for you to examine and evaluate.

If you already have a business and want to grow it, of course you will want to buy another company only if it will make your operation stronger because of a better distribution channel, enhanced market share, unique product, or some technology that benefits your business.

The success rate for those who buy an established business is higher than that for start-up entrepreneurs. Still, due diligence is required. When buying an existing business, you must carefully check out every aspect of the operation. You need to know why the owner has decided to sell. It could be that the owner simply wants to retire; on the other hand, perhaps the owner is fleeing a declining market, a lawsuit, or a bad partner. You might want to bring in a professional investigator who does background checks for business acquisitions by looking at public records and talking to former employees, suppliers, and customers.

The process of acquiring an existing business takes time and patience. You need to decide what sort of business you want to buy, of course, and then establish the standards that must be met.

Any business you buy should meet or exceed basic standards. A general profile is hard to come up with since every situation is unique, but experts recommend that any business you purchase meet at least some of these basic criteria: a profit margin above 12 percent of sales before taxes; average annual sales growth of at least 12 percent; proprietary or branded products or technology or some other sort of competitive advantage; a significant share of a growing, defined market; sales over $20 million; a diverse market; and a strong, stable management team.

DUE DILIGENCE

Like a real estate agent presenting a house to potential buyers, a business seller will gladly show you the new kitchen, the renovated pool, and the bonus room over the garage. Yet he or she may neglect to point out the mold in the basement or the family of squirrels nesting in the attic.

As with most homes, all businesses have their hidden problems. Many of them can be fixed, but you need to factor in the cost of the fix when you negotiate the purchase price. If you can't do that, you may need to walk away. Buyer's remorse isn't restricted to the housing market. There are countless examples of major corporations rushing into deals, buying up businesses, and then discovering major problems after the deal is done.

We saw an example of that here in Southern California when the Tribune Company in Chicago purchased the *Los Angeles Times* from the Times Mirror Company. After completing the $8 billion deal in 2000, Tribune executives discovered that their company was facing an Internal Revenue Service bill of as much as $1 billion in back taxes and interest penalties because of two

1998 Times Mirror transactions whose tax-free basis had been disallowed by an IRS audit. The Tribune Company eventually reached an agreement with the IRS that resulted in a net cash payout of $286 million—still a very costly mistake.

When you buy an existing business, you can end up inheriting lawsuits and tax problems unless you are extremely careful in checking it out before the purchase contract is signed. The Tribune Company isn't the only one to get burned in a big way. Halliburton, for example, had to pay $5.1 billion to settle asbestos-related claims that came with its 1998 purchase of Dresser Industries.

Buying another company with serious legal or tax problems is like marrying into a troubled family. Once you've done the deal, its problems are your problems. Love may conquer all, but huge IRS bills and multimillion-dollar lawsuits can drive your business into bankruptcy. You don't want your hard work and investments to go down the drain because you didn't do your homework.

Talking to the target company's customers, creditors, suppliers, and present and former employees can help you put together a true picture. At Magic Johnson Enterprises we put each potential purchase through several layers of analysis by members of our team. We even check the court records in the county where the existing business is based to determine whether there have been lawsuits against it and whether there is any ongoing or pending litigation or liens. The Better Business Bureau in the area can be a good source if complaints have been lodged against the business.

Once we have done our homework, we double-check everything with our friends just a few floors away in our office building: my longtime business and investment advisers Warren Grant and Corey Barash. They look at every aspect of the business and its relationships and then run the numbers again.

INSIDE LOOK

It is also important to look inside your own business when you are thinking about purchasing another one. We step back and look at where our own company stands and where it is headed. We ask ourselves how this deal would impact not just our bottom line but our brand image, our employees, our vendors, our joint ventures, our partners, and everyone else we do business with.

We consider purchasing only companies that we can grow or leverage into a bigger and better business. We are on a mission. We have strong values. I would never compromise either of them for a good deal or a fast dollar. Neither should you.

Another consideration is whether our team should run the new company or leave the existing management in place. Not all executives are fit to run all companies in all industries. Sometimes two perfectly good companies with no problems fall to pieces when they merge, because of conflicting cultures. Such clashes are all too common. Often, one group feels the other is favored, and resentments flare.

When we bring new companies into the fold, I lead the welcoming committee. I visit their offices to become acquainted with the employees and to let them know that they are valued. We have a very close-knit family in the headquarters of Magic Johnson Enterprises. We've grown so much and in so many directions that I can't possibly spend one-on-one time with everyone who joins us. Still, we make certain that the companies we purchase understand and share our goals, our values, and our mission.

BUSINESS SHOPPING

If buying an existing business appeals to you, where can you find one for sale? Most of our acquisitions have come to us through our ever-growing network of contacts. Still, if you are just starting out as an entrepreneur, you may want to work with a well-connected business broker who knows your field, a business accounting firm in your area, or an investment banker.

Brokers or bankers charge an up-front fee atop a contingency fee if you purchase a business they recommend. The contingency fee varies depending on the size of the deal. It can range from 5 to 10 percent for smaller businesses to as low as 1 percent for multimillion-dollar purchases.

Professional organizations and industry groups in your field may also offer information about businesses for sale. The Association for Corporate Growth, headquartered in Glenview, Illinois (www.acg.org), is a global networking group of 11,000 members involved in corporate development, mergers, and acquisitions. Local chapters meet to discuss opportunities in their areas.

Your local Chamber of Commerce can also steer you to sources of information on businesses for sale. The Internet has many resources for business shoppers, including these sites:

- BizBuySell: www.bizbuysell.com
- BizQuest.com: www.bizquest.com
- MergerNetwork: www.mergernetwork.com

DEAL MAKERS

When the time comes to purchase a business, you will need an accountant, a lawyer, and a financial adviser with practical experience in business acquisitions and due diligence. You might also want to get an independent appraisal of the business you plan to buy. Both the American Society of Appraisers (www.appraisers .org) and the Institute of Business Appraisers (www.go-iba.org) offer directories of their members. Appraisers charge $200 to $300 an hour or more, so their services can get expensive if the business is complicated.

Once you have done all of your initial due diligence, looked in every closet for skeletons, and checked out the seller's reputation, you will need to have a lawyer write up a letter of intent to purchase—subject to your conditions. This prevents the seller from soliciting other offers and may also include conditions that allow for arranging financing and doing any final analysis and checking. The seller then has to agree to provide access to all company records—so this is where serious scrutiny is needed.

At this point, you call in the lawyers and accountants to go over every detail of the company's financial records. They should look at trends in revenues, profit margins, sales, and market share. The condition of equipment and technology is also important. Your accountants should review the last five to seven years of tax returns, because it is hard to conceal things from the IRS.

Make certain that the letter of intent also requires the seller to operate the company normally until the deal is done. That is important because you don't want the seller to let the business fall apart just before you step in. It also prevents the seller from taking on huge loans or promising employee bonuses that will affect your bottom line. You may want to include a no-compete clause so that the seller doesn't open up a new business just down the street to steal away your customers.

Buying an existing business can take your own company to new heights with minimal risks, but only if you do your homework. Once the deal is done, you can then focus on growing both enterprises and reaping the rewards.

Minority Vendors

Reach out and support minority entrepreneurs.

Kairi Brown, a vice president for Warner Bros. Records, went to his first NASCAR race in 2004 when one of the artists on his label, Kiley Dean, was to perform the National Anthem there. Since he'd never been to a NASCAR event, Kairi was eager to see what all the excitement was about. He walked around the Richmond International Raceway, taking in all of the sights and sounds, and two things stood out.

First of all, Kairi realized that there were not many black fans in the crowd, and second, "there was no place to get barbecue."

Kairi, who grew up working in his father's chicken and ribs restaurant, decided that a southern-born sport like NASCAR needed BBQ on the menu. Since he loved cooking just as much as he loved making music, Kairi had always hoped to open his own restaurant someday. He saw an opportunity at barbecue-deprived NASCAR tracks.

He didn't know much about auto racing, but he figured the tracks would make great test kitchens for his BBQ recipes—and save him a bundle in start-up expenses. Since NASCAR events often attract hundreds of thousands of fans over three-day weekends, it was also a smart way to build a brand.

Kairi came to me with his idea because we had known each

other for more than ten years. We'd hung out in the same places in Los Angeles, and we'd gotten to know each other through mutual friends.

As it turned out, Kairi's timing was perfect. He pitched his idea for bringing barbecue to NASCAR events just after I had signed on to be cochairman of NASCAR's Executive Steering Committee for Diversity. NASCAR's leaders had asked me to help them attract more African Americans, Hispanics, and women to its sport, as employees, racers, suppliers, vendors, and fans.

Kairi and his Bubba's Q barbecue start-up became our first project with NASCAR. I called Brian France, the CEO of NASCAR, and told him about Kairi's proposal. Brian said it fit his plan to attract a wider range of fans and participants to NASCAR, so he provided us with contacts at Americrown Service Corporation, the food division of NASCAR, and with SMI, the racetrack operators for many events.

After a year of planning and preparation, Bubba's Q made its first appearance at the Auto Club Speedway near Fontana, California, in September 2005. They were expecting more than 100,000 people for the race, but I thought it wouldn't hurt to bring a few more. I invited everyone in the office to bring their families and friends to help get Kairi off to a good start. We loaded up about 150 people for the NASCAR race and for Bubba's Q barbecue. We were joined over the weekend by NBA star Grant Hill and his wife, Tamia, a singer who had worked with Kairi in the music business.

Kairi was the star that day because with that event he officially became NASCAR's first minority contractor. Bubba's Q now serves barbecue chicken, ribs, pulled pork, hot links, and baked beans at nearly twenty NASCAR events each year. Kairi is also working with NASCAR to sell three flavors of Bubba's Q sauce and seasonings at racetracks and other outlets. He plans to open his first Bubba's Q restaurant in the Santa Clarita Valley, about thirty-five miles north of Los Angeles.

I admire Kairi's ambition and courage. He had a great career in the music industry, working with Quincy Jones, Jaheim, and other recording artists, but he was willing to make the leap into the food business so that he could control his own destiny. I was glad to help such a hardworking entrepreneur, and believe me, he has had to put in many long hours to get Bubba's Q up and running.

BILLIONS TO BELIEVE IN

Kairi serves as a great example of an entrepreneur who saw an opportunity and seized it. Once he understood that NASCAR was eager to bring in qualified minority vendors, Kairi jumped on the opportunity. He would be the first to tell you that it was not an easy process.

"I've learned that there are a lot of contracts and opportunities available for minorities but people either aren't aware of them or they don't want to put in the time and effort to take advantage of them," he said. "There is a lot of paperwork involved in getting certified, sure, and I had a huge learning curve in that first year. Still, I found that when you commit to your dream, people buy in to it and reach out to help you."

Nearly 18 percent of all U.S. businesses are owned by minorities, according to a 2008 federal study by the Small Business Administration. Thanks to avid entrepreneurs such as Kairi Brown, who is working on three different businesses, that figure is expected to keep growing. Major corporations such as NASCAR, Starbucks, Best Buy, Lexus, and other powerful brands are increasingly aware that doing business with minority firms makes good business sense.

I tell everyone who will listen that doing business with well-run minority-owned vendors and contractors is a winning formula for all parties and for the country. These businesses provide jobs and pay taxes that help stabilize communities. They take people off the welfare rolls, reduce crime, encourage other minorities to launch start-ups, and serve as positive role models.

I'm a believer. I've built my entire business around my mission to make life better for underserved minority communities. I'm not alone. Minority business owners and entrepreneurs need to understand that many of the most powerful corporations in the country believe that what is good for minority businesses is good for them.

AT&T, Boeing, Chrysler, Ford, General Motors, and IBM are among the members of the Billion Dollar Roundtable, which was created in 2001 "to recognize and celebrate corporations that achieved spending of $1.0 billion or more with minority and woman-owned suppliers."

The mission of the Billion Dollar Roundtable (www.bdrusa .org) is to encourage excellence among diversity suppliers at a global level. Members of the roundtable also encourage other corporations to increase their commitment to and spending on minority contracts. Most business leaders understand that a diverse group of suppliers is just as important as diversity among their employees. Nearly all government agencies and most major corporations now have diversity supplier programs, so the opportunities are there, but you have to make the effort to obtain certification so you can take advantage of them.

Kairi jumped on the opportunity to become a minority contractor with NASCAR. I've done it in a number of my businesses, including my joint venture with Sodexo that is winning minority contracts across the country. Government agencies and private companies with diversity or minority supplier programs require you to be certified as a qualified Minority Business Enterprise (MBE) through federal or state programs or professional councils.

Certification requires patience and effort. The standards keep getting higher and higher. Yet the rewards can be incredible.

Still, getting certified as an MBE only puts you into the game; it does not guarantee that you will win every contract that you go after. You are still competing against other businesses, so you've got to keep working at being the best in your field.

GOOD BUSINESS

Minority supplier programs were first created in the 1960s under growing pressure from blacks and women who felt they were being shut out of the bidding for contracts with government agencies and major corporations. In the early days, enforcement was lax and enthusiasm was very limited, especially in the business community. Some people regarded them as token propaganda tools rather than true economic programs that would benefit all parties.

But slowly those perceptions have changed because minority groups and women are becoming business owners at a much higher rate than the national average, according to the U.S. Census Bureau's "2002 Survey of Business Owners (SBO)" released in July 2005. The number of U.S. businesses increased by 10 percent between 1997 and 2002, to 23 million. Yet the rate of growth of minority- and women-owned businesses was much higher, ranging from 67 percent for native Hawaiian– and other Pacific Islander–owned businesses to 20 percent for firms owned by women.

Even so, we need to encourage more minorities to become entrepreneurs. Minorities currently make up 28 percent of the United States population, according to U.S. Census statistics. Still, minority businesses make up only 15 percent of total businesses, 3 percent of gross receipts, and 4 percent of total corporate purchases.

The Census Bureau also estimates that minorities will make up about 40 percent of the U.S. population by 2050. There is

power in those numbers. Big corporations increasingly understand that minority customers will buy brands that buy from them
and invest in their communities. The nation can no longer afford
to limit opportunities and remain healthy economically. Thanks
to the global economy and growing numbers of entrepreneurs
among blacks, Hispanics, Asians, and women in business, what
was once "politically correct" now makes economic sense, particularly when minority consumers show their support of minority-
owned businesses and brands.

Most major companies have full-time administrators who are
held accountable for meeting minority contracting goals. They
recruit minority-owned suppliers and often provide them with
substantial financial support and training programs to help them
make their businesses stronger.

These are not charitable programs. More and more, major
corporations and government agencies understand that while
contracting with minority-owned businesses may be the right
thing to do, it is also a smart business move.

America's largest corporations hold their minority suppliers
and contractors to the same standards required of every other
business they deal with: they are required to be competitive in
their pricing, and they must meet the same quality standards.

With government agencies and large corporations hiring
more and more independent contractors and outsourcing everything from employee benefit programs to billing and IT services,
the opportunities for minority contractors and suppliers are
growing. At Magic Johnson Enterprises, we are often approached
by major companies aspiring to qualify for minority contracts
through joint ventures. That works to our advantage because it
helps us jump on business opportunities that we otherwise might
not have the expertise or infrastructure to support. The growing
demand for minority firms is also inspiring other minority business owners to form alliances with one another so that they can
compete for the bigger contracts.

OPPORTUNITIES AWAIT

One of the best resources for minority business owners is the National Minority Supplier Development Council (NMSDC; www.nmsdcus.org). Since 1972 its mission has been to help American corporations connect with qualified minority-owned businesses. Its headquarters is in New York City, but you can go to its Web site to see which of its thirty-nine regional councils is nearest you. More than 3,500 corporations belong to the NMSDC network, which also includes universities, hospitals, and other major institutions looking for minority-owned suppliers and contractors. The NMSDC has certified more than 15,000 businesses as "minority-owned" or "minority-controlled." Those MBEs have reaped hundreds of millions of dollars' worth of contracts thanks to the bridges built by the NMSDC.

The U.S. Small Business Administration (www.sba.gov) also certifies minority-owned businesses. The Women's Business Enterprise National Council (www.wbenc.org) does the same for women-owned businesses. Once your business is certified, you can register it with Diversity Information Resources (www .diversityinforesources.com), which tracks contract opportunities for minority firms and also connects them with corporate purchasing departments.

The U.S. Small Business Administration's 8(a) Business Development Program is the largest program that provides the same service for government contracts. This is serious business, amounting to billions in set-aside contracts each year for minority- and women-owned businesses. Another source for federal contracts is the Federal Business Opportunities Web site (www.fedbizopps.gov). There are similar Web sites for most state and local government agencies with set-aside programs for minorities.

GO BIG, STAY FLEXIBLE

The trend among U.S. corporations and also many government agencies is to reduce the number of suppliers and to have bigger contracts with those that they do deal with. That means you may have to go big or stay home. That can be a scary prospect for a small-business owner. There are ways to do it without taking on huge debt. By forming joint ventures or strategic alliances, or merging with minority-owned businesses, you can bulk up to step up your game. The Small Business Administration has a "Mentor-Protégé" program that pairs non-minority-owned companies with smaller minority-owned companies so that they can bid together for minority-targeted federal contracts.

To succeed in today's rapidly changing global business environment, minority entrepreneurs—like all other business owners—have to be imaginative and flexible, adapting based on the opportunities that are available. The one thing you can count on is that just when you think things are going smoothly, a change in the market, a new technology, or a great opportunity will send you scrambling. I see this in my own businesses and in those that we deal with.

One of those adaptable businesses I've come to admire is Uncle Darrow's, which was started in 1988 by four Louisiana cousins, Norwood J. Clark, Jr., Samuel Small, Jr., Ronald Smith, and Ronald Washington. They started out making New Orleans–style sweet treats based on family recipes dating back to the 1800s. Their pralines and Cajun pecan candies, in particular, were so good that they landed contracts to supply them to Nordstrom and Neiman Marcus in Beverly Hills.

We learned about Uncle Darrow's when they had a booth at a Black History program in the Baldwin Hills Crenshaw Plaza, where we were opening the first Magic Johnson Theatre. Ken Lombard sampled their sweets and thought they would be a great addition to the line of confections offered to our movie clients. We were eager to do business with other local minority-owned companies, so Uncle Darrow's looked like a great fit.

Norwood Clark, the president of Uncle Darrow's, met with us and with executives of Sony and Loews to see what they could do for us. As much as we all wanted to make it work, Uncle Darrow's decided it wasn't cost-effective for them to reformulate their products and packaging for our market. Their confections are high end, and they just couldn't find a way to make it work.

But that wasn't the end of the story, and that's a point worth noting. The discussions with our partners and the Uncle Darrow's leadership were all about trying to find a way to work together for the benefit of all parties. We liked them. They liked us. It was frustrating that we couldn't get their sweets into our theater, but nobody got angry or upset when that door closed.

Instead, Norwood Clark and his team came back with another plan. They proposed that we sell a new product that they would develop, Uncle Darrow's Bigg Dawg, a turkey hot dog treat. It turned out to be a phenomenal seller in our theaters and a great product for Uncle Darrow's.

And then when we did our deal with Starbucks, guess who got another call from us? Actually, we pitched the idea to executives at Starbucks first, because we wanted to offer special items for our customers in the UCO Starbucks stores. Once Starbucks officials bought in to the idea, they made the call to Uncle Darrow's, which caught Norwood Clark and his partners completely by surprise.

"I had no idea that Magic Johnson Enterprises was involved with Starbucks until I got a call from the Starbucks corporate office in Seattle and they told me that Magic's associates had suggested that we talk," Norwood recalled. "They flew us in to check us out, and then their people from Seattle came and spent several hours touring our commissary in Los Angeles. I had to show proof of this and that, and I had no problem doing it."

Starbucks doesn't play around. Neither did Nordstrom and Neiman Marcus. Uncle Darrow's had proven itself again. Like everyone else, Starbucks walked away impressed with its operation. Uncle Darrow's began producing four desserts—a peach cobbler, a sweet potato cranberry pecan cookie, a sweet potato pie turnover, and a southern-style tea cake—for the UCO Starbucks stores in the L.A. area.

For four years, Uncle Darrow's produced those treats for our Starbucks customers. They were a great supplier and we had a terrific relationship with them. In fact, when we began to expand our Starbucks holdings across the country, we asked Uncle Darrow's to supply our other stores with their products. Guess what? They decided that our expanded business needed more goods than they were equipped to provide. Once again, they took a hard look at the numbers and made a business decision.

Every successful entrepreneur is faced with similar tough decisions from time to time. Norwood Clark wanted to continue his relationship with MJE and Starbucks, but for him to maintain the high standards of his product, he would have had to open commissaries around the country to serve our stores. That was just too big a step, requiring too big an investment at that point in the history of Uncle Darrow's.

"We've had a good run," Norwood said.

Uncle Darrow's leadership decided instead to cash in on the brand recognition and the respect they had earned with their Starbucks, Nordstrom, and Neiman Marcus deals and go in a different direction. Today, you can join me, many of the Lakers and Dodgers, all sorts of Hollywood celebrities, and stars of the music industry at Uncle Darrow's Cajun/Creole Eatery in Marina del Rey. This is actually the second Uncle Darrow's location; the original was on Venice Boulevard in Los Angeles, where it was praised as a "gastronomic treasure trove" of southern cooking, with fresh seafood flown in daily from New Orleans.

When Norwood Clark and his partners decided to move their

successful restaurant from Venice Boulevard to Marina del Rey, they went to several banks for financing. Even with their successful track record, they found that most banks were unwilling to lend them the money they needed to move their restaurant to a more upscale location.

Did Norwood Clark give up? No, he kept going until he went to the right bank: Founders Bank, where I happened to be one of the stockholders. We arranged for a $150,000 SBA loan. Uncle Darrow's got the money it needed for a thriving restaurant that provides jobs for the community while serving up great food for loyal customers. I was known for my assists as a point guard for the Lakers, but I've got to tell you, there is no bigger thrill for me today than giving an assist to hardworking, creative entrepreneurs like Norwood Clark. I encourage all entrepreneurs to reach out and help others create and grow their businesses. When businesses help one another, everyone wins.

Web Wisdom

The Internet is an entrepreneur's best tool.

When we first considered forming a joint venture with Starbucks in 1997, one of our staff members suggested that I check out its "amazing" corporate Web site. I went to my office computer, jumped on the Internet, and was just floored by the amount of information I found there.

Now it happens nearly every day. Someone on our team will tell me about a potential new partner or client and then say, "Go to their Web site and check it out."

It works both ways. Not a day goes by without someone talking to me about something they saw on the Web sites of Magic Johnson Enterprises or the Magic Johnson Foundation.

Nobody has to convince me that Web sites are crucial for any business, big or small. From first impressions to final purchases, more and more business is done on the Internet. Just ten years ago, business Web sites were not all that common and most entrepreneurs relied on print and broadcast advertising, trade shows, telemarketing, direct mail, and other traditional methods of marketing their companies.

Now all that has changed. Online and e-commerce retail sales now exceed $100 billion annually, according to the U.S. Census Bureau. Your customers and clients go looking for what they want by "Googling" or using other search engines. Whether buying a house, a car, or a vacuum cleaner, their shopping begins at home, on the computer. They can make decisions and purchase products without ever talking to you or your sales team. If they do come to you, it is usually with a whole lot of information to inform their buying decisions.

Just look at how Web sites such as www.edmunds.com have changed the way people buy and sell cars. Now car shoppers walk into dealers knowing exactly what the dealer pays for the car and for every option on the car. They can even find out about special incentives that the car manufacturers are offering their dealers on specific models. That sort of information has changed the way that that industry operates.

Business-to-business shopping has changed too. Marketing-Sherpa reports that 98 percent of business-to-business buyers search Google. It is essential, then, for every business big and small not only to have a first-class Web site but to find ways to drive potential customers and clients to it and then to keep them coming back.

The great thing about the Web is that it levels the playing field. With a strong Web site your mom-and-pop business can compete with the giants of your industry and maybe even become one of them. After all, eBay, which has annual sales of more than $59 billion, started as a Web site created by a collector of Pez candy dispensers looking to hook up with other collectors! You just never know where the Web can take your business until you get a site up and running.

SMART POLITECHS

The 2008 presidential campaign served as a great example of the importance of a strong Internet presence. Once a long-shot candidate, Democrat Barack Obama raised the bar with his campaign's skilled use of Web sites, social networking, user-generated video, and targeted e-mails to build community, rally support, and bring in donations.

The New York Times reported that early in the campaign, Obama's team invested $2 million in software and hardware so that it could leverage the power of the Web. It didn't hurt that a key member of his team, Steve Westly, cochair of Obama's California campaign, was formerly an executive at eBay.

Obama used state-of-the-art online fund-raising tools to build early momentum. Through his Web strategies, Obama drew supporters close to his campaign by asking for feedback and for personal information including occupations, church affiliations, and volunteer histories. He attracted more money than any other candidate by sending out regular e-mails asking for it in an inoffensive way that made donors feel as though they were part of an important mission.

The Obama campaign pioneered the "small donors" approach, with 90 percent of his money coming in donations of $100 or less. This allowed donors to give again and again during the campaign before they hit the $2,300 limit. Even before the Democratic Party decided on its candidate, Obama's campaign had registered 1 million donors, with more than 90 percent of $50 million in contributions coming through his campaign's Web site. His donor list was more than three times the size of the largest list compiled by candidate Howard Dean in the previous presidential election.

WEB WISDOM

To build momentum and grow your business, you have to reach out with a Web site that will attract attention from the millions of people who go online to shop, find information, and find the products and services they need. It is so important that one of the key questions we now ask all potential partners and suppliers is how they intend to use the resources of the Web to build their brands and their businesses.

In the past, if you wanted to learn about a business or a corporation, you had to go to the library or to its bricks-and-mortar location. Now the company's Web site serves as the front door you walk through to check out the brand and the business. You want to keep customers coming through that door by creating a dynamic and inviting Web portal.

Print ads and telemarketing still have their place, but the newest marketing tools include search engine optimization (SEO), pay-per-click (PPC) advertising, blogging, forums, buzz marketing, targeted landing pages, conversion tools, and sophisticated analytics. Google Analytics (www.google.com/analytics) and Site Meter (www.sitemeter.com) are among the free tools available on the Internet that can help you find out how people are finding your Web site and which keywords are luring them.

Unless you are a Web guru, you will have to hire someone to design and maintain your Web sites for you. Advances in methods of drawing people to your Web site have also added to the complexity and heightened competition for "hits" from the major search engines. Search engine optimization (SEO) is a process for increasing the volume and quality of online traffic directed to a Web site from Google, Yahoo!, and other search engines.

The goal is to get your site's link to appear at or near the top of the results page of those big search engines. The higher your site rank, the more people are directed to your Web site. SEO masters also have methods of rating the accuracy of site content, tracking updates, and attracting links from other sites. Web site developers, Web designers, and Internet directory companies can help you find other ways to help you draw attention to your site.

ONLINE BASICS

Your business Web site will need an Internet service provider to put it online, a distinguishing domain name, a home page with a basic description of your products or services, and a company e-mail address. Small businesses on a budget can get help for a basic Web site from inexpensive packages offered by Yahoo! Small Business, Web.com, GoDaddy.com, and others found online.

These services can get your Web site up and running and help you learn the ins and outs for as little as $12 a month. If you want to sell things and accept credit card charges on your site, the technical aspects become more complex and more expensive in a hurry. For small businesses, Yahoo! has a Merchant Solutions package that starts at $40 a month. Other services that offer similar packages include ShoppingCart.com and GoDaddy's Business Hosting Solutions.

The Web sites of Magic Johnson Enterprises and the Magic Johnson Foundation have become more important and complex as we have diversified our businesses and increased our philanthropy. Our mission to serve urban America has attracted attention from around the world. We track visits, and though most of our Web site guests come from the United States, we have substantial international viewership from guests in Italy, Mexico, South Africa, China, and elsewhere across the globe. Many of them want to do business or to inquire about opportunities.

Customers of our retail chains and foundation contact us through our Web sites to make suggestions and offer feedback. If there is a dirty towel on the floor in one of our locker rooms or a trash can that needs emptying at a Starbucks, we hear about it. We also use our Web sites to respond to our customers, to stay connected, to explain our mission, and to make major announcements about our brand.

The challenge for our Web team is producing and maintaining one all-encompassing Web site that reflects everything we do while serving an incredibly diverse audience of consumers, customers, corporate clients, basketball fans, and the general public. Just keeping up with the day-to-day changes and news emanating from a dynamic business requires a continual process of updating, upgrading, and improving our site. Just when we think we've got our site in perfect shape, our Web team has to go back in and add something new or remove something that has become outdated. They are constantly looking for ways to improve our site, to take advantage of the newest technologies, and to make sure that our Internet presence, like the rest of our company, surpasses expectations.

For a while, we had three or four independent Web sites devoted to our varied business and nonprofit endeavors, and we had several different vendors managing them. Lisa Meyers, our senior vice president of communications and branding, wisely saw that we needed to refresh and redefine our Web presence and, more than anything, take ownership of our Web site by managing it ourselves on a day-to-day basis. We view the Web primarily as a communication medium, with an incredible power to build our brand.

As Lisa noted, potential customers, business partners, and others visit our Web site for a wide range of reasons: to find information, donate to our nonprofit projects, and seek employment too. Our goals in revising and centralizing our Web sites were to streamline management while providing up-to-date information about our brand. We also wanted to build a foundation for Web growth and development so that we can begin to take advantage of new media and social networking opportunities. Before we began our Web site revisions our primary site, www.magicjohnson enterprises.com, was amazing graphically, but it was difficult to navigate and lacked substance. We also had problems with the site's daily management and maintenance because we did not have the ability to manage content quickly in-house through a basic content management solution.

My in-house Web team is always updating and improving our online presence. They are constantly adjusting to new technologies. They also have the challenge of updating as we grow rapidly. We've gone from a small company with just a handful of people to a multifaceted corporation with thousands of employees. The Magic Johnson Foundation has grown to include HIV/AIDS education and research, college scholarship grants, and computer and career training for residents in both urban and rural areas.

Like many businesses, we have experimented with different Web designers to get the appearance and feel that we want. You will be working closely with your designer for long periods, so it is important to find someone who "gets" your business and your brand. It is not an inexpensive proposition. Depending on the size of your business and your Web site needs, creating and maintaining a business Web site can add thousands to tens of thousands of dollars to your annual budget.

According to Stefannie Bernstein, senior manager of public relations for Magic Johnson Enterprises, "One lesson we've learned is that you should always have full access to manage your online content. You should never turn over complete control of your Web site to an outside contractor. We keep the content management tools in-house so that people in our organization can control and contribute to the site daily." Lately we have been adding tools that allow us to update the Web sites as easily as writing and sending e-mails.

Business and corporate Web sites must convey the mission and culture in unique and enticing ways so that they don't look like every other company site. There are additional challenges for our foundation Web site. We compete with other nonprofit organizations for donations, so we have to lure visitors to that site and sell our appeal to them tactfully but convincingly. Our Web

team is always looking for ways to add more video, online mer-
chandising, and more sophisticated methods for attracting and
processing donations to the foundation site.

UP AND RUNNING

The key to having a successful Web site or Web business is the
ability to aggregate your audience, or potential audience, to your
Web portal. There are millions of Web sites and Web addresses
and millions of blogs (which stands for "Web logs"). Competition
for visitors or viewers is intense, so you have to master methods
for attracting your target audience.

Once your Web site is up and running, you will want to promote your URL (Web address) on your business cards, press re-
leases, letterheads, envelopes, brochures, flyers, and newsletters.
You might also want to make reference to your Web site address
on your phone system message. Promoting business Web sites
and "attracting eyeballs" has become a major business in itself as
those who sell their goods and services and market their companies on the Internet look for ways to grow their companies online. It is not enough for your Web site to attract visitors directly;
it must also rank favorably with search engines.

The key to search engine optimization is something called
the Google Index. This index explores how many times your specific name, brand, or company appears on the front page of
Google when it is placed in their search box. Because Google is
the most popular search engine in the United States, and because of the millions of visitors that log on daily, it is imperative
that your brand appear on the first page of the search results.
The Google Index explores steps on how you can get this done.

The tricks of this trade include providing the right meta tags
and beta tags so that search engines can determine what sort of
products and services your site is offering and what types of cus-

tomers and clients you serve. That means having the right page titles and keywords on the page and in your Web address too.

It has also become important to lure targeted traffic to your Web site by having other sites link to yours. Each link to your site is considered a vote of confidence by the search engines, but you have to be careful to link to only trustworthy sites.

Blogs, which entered the mainstream around 2002, are now considered link magnets because search engines tend to look for fresh content, according to our Web gurus. A well-written, informative blog that offers insights, unique information, commentary, or a fresh perspective can bring more readers who will link to your site, helping create a sense of community and enhancing your brand. Only about 5 percent of small businesses with fewer than one hundred employees have blogs on their Web sites, according to a 2008 American Express survey. Some professionals and types of businesses seem to embrace them more than others. So many lawyers have blogs that they have their own name: "blawgers."

Blogging can be an inexpensive form of guerrilla marketing if you do the blogging yourself or have someone on staff with the writing skills and time to do it. Blogs can run just a few sentences to a few paragraphs—many times not reaching over seven hundred words, according to our Web masters. They say that the challenge is to keep the information fresh day after day, and to give people a reason to come back for more. For example, in 2007 Doug Melville, my vice president of marketing and business development, was invited by *Advertising Age* to write a weekly blog on multicultural marketing and various new techniques. Our participation in this kind of blogging has helped keep viewers tied to our site while keeping us current on new trends and business opportunities.

If you provide products or a service and qualify as an expert in your field or as someone with intimate knowledge—whether it is law, politics, the great outdoors, or pet care—you would probably have little difficulty writing a daily blog for your Web site. Blogging is similar to writing a guest column for the local newspaper and a subtle way to market your business. I have yet to figure out a way to write a blog myself because my days are so heavily booked and because I travel so much. Our Web team advises that the best bloggers are authentic and authoring their own blogs, but some business owners do hire staff to write blogs based on information they provide. Bloggers have to work at keeping their blogs interesting, entertaining, and relevant; otherwise, don't expect people to keep coming back to read them. I'm told that physicians do this by offering health tips on their Web sites. Lawyers offer legal advice. Veterinarians feature the latest in pet care news. Viewers return to Web sites that give them information they can't easily find elsewhere.

MAKING THE GRADE

The power of search engines to generate revenue has created a whole new form of competition as online businesses jockey for position. They ride rapidly changing technologies to stay ahead in this race for high standings with Google, Yahoo!, and MSN that can bring people to a Web site.

An inexpensive way to check your Web site's effectiveness in this arena is by using Website Grader at www.websitegrader.com. You simply plug in your Web address (URL) and the grader gives you a report that grades your site on a scale of 1 to 100; the higher the grade, the better your rating.

The grader provides explanations for why the search engines might be missing or ignoring your site and offers suggestions that can help your site get more respect from Google and the gang. It tells you how many of your Web pages are indexed by Google, how many other sites link to yours, and how many times you have been bookmarked on Delicious (del.icio.us), the popular social-bookmarking Web site. Grader will also analyze whether your Web site is stressing the right terms to get the sort of attention you want from the online search engines.

While writing this chapter, our Web experts plugged "www.magicjohnson.com" into the Website Grader, and it came up with a score that we will work to improve upon. (I'm still competitive, remember.) We scored 73 out of 100, which meant that our site scored higher than 73 percent of all others tested in terms of its marketing effectiveness. This score is measured by examining more than fifty variables, including search engine data, Web site structure, approximate traffic, site performance, and readability level, according to the report.

Another tool that is very informative for checking the health of your Web site is www.Quantcast.com. Quantcast measures your Web site's overall rank and data based on the amount of hits and Web traffic that it garners; it's used by many of the top technology and marketing executives as a quick way to get the lowdown on a particular site. To use Quantcast, simply type in a URL to see how it ranks. You should also realize that checking out a site on Quantcast is the industry standard, so it's very likely that your competitors, partners, and potential investors will all be using it to peek at your online results and presence.

TECH TIPS

Your Web site has between fifteen and thirty seconds to capture the attention of each visitor, according to studies on Internet traffic. To get them to stick around and do business, here are a few suggestions from the Web wizards at Magic Johnson Enterprises.

- **PAY A PRO.** A professional Web designer will update design, layout, and functionality so that your site can compete with the latest tools and technologies, such as podcasting and videos. Make sure you have the ability to get into your Web site and change material whenever you feel the need to do it.

- **KEEP THE LAYOUT SIMPLE AND CLEAN.** Make it easy to read and to search by putting a search box near the top. Viewers should also have easy access to your site's About Us, Frequently Asked Questions, and Contact Us links.

- **FORGET THE FLASH.** Web designers may be enamored of flashy features such as "splash pages" with music and videos that pop up before your home page, but most viewers are looking for information, not entertainment. They should be able to get to the goods within ten seconds without distracting bells and whistles.

- **PERSONALIZE YOUR SITE.** Your goal with any marketing tool is to create a connection, so give your site the human touch with photographs, contact information, and bios of key people in the company.

- **KEEP THEM COMING.** Studies have found that 85 percent of online shoppers arrive via search engines, so make sure your Web site is a search-engine magnet with the right keywords and phrases and constantly updated content.

- **STAY ON TOP OF IT.** Even if you hire professional firms to create and maintain your Web site, pay attention to the latest developments to make sure they are staying on top of new technologies and giving your site all it needs to draw viewers.

- **INVITE VISITORS TO STAY.** Blogs, forums, podcasts, and Webinars (seminars on the Web) create a dialogue and encourage viewers to stick around to learn more about you and your business.

- **BE RESPONSIVE.** Make sure you respond to e-mail inquiries and questions from visitors to your Web site. Every one of them is a potential opportunity to turn a visitor into a customer or client.

PART IV

BUSINESS LEADERSHIP

Leading Versus Managing

True leaders don't just manage a business team, they inspire it.

I played "the point" most of my basketball career. I was the leader on the floor—the point guard—setting up plays and distributing the ball on offense. Now I call the plays for our businesses at Magic Johnson Enterprises and for our philanthropic work at the Magic Johnson Foundation.

Playing point is a bigger job now, and it's a lonely job because there is no coach on the bench giving me direction. Nor is there a general manager sitting above the coach to give us a master strategy.

Like most entrepreneurs, I have to figure it out myself, every minute of every day. I choose the team members. I set the game plan, and I keep everyone hustling toward our goals.

The responsibility for our success or failure is mine and mine alone. In living up to that responsibility, I face the same quandary that confronts every entrepreneurial business leader sooner or later: *Am I the leader or the manager?*

Management and leadership experts note that the two roles are often conflicting. Managers keep order by solving problems and ensuring that businesses operate smoothly. They make sure tasks are done and goals are accomplished. They are supposed to stay cool emotionally and professionally.

Entrepreneurial leaders run hot. We are driven by passion, and we tend to create chaos as we push for innovation and change to keep our companies competitive and ahead of an ever-changing market.

There are other differences between leaders and managers:

- Managers are reactive; leaders are proactive.
- Managers seek compromise and consensus; leaders challenge the status quo.
- Managers meet expectations; leaders create them.

Every business needs both managers and leaders. The question for the entrepreneur is: Can you be both?

Earlier, I noted that role models and mentors are invaluable resources for entrepreneurs. When I was trying to sort out my role as a business leader and manager, I often looked to Lakers majority owner Dr. Jerry Buss because he was a passionate leader who also paid attention to details. In fact, he transformed the Lakers and the entire league.

DETAIL MAN

Dr. Buss cultivates the image of a gregarious, hard-partying guy, but I learned early on that he didn't miss a thing that went on with his businesses, his team, or his players.

Shortly after I reported to training camp in 1979, my rookie year with the Lakers, I went to a party in Malibu with Dr. Buss, who had just purchased the team from Jack Kent Cooke. The party was at a beautiful home on the ocean, packed with celebrities and wealthy people. I felt lost. This was a long, long way from Lansing.

A cocktail waitress approached me while I was standing alone. She asked if I wanted a drink. Dr. Buss was nearby talking to friends, and he looked over when he heard the waitress offer me a cocktail.

"Yes, I'd like a cranberry and orange juice on the rocks," I told her.

Dr. Buss caught my eye, lifted his glass my way, and smiled.

I'd forgotten about that moment until Dr. Buss brought it up at my forty-seventh birthday party in 2006. As usual, he was the first person to arrive.

"I'm glad you could make it," I told him, holding up my cranberry and orange juice drink for a toast.

"You know, twenty-seven years ago, I took you to a party and saw you order that same drink. I knew then that you were going to be successful no matter what you did after basketball," Dr. Buss said.

I asked him what he meant by that.

"Even as a young guy, you kept it under control, always with a smile on your face. You stayed focused. You took care of your money. Most of all, you understood that the best way to learn was to listen."

Dr. Buss and I had a special relationship and a closeness that you rarely see today between an owner and one of his players. He treated me like a son. I was just a few years out of high school when I joined the Lakers. Yet when I told him that I was interested in business, he took me seriously. He invited me to sit in on meetings so that I could see how he dealt with bankers, sponsors, lawyers, and other aspects of his businesses.

I learned a great deal just by hanging out with Dr. Buss. He is the most successful owner in any sport, and he is always a step ahead of the competition. Yet he was a late bloomer as a businessman.

Dr. Buss grew up in a rural area near the small town of Kemmerer, Wyoming, known as the "Fossil Fish Capital of the World."

The population was only a couple thousand people, along with "103 Pronghorn Antelope and 113,000 Fossil Fish." He graduated from the University of Wyoming and then earned a doctorate in physical chemistry at the University of Southern California.

He became a teacher after college. It didn't pay much, but he loved it. To help pay the bills, he began investing in real estate just as the boom times hit. He and his partner bought their first apartment building with a $1,000 investment in 1959 and later sold it for a big profit. They were off and running, and soon Dr. Buss left teaching to become a major player in the real estate market. His earnings enabled him to buy the Lakers, the Los Angeles Kings, the Forum, and a 13,000-acre ranch for a total of $67.5 million in 1979.

Today, the Lakers are worth $560 million or more, according to *Forbes* magazine. The unprecedented success of the franchise is due mostly to Dr. Buss's leadership. He transformed the team into one of the most popular sports franchises in the country by embracing the diversity of the city and blending entertainment with sports. Lakers games are the hottest ticket in sports, and being seen at courtside is like walking the red carpet at the Oscars.

LEADING CHANGE

Shortly after he bought the Lakers, Dr. Buss went to a favorite lounge owned by a musical director for MGM Studios. The owner often staged musical shows, and that night, the people in the bar started chanting "Showtime! Showtime!" before the opening curtain.

Dr. Buss decided he wanted Lakers fans to be that excited about their team. He set about transforming home games into "Showtime!" He stepped back and saw that the Lakers were going to have to compete with a rapidly expanding number of entertainment options. So he became a change agent, transforming the Lakers and the entire league. He revitalized the Forum as the sports version of a Broadway show or a Las Vegas revue.

He served as a visionary leader while also attending to the fine details. He created the modern Lakers brand by adding critical elements such as the Laker Girls and a house band. He invited Hollywood's biggest stars to sit courtside. Word quickly spread that the Lakers hosted parties where games broke out.

It was a joy to be a player when everyone in the stands was having so much fun, but it was tough to go to the locker room because the Lakers halftime entertainment was as good as anything you could see in Las Vegas.

Dr. Buss was the host and master of ceremonies. He created the Forum Club as his own private nightclub and hosted pregame dinners there with Hollywood stars, business leaders, and politicians.

Under his guidance, the Lakers went from being just another sports franchise to being an integral part of the city and the hottest ticket in the NBA. Dr. Buss's success with the Lakers took the NBA to new levels and really merged the worlds of sports and entertainment. He pays attention to details while always advancing his primary mission: to give Lakers fans a great experience.

SHARING THE LEAD

When I shake things up in my businesses to keep us moving forward, my staff calls it "Magicizing," but it is just my version of Dr. Buss's continuous efforts to give customers what they want—and to exceed their expectations in the process.

Our goal with both our customers and our partners is to serve their needs so that we can thrive together. In our partnerships and joint ventures, I study the details of each business with the intention of adding value by providing expertise on the wants and needs of urban and rural minorities.

I recommended, for example, that all of our Magic Sport 24 Hour Fitness centers include basketball courts, because so many public courts have deteriorated or become dangerous. Those basketball courts, which are run with strictly enforced rules to allow equal access, have become one of the most popular areas in our clubs.

Similarly, my staff and I developed a ten-step program to prepare aspiring home owners for their loan applications for our former partner WaMu because many urban residents were easily discouraged by that process. The program helped them understand how to prepare their finances so that they can meet bank requirements.

In the spring of 2008, we launched a consulting and licensing partnership with Best Buy to help this leading brand retail chain strengthen its relationship with minority consumers. One of my first suggestions as the leader of the new partnership was that we hold special meetings to improve networking among the managers of Best Buy's urban market stores. When I met with them, I quickly grasped that they shared unique challenges in trying to serve their customers. Some of them offered great ideas when I spoke with them, but they had no process for sharing those ideas with one another.

One of the problems faced by Best Buy urban store managers is that their customers have very specific tastes in music but their stores were expected to offer the same selection with the same marketing as suburban stores. I suggested to Best Buy officials that displays of Mick Jagger were just fine in affluent neighborhoods populated by aging baby boomers, but they were not likely to inspire sales in minority communities such as Compton or the

South Side of Chicago. Best Buy listened, and it is working on giving greater autonomy to its urban store managers.

Small details can add up to big sales. Today's entrepreneurial business leaders have to be able to listen to their team members and make adjustments when they make sense. Shaking things up is a great way to get rid of the cobwebs and keep a business fresh.

Motivating Employees

Think of your employees as fellow entrepreneurs.

I got some unsettling news while preparing for our annual young scholars leadership conference a few years ago. One of our top scholarship students wanted to quit school. I made it my mission to change her mind.

Muriel is a strong-willed young lady and a very smart one too. A natural entrepreneur, she had grown impatient with college classes. She told the foundation staff that she wanted to get out and start a business immediately.

She had the drive, but she was not ready. She did not have the tools she needed to survive. We didn't want her to look back one day and realize that she had walked away from an incredible opportunity to have most of her college education paid for.

I give a welcoming speech at the opening of the conference for young people in our Taylor Michaels Scholarship Program each year. There are usually 150 students in the program. We provide them with partial scholarships ranging from $3,000 to $10,000 annually, along with a laptop and a printer for the freshmen. Students in the program come from communities across the country where we have business interests and from my hometown, Lansing, Michigan.

We choose students who have had challenges to overcome

but have proven themselves to be determined, strong-willed, and leaders. Muriel was all of the above, with ample doses in every category. She was impatient with school and yearned to be free. I admired her ambition, but the consensus was that Muriel needed to finish her last year of schooling. My goal was to convince her to stay in school. To do that, I departed from my prepared speech that day.

A few minutes into my speech to the scholars, I asked Muriel to join me at the podium. Then I called her out. I praised her for her intelligence, her hard work, and her drive. I told her that we cared deeply for her and that we felt she had a lot to offer the world.

"You are going to make big contributions one day," I said. "But you need to stay in school, get your education, and then get out there and tear it up."

Then I called for a vote. I asked all of her peers to raise their hands if they thought Muriel should quit school. Nobody raised a hand. Then I invited everyone who wanted her to stay to come up and give Muriel a hug. They swarmed her. I also told all of the other students to make sure they kept encouraging Muriel to finish her education.

Muriel cried. I cried. The whole room was one big eye-wiping, nose-blowing mess by the time I finished the speech. Then Muriel and I shared a big hug. She promised to continue her education, and she lived up to her pledge by getting her degree. She thanks me to this day for motivating her to stay on track.

COACH AND CHEERLEADER

I think of myself as both coach and cheerleader of my businesses. Now, there certainly are coaches who operate in the command-and-control management mode. They shy away from any personal involvement with their players, treating them like replaceable parts. But I preferred playing for coaches who were passionate about the game and bonded with their players. Scorebooks indicate that I had a pretty decent career.

My favorite coaches were good managers, but they were even better motivators and leaders. They encouraged us to develop our talents fully. We felt they wanted us to succeed as individuals and as a team, and they gave us a sense of mission. It was us against the universe.

If managing the bottom line is all that matters to the person at the top of a company, you can rest assured that everyone else will be driven by the same sort of single-minded self-interest. That sort of narrowly focused management may sustain a business for a while, but eventually it will fall apart. The fall of Enron is a perfect example. The collapse of the entire subprime mortgage industry is another.

In both cases, those businesses were characterized by everyone grabbing for as much profit as they could get their hands on, even when they saw that their business models were corrupt and doomed to failure. They lost their bearings, and their worlds imploded because their leadership failed them.

I am all for making a profit and building wealth for myself, my employees, and the greater community. Still, my deepest satisfaction is in creating jobs and opportunities for others. That may not suit your personality. You have to be true to yourself. You can't fake it. If making money is your primary focus, I wish you the best. You may well achieve your goal. For me, the important thing is to enjoy what I do every day and to help others achieve their goals in the process.

I have always motivated my team based on instinct. To keep your team engaged and on task, you have to serve their needs, not yours. We are all essentially self-centered, but we are also capable of working unselfishly for the greater good. Here are my tips for being a leader who motivates and inspires your team.

1. Carry the flag

We are the communities we serve. That's our motto, and I make sure no one forgets it. Everything we do is aimed at serving people who have not been well served by the business community in the past. Call them urban Americans, emerging markets, or minority communities; they are why we do what we do—in everything we do. I remind team members every day of our mission because it helps them understand that they are part of something important, something that can change the world.

2. Share the blessings

My name is on the company and the brand. I get plenty of attention everywhere I go. I think it is important for me to recognize the contributions made by the rest of our team. I want everyone in our headquarters to know that I care about them and that I am invested in their success. One way I show that is by organizing potlucks or buying lunch.

There are more than thirty team members in our corporate headquarters. Every day that I am in the office, I buy them lunch and I eat with them. Not everyone can be there every day, but each of those present gathers in the lunchroom and shares with me what is going on at work and in their lives.

Sometimes I phone for a delivery, but most times, I'll go out and get it myself. My staff says I've checked out every restaurant in Beverly Hills. I do it because I enjoy it. I see it as a small perk that I can provide. The important thing isn't that I buy lunch—although it's not a bad perk—it's that our little lunch sessions help us bond as a team.

I've been known to treat my other audiences too. I recently put on a basketball clinic at the U.S. Marine Corps base at Camp Pendleton in Southern California for children whose fathers or mothers are soldiers stationed in Iraq or Afghanistan and around the world. Many of these kids have a tough time because their parents are serving their country. I wanted to do something that would lift their spirits and get them excited. A couple days before the clinic, I went on a shopping spree at the Lakers Store in the Staples Center. I bought a truckload of the latest Lakers caps, jerseys, and T-shirts.

When I arrived at Camp Pendleton, I passed out all those Lakers goodies, and from that point on, I had their full attention. I encouraged them to dream big and to remember, whenever they put on their Lakers hat, jersey, and T-shirt, that they should always feel free to pursue their dreams.

3. Get away together

It is important for me to be close to the members of my team. I want to know what is going on in their lives. I pay attention to who is up, who is down, and who may need my help or guidance or a little motivation.

To help keep our bonds strong, I have a company retreat to Hawaii, Mexico, or some other beautiful location each year. These are fun getaways, but they aren't all relaxation and recreation. We do a lot of soul-searching both personally and professionally. My purpose is to receive feedback, to reinforce the vision, goals, and mission of the company, to recognize achievement, and to help our team members keep growing.

4. Make them stretch

At a recent company retreat, I delivered a change-up. I had prepared a rousing motivational speech built around the concept of "one band, one sound," from the 2002 movie *Drumline* about a legendary marching band at a historically black university. The idea was that while we are a group of individuals, we are working together toward a common vision and purpose.

Stefannie Bernstein, senior manager of public relations, helped me put together a PowerPoint presentation showing a breakdown for each quarter of the previous year. There were scorecards of where we were, where I wanted to go, and what I expected for the year ahead. I intended to include a lot of humor because I wanted this to be a playful session.

I worked harder on that presentation than on any I've ever done in-house. I locked myself in a conference room for several hours with Stefannie, to refine it.

The next morning, I went through the whole thing one last time and decided to completely change it. Earlier that morning, my executive team had taken me through a Strengths, Weaknesses, Opportunities, and Threats (SWOT) analysis of our company. It evaluated Magic Johnson Enterprises in terms of our internal strengths and weaknesses and identified external opportunities and threats that might impact our company. We use the SWOT analysis as a tool for adjusting our business plan as we move forward. It is a method of organizing information and looking at the possibilities so we can come up with strategies for growing our business and protecting our brand. We also do SWOT analysis from time to time to help us understand the company's strengths, correct its weaknesses, and plot its future.

Hearing the results of the SWOT analysis that morning really fired me up. It gave me such a clear picture of our strengths and weaknesses and the opportunities and threats that I had to throw my entire prepared presentation out the window, including the *Drumline* theme.

Instead, I built my presentation around an internal memo from someone I greatly admire, Starbucks founder Howard Schultz. The memo had just become public. It was Howard's honest and straightforward assessment of what he believed had gone wrong with the company he created. He felt it had lost touch with its core customers and its purpose. The memo was Howard's passionate manifesto for reclaiming Starbucks's greatness. I decided to incorporate it into my revised presentation.

I scared everyone at first because I was so passionate. I had Stefannie read Howard's memo. I then talked about how much I

believed in our commitment to making life better for people in
urban America. Then I told them what I had learned in the analysis of our strengths and weaknesses. Finally, I listed the opportunities and also the challenges we faced in carrying out that
commitment.

It was an intense presentation. I was concerned about both
the weaknesses and the challenges. Yet the strengths and opportunities that were identified thrilled me. Reviewing where we'd
been and looking at where we wanted to go proved to be a very
emotional experience. We laughed. We cried. We agreed that we
all needed to work harder and reach higher. I homed in on several key people, noting strengths and weaknesses and letting
them know that I wanted them to succeed.

One of our younger staff members was surprised when I
served him up as an example. I had overheard another employee
challenge him to a race on the beach earlier in the week. They
had made a bet. A day later, I asked how the race had gone. It
hadn't. The challenger had showed up for the race, but his opponent had not. I told the no-show, "If you run from competition in
your personal life, you may do it in your career too. I don't want
you to ever run from competition again. If you tell someone you
are going to do something or be somewhere, I expect you to live
up to that promise."

It was a tough-love moment, but there was no resentment because he knew I was trying to make him a better person and a
stronger employee. Still, there was a lot of buzz about it because
no one knew that I'd been listening when the bet was made. It
helped make the point that I pay attention and that I care.

At that retreat, we bonded in our mission to be the best individuals and the best company that we can possibly be. Afterward,
we videotaped responses from each employee as to what was
learned that day and the feelings and thoughts it inspired. The
responses were incredible, and they inspired me.

5. Surprise them

I try to put myself into the shoes of the people who work for our companies. Although I don't like to receive surprises, I like to give surprises. So I like to surprise them with Lakers tickets and other treats. I've been known to call the office on a Friday morning and announce a special holiday: "Tell everyone to take the rest of the day off. Turn the lights out. Lock the door. Go home."

We have a lot of working moms and dads at MJE, so when things get hectic around my house, I know it must be the same for them. I encourage people to take off early to go to their kids' Halloween parties or their school plays and holiday pageants. I don't have to worry about them falling behind on their work because they come back and work twice as hard the next day.

6. Pray with them

This one may surprise you. I don't make a big deal about my faith. Yet I have a lot to be grateful for, and before every meal and meeting at our office, I invite all those present to say a little private prayer. I don't care whom they pray to or what they say—as long as they put in a good word for the boss. Is there a place for faith in the office? It seems to be working for us!

Change Management

A wise boss isn't afraid
to shake things up to stay on top.

I have many boxes of athletic ribbons, plaques, and trophies, but I may be just as proud of a few words printed in December 2001. It wasn't the usual source; not the *Los Angeles Times*, *Sports Illustrated*, or ESPN. This was a report in the *Harvard Business Review* entitled "The Work of Leadership."

Here's an excerpt:

Earvin "Magic" Johnson's greatness in leading his basketball team came in part from his ability to play hard while keeping the whole game situation in mind, as if he stood in a press box or on a balcony above the field of play. Bobby Orr played hockey in the same way. Other players might fail to recognize the larger patterns of play that performers like Johnson and Orr quickly understand, because they are so engaged in the game that they get carried away by it. Their attention is captured by the rapid motion, the physical contact, the roar of the crowd, and the pressure to execute. In sports, most players simply may not see who is open for a pass, who is missing a block, or how the offense and defense work together. Players like

Johnson and Orr watch these things and allow their observations to guide their actions.

The study went on to say that business leaders too must have
the ability "to view patterns as if they were on a balcony." Whether
leading a sports team or a company, the person in charge has to
have the ability to assess the company's progress in relation to its
goals at any given time.

I am flattered that the *Harvard Business Review* recognized my
ability to step back and make corrections in the flow of a game. I
do the same thing in my businesses. The talents and skill sets required of you as a business leader can vary greatly depending on
the field you are in and market conditions, but the ability to step
back, measure the progress of your business, and then make the
necessary corrections to stay on course is essential for every top
executive and entrepreneurial owner.

No business operates in a static marketplace. A surge in the
price of oil, a drop in housing values, a terrorist strike, a tainted
or flawed product, a new technology, so many major events can
cause tidal shifts in our markets. Local events may impact small
businesses in a big way: street repairs block access to your store,
or an aggressive competitor slashes prices. A business owner must
adapt and adjust on the run when the market shifts.

I keep an eye out for challenges. Yet I also try to focus on solutions and opportunities rather than dwelling on problems. Bobby
Turner and I did this when we saw that the housing bubble was
going to burst. We were monitoring and reading the conditions
that caused the downturn even before it occurred. We recognized that the decline in the housing market and the tightening
of mortgage loans were going to impact urban communities. We
saw that residents there were likely to shift away from buying
homes to renting apartments. We then reacted to what we read
and recognized, and we didn't do it in a small way.

We created a new Canyon-Johnson fund by raising more than

twice the combined amount of our two previous funds. The new Canyon-Johnson Urban Fund III has equity of $1 billion, compared with the combined total of $400 million in our two other funds. That $1 billion is just seed money. We plan on using it to bring about more than $4 billion in new development and urban revitalization in the top forty U.S. metropolitan markets.

Our first two funds were aimed at commercial and industrial, and some housing, developments in urban America. The focus of the third fund is to build and renovate apartments in ethnically diverse neighborhoods.

When the housing bubble burst and financial markets experienced turmoil in 2006–2008, we adjusted our strategy. We looked at the fundamentals and saw that the drop in home prices did not mean a long-term drop in demand for places to live. Our research indicated that over the next ten years population growth will generate demand for 14.6 million units of housing, with minority populations projected to account for 70 percent of that demand.

Based on our findings, we created the Canyon-Johnson Urban Communities Fund to focus on acquiring, improving, and greening residential rental and mixed-use properties in urban communities across America. We read the market, reflected on the changes under way in society, and recognized that more and more people would be renting instead of purchasing their own homes as it became more difficult to obtain mortgages.

The new reality caused by the collapse in the subprime mortgage market called for a new strategy. The Urban Communities Fund will invest more than $2 billion to acquire at least ten thousand existing residential rental units in major U.S. markets. Our goal is to upgrade them with "green" features such as energy-efficient appliances, add amenities, improve management, and provide residents with a secure, high-quality place to live.

These are not luxury lofts. These are intended to serve as homes for the hardworking men and women who form the backbone of urban communities: firefighters, police officers, bus drivers, construction workers, and others who bring stability to their neighborhoods. We believe that urban populations will grow through immigration and demographic shifts, so that the demand for this "workforce housing" will only increase. We want to meet that demand and serve the needs of those valuable members of society.

We are particularly interested in building and redeveloping apartment complexes near public transportation so that urban residents can easily get to schools and jobs and shopping places. Because of the surge in oil prices and growing environmental concerns, Bobby and I adjusted our business by trying to put our urban renters within walking distance of public transportation.

READ, REFLECT, RECOGNIZE, AND REACT

I first developed my leadership skills on the court. I learned to play to the strengths and weaknesses of my teammates and our opponents in the flow of each game, the regular season, and the play-offs, as well as a few championships. Leadership is one of those basketball skills that translates well to business because I had to constantly "read" the floor, which included not only knowing the score but also monitoring the effectiveness of the game plan, evaluating the performances of each teammate and opponent, and keeping an eye on the game clock.

The *Harvard Business Review* report advised that organizational leaders work smart. I do that by practicing "The Four Rs." I stay engaged in the day-to-day flow of things. I pay attention to the details.

I also step back at regular intervals—daily, weekly, monthly, yearly—so that I can *read* the market and where we stand in it. Then I *reflect* on where we have been, where we are now, and what we need to do to keep moving ahead. Next, I *recognize* what the trends are and how we measure up according to the guiding vision and the mission we set for our businesses. Finally, I *react* by adjusting my strategies.

I may go through "The Four Rs" three or four times during a workday. I always run a checklist against my goals and our mission when we are discussing a new project. This process might take only thirty seconds or a few minutes during the day. Later, near the end of each workday, I take some time to do it more deliberately and thoughtfully—looking at things from every possible angle—taking maybe a half hour or longer to pick up on something that needs fixing or an idea worth exploring. At the end of each week or over the weekend, I'll devote even more time to "The Four Rs," and I usually set aside some time at the end of each month to take an even more complete measure.

Of course, I have more formal quarterly and annual staff meetings in which we all assess our mission and how we are doing. But the daily measuring of progress has become an almost unconscious process with me, and I have talked to other business executives who do the same thing. It is an essential part of being a leader.

CHANGE AGENTS

Business schools, management programs, and leadership coaches encourage entrepreneurs and business executives to be "change agents" who are quick to see shifts in their markets, recognize the need to make adjustments, and then enable their employees and their businesses to react swiftly.

I don't think anybody would disagree with the notion that for thirteen years I was a change agent in basketball shorts and sneakers. I played point guard for most of my NBA career even though I was built more like a typical forward. My coaches gave me that role because I had a knack for leading my teammates and making adjustments to whatever our opponents threw at us.

The point guard is considered the quarterback of a basketball team's offense. You set up plays and constantly make changes in your offense as you read, recognize, and react to what the other team is doing.

We had offensive strategies and plays designed for every sort of defense that our opponents played. I also made my own personal adjustments depending on an ever-changing set of circumstances, including who was guarding me at any given moment, what sort of defense the other team was playing, how much time was on the shot clock, the game score, and a hundred other factors.

AHEAD OF THE GAME

Your success as an entrepreneur or within a business organization will depend to a large degree on how well you *read* changes, *reflect* on their impact on your business, *recognize* the patterns and trends, and *react* to deal with them. It won't do you any good to read about changes in your industry in *The New York Times* or *Business Week*. You have to recognize the signs *before* they become major topics in the media; otherwise, you will never be able to recognize the impact and react in time.

Even while I was still playing, I had to make some major changes early in my business dealings. In 1986 my teammate Kareem Abdul-Jabbar discovered that his business manager and adviser had apparently taken out more than $9 million in loans and made investments that Kareem knew nothing about. Kareem told me that there had been warning signs of trouble in his finances; his agent had not provided monthly financial statements and had not paid Kareem's taxes for two years.

Kareem is one of the most intelligent people I know, but he did not have a business background and he was focused on playing basketball. By the time he recognized what was going on with his finances, the damage had already been done.

His misfortune was a wake-up call for me. I'd been feeling as if I were missing opportunities in my own business affairs at that point, and even though I had good personal relationships with my business manager and advisers, I decided to make a change. I fired my entire business team and built a new one. It wasn't an easy thing to do. Change is often difficult, and the bigger your company becomes, the harder it can be—unless you make "The Four Rs" part of the culture.

How do you do that? Well, as the point person for your company or your team, you make sure you teach "The Four Rs" to every one of your employees or team members. You instill in them a sense of urgency and flexibility so that they aren't afraid to alert you to shifts in the markets and suggest changes. Your employees and team members are your best sources of information. You want them to develop a sixth sense so that they can adapt on the run.

Once you have them alert and reading the signs, you have to keep them informed and motivated so that they reflect on the information they gather, and recognize how it will impact your business. It's your responsibility to train them so that they understand how a new technology, economic shifts, the emergence of a strong competitor, and other possible changes may impact your business. Then you must help them understand how to react swiftly to those changes with internal and external strategies.

This isn't just about reacting; it's crucial to create a culture in which your employees are always thinking ahead so that they are always making adjustments in a proactive way to move the business forward according to the vision you establish.

Jack Welch is known as one of the great change agents among corporate leaders for his transformation of General Electric. His philosophy was that a company will never be able to change quickly enough unless everyone buys in to a common vision. When a business leader establishes a common vision and builds "The Four Rs" into the company's culture, employees are more accepting of change. It's only natural that people get comfortable in a successful company, and that can make them resistant to change. So you have to make reading, reflecting, recognizing, and reacting part of the daily culture.

Business psychologists have identified the stages that employees go through during times of change. They will initially be fearful and resistant, but if you give them the support and information they need to adjust successfully, each little victory builds confidence in the new strategy. You can't expect everyone to buy in immediately, or demand that they do.

It helps to let everyone know that while there is always risk in making changes, the biggest risk is *not* to change. Either you change and grow, or your business becomes stagnant. The three-hundred-year-old newspaper industry did not read, recognize, or react to advertisers shifting to the Internet in the 1990s, and as a result, newspapers saw their long-term profit margins of 20 and 30 percent drop rapidly. Even today as newspapers try to shift their revenue online through Internet ads, they still cannot garner the money they used to in print. Online portals such as CNN.com and Fox News have dominated the online news marketplace and have taken the bulk of the revenues that used to belong to newspapers.

As my business ventures have grown, I have encouraged my team members to look down the road so that we get out ahead of change and give ourselves a competitive advantage. When my company was just starting, we tried to plan three years out. As we grew, our strategy was to look five years ahead. Now we strategize ten years out, looking at the trends and mapping our "plays" so that we can react instinctively rather than panicking when change comes. There are no time-outs in the business world. We can't stop the action so we can devise new strategies. We have to think ahead so we react in real time.

We have led change in South Central, Harlem, and other urban neighborhoods around the country because we read the market and saw that change was coming. The change that we led by following "The Four Rs" has increased jobs, reduced crime, and improved the quality of life in communities across the country. Change like that benefits everyone!

Making Presentations

Sealing the deal is a skill that you must master.

In the summer of 2008, I called a top executive at a major-brand apparel company and suggested that we meet to discuss the services offered by Magic Workforce Solutions, my company's strategic alliance with the global staffing giant Adecco.

The apparel company executive agreed to the meeting and offered to fly to Los Angeles.

"No," I said, "we will come to you."

Basketball was my game, but I've learned the value of a good pitch. I wanted to set the tone for my presentation by letting the head of procurement know that I valued his time and the opportunity to talk to him.

I've made scores of important business presentations over the years, and I've learned that no matter how much you prepare, there are always some surprises in each meeting. My trip to the apparel company's headquarters was no exception.

This was an introductory meeting. There were no contracts on the table. At that point, Magic Workforce Solutions was a new player in the staffing industry, even though Adecco had been a major force for decades. My goal was to let this potential client know what we offered and that we were excited about serving its staffing needs.

I was eager to do that, and I was prepared to make a dazzling presentation to all of the assembled executives in the meeting room. The surprise came as everyone in the room introduced themselves. Their key people were there, which thrilled me. But I was shocked to discover that a couple of people in the room were from a competing staffing firm that already had a contract with them.

This will be interesting, I thought.

Needless to say, I had to rewrite my presentation a bit due to the competitors in the room. I improvised a joke comparing them to Michael Jordan sneaking up on me.

They laughed.

We bonded.

On the return flight to Los Angeles, I received a phone call from the CEO of Adecco Group North America. I thought he was calling to ask how my presentation had gone, but he already knew.

"They just called me and said they are looking forward to doing business with us," he said.

As this book was going to press, that relationship was off to a great start . . . So stay tuned.

SEALING A DEAL

Many businesses and business deals are sparked by a simple thought: the recognition of a trend or a need or a new technology that opens up opportunities. Then the real work begins. Months of research, meetings, and deliberations take place. Crunch time comes when you have to make your final presentation or pitch.

In my transition from basketball to boardroom, making critical presentations was the part of business that scared me the most at first. Every possible insecurity, feeling of inadequacy, and nagging self-doubt came rising up through my pores. My stomach too.

In my first few business presentations, I walked in as Earvin "Magic" Johnson wearing extra-long pants and a custom-tailored suit, but I felt like little Earvin "Junior" Johnson in hand-me-down jeans back in third-grade English class in Lansing.

Most of my fears played out before I began my speech. Even in the early days, I worked as hard at preparing for business presentations as I had for championship games. I studied every aspect of the group I was addressing, from their executive biographies to their news clippings, favorite vacation places, and sports teams. I tried to know as much about their businesses and markets as they did.

Still, in the beginning, I worried that I didn't know enough; that I wasn't yet the savvy businessman that I wanted to be. It struck me that there was nowhere to hide during these presentations. When I hit a rough spot during a basketball game, I could always count on my teammates to step up while I got back into the flow. That wasn't the case in business meetings. You can't hide along the baseline and catch your breath while someone else moves the ball up the court.

Making presentations to business and investment groups terrified me at first. Still, I used that fear to drive myself to keep learning and preparing so that by the time I actually stood up, started talking, and hit all the right buttons, it flowed. I learned to overprepare and overdeliver, and that is how everyone in our company approaches our key presentations to potential partners and clients.

We discuss our approach strategy, the topics we will cover, and the "hot buttons" that we'll need to push to make the deal. We put together a brief PowerPoint presentation to provide essential facts and figures for the visual learners in the crowd.

MAKING THE CASE

I sat through many business presentations before I conducted one myself. I benefited from seeing how top-notch business leaders performed in those situations. I came to appreciate how important such meetings are and what a difference there is when they are done right.

Since I did not go to business school, I had to learn through my observations and experience, and from my mentors. I am a stickler for details. I look at the backgrounds of everyone attending the meeting. I determine what their goals are individually and as a group. I find out what their chief concerns are and prepare to address them.

My staff teases that I even have to know what the room temperature will be in critical meetings. It's true. I want everyone to be comfortable and thinking about what is being presented rather than worrying about catching pneumonia or sweating through our business jackets.

Presentations to potential clients or partners should answer the key questions: What's in this for our side? And what's in this for your side? Motivation is critical too. If our goals are at odds, the deal will never work.

PREPARATION

Toastmasters International offers excellent tips on business presentations on its Web site, www.toastmasters.org. I recommend that you take a look even though you may think that you learned all you need to know in high-school speech class.

I've seen entertainment moguls, community leaders, and business powers such as Michael Ovitz, Victor MacFarlane, and Bobby Turner make presentations. Believe me, at that level there is a lot more to it than anything you learned in Speech 101.

The underlying goal of business presentations is to persuade the other side to do the deal. The better your presentation, the more inclined they will be to buy in. Here are a few tips I've picked up from the pros.

1. Set goals for each presentation.
2. Figure out what the other side wants and needs.
3. Decide how you are going to make your case and support it by showing how the other side will benefit.
4. Determine how to seal the deal by getting the other side to act.

The key to effective business presentations is to deliver the most important information up front so that you claim everyone's attention right away. Then you go for the buy-in by making your case. You can't relax yet. You have to be ready for every tough question thrown your way.

I prepare by having my staff grill me in practice sessions. I want to know who will be in the room and what each person's responsibilities are within the company. I make sure that I've got all the information I need to answer anything that could be asked. Self-interest rules every decision. My audience is focused on how their organization will benefit and how each of them will be affected personally and professionally. My job is to convince them that they will profit from the venture at every level.

GETTING THE WORD OUT

The president of Adecco, our strategic alliance partner in Magic Workforce Solutions, was not surprised that my presentation to the big apparel company had gone well, because I'd sold him in an earlier presentation.

My company joined forces with the world's largest employment staffing and human resources company after a series of interesting coincidences that became opportunities.

As mentioned earlier, in the spring of 2006, I'd met a corporate CEO who'd told me he was frustrated because he couldn't find enough qualified minorities to meet the needs of his business.

I'd been hearing the same thing from some of our corporate partners and other business contacts over the last several years. Often, they would ask us to recommend someone for openings they had. We would try to help them out through our network. On a couple occasions, they hired away my own top people by offering them great opportunities.

At the same time, résumés and job applications from highly qualified blacks, Hispanics, and Asians were pouring into our offices at Magic Johnson Enterprises and the Magic Johnson Foundation every day. I was struck by the contrast between the demand for qualified minorities being expressed by other business leaders and the piles of impressive résumés flowing into our office. Somewhere there was a disconnect between the supply and the demand—and maybe an opportunity.

That thought kept popping up over several months. I brainstormed about it with Kawanna Brown, the COO of Magic Johnson Enterprises. We decided that she should look for opportunities to address that gap by forming some sort of alliance with one of the major human resource or staffing companies, such as Adecco, Manpower, or Kelly Services.

Kawanna took that thought and ran with it, as usual. She spent the next five months researching those companies and laying the groundwork in meetings with their executives. In the meantime, I kept running into some of the same people Kawanna was courting.

In mid-October 2006, I gave the keynote speech at the National Minority Supplier Development Council conference in San Diego. In my speech, I talked about the importance of diversity in hiring and contracting and our successful, groundbreaking efforts to bring economic development to urban markets.

Adecco's vice president of supplier diversity in North America was in the audience. Adecco, based in Switzerland, is a Fortune Global 500 company with annual sales of more than $21 billion and 7,000 offices in more than 60 countries and territories. It puts 700,000 people to work every day. It is the leader in its industry. We strive to team with industry leaders.

At that point, the Adecco vice president and other executives had already met with Kawanna. She later told her that she'd been impressed to hear me talk so passionately about the very things they'd been discussing.

Then, just ten days later, Cookie and I were guests on *Oprah* in Oprah's Chicago studio. The president and COO of Adecco General Staffing in the U.S. and Canada just happened to be in the audience for that show. Kawanna told me that the president and vice president of Adecco were bowled over by the fact that I seemed to be in the spotlight and leading the charge everywhere they went. This was beginning to seem like fate.

DESIGNATED CLOSER

I serve as the host for most of our presentations to potential clients and partners. We changed that for the Adecco meeting in

May 2007. Kawanna had been leading the charge on this deal, so we decided that she should open the show. I was the designated closer.

Adecco had just welcomed a new country manager for its U.S. and Canada group, former IBM executive Theron "Tig" Gilliam, so this was my first meeting with him and his top executives. I knew that he had expressed support for diversity in the workplace. I was about to give him the opportunity to walk the talk.

I also went into the meeting aware that the U.S. labor market was shedding thousands and thousands of jobs because of the economic downturn. Adecco was hungry for opportunities to develop new business. We were in a great position because our plan was devised to open doors that Adecco could not get into without us.

Kawanna set the stage with a PowerPoint presentation that reviewed key points in the discussions she had had with Adecco's team. She noted the shared mission of our two companies. Then she carefully laid out the reasons why an alliance between our two brands would serve the goals of both companies while enhancing our bottom lines too.

Kawanna knocked them out. I was so proud of her. She provided example after example to show the power and credibility of our brand. Then she called in "the closer." To tell you the truth, though, Kawanna had already done most of the heavy lifting, so my fears evaporated. By the time I stood up, there was nothing for me to do but have fun. I talked about my transition from basketball to boardroom and how we had worked to build our brand while bringing economic development to underserved urban communities.

I told them that we had approached Adecco as the global leader in employment staffing after realizing that the corporate world had a growing demand for talented and skilled minority workers but did not know how to reach them. We know they are out there, I said, because they call, write, and e-mail us every day, by the hundreds and thousands.

They nodded and smiled as I explained that Magic Johnson Enterprises was positioned to connect the growing supply of diverse workforce talent to the ever-growing demand for it by joining forces with Adecco.

"Since you are number one in your industry," I said, "I would like you to join my newest team."

Then I laid out the synergies between our companies one more time.

Kawanna had established in earlier discussions that we were not proposing a partnership. We wanted Adecco to join us in a strategic alliance, a formal relationship to combine the strengths of our two companies so that we could create new opportunities.

We proposed a new company that Magic Johnson Enterprises would own, operate, and financially control 100 percent, allowing the business to be certified as a true minority-owned business. We called for an arrangement in which Adecco would provide mentorship and development by leveraging their proven systems and processes that are critical to successfully supporting Fortune 500 companies.

Magic Workforce Solutions, our strategic alliance with Adecco, would be positioned to qualify as a preferred minority vendor to American corporations seeking qualified, diverse employees, I explained.

There were other ways for us to work together as well. One of them involved giving Adecco access to the men and women trained for careers in the twenty Community Empowerment Centers in underserved communities around the country established by the Magic Johnson Foundation. (Later I will tell you more about these great places.)

Our presentation was scheduled to last for a couple of hours. Adecco's executives said they were on board after just thirty minutes!

Today, Magic Workforce Solutions is on track to become a billion-dollar business. It is a win-win for both Adecco and our companies. It will prove to be an even better deal for the communities and people we want to serve because it will provide more job opportunities for the people who need them the most. That's the sort of deal I just love to close!

Training

Employee training begins with the boss.

I walked into my Starbucks in the Ladera Center early one morning, and things got a little crazy in a big hurry. It was crowded, as usual. The tables were packed. A half-dozen customers were lined up to order at the front counter.

Just as I got inside the door, an older gentleman seated at a table with some friends rose from his chair to say hello to me. As he stood, he knocked over the whole table and all the coffee cups on it, soaking his shirt and pants.

Clean up aisle one!

No problem. I was on it. I went to the back room and grabbed some cleaning supplies and towels. First I tried to help the gentleman who'd gone from drinking the brew of the day to wearing it. I helped him clean up, and I made sure he and his friends got fresh cups of coffee.

Then I mopped up the spilled coffee so no one would slip on it. The store's manager hustled over.

"Mr. Johnson, let me do the cleanup," the manager said.

I waved him off.

"I worked my way through high school mopping floors," I said. "You take care of the customers in line. I've got this covered."

I got a bucket and put down some cleanser and had most of the mess cleaned up before I realized that I had an audience. I looked around, and there were a lot of smiling faces. Some of the customers started teasing me about the "high-priced help." One commented that I had a future as a custodian.

The gentleman who had accidentally made the mess walked up with his cell phone in hand and said, "I've been after my lazy son to get a job. I'm going to call him right now and tell him that Magic Johnson isn't afraid to get his hands dirty, so he doesn't have any more excuses."

TRAIN THE BOSS FIRST

When I invest in a business or any opportunity, I want to know how it works from top to bottom. Part of it is just curiosity. I love to know the nuts and bolts of businesses. It's also due partly to my obsession with details. The real driver is pride. I would be embarrassed to walk into a place that I owned if I were clueless about its operations. I have to know the right way to do things in order to judge whether my employees are doing a good job.

As a result, I make a killer cappuccino and can run an end loader like nobody's business. Good training starts with the boss. I am a proud graduate of both the Starbucks Barista School and Burger King University—and I have aprons with the coffee and ketchup stains to prove it.

Thanks to my own training, I can tell you that there are more than 200,000 ways to build a Whopper, and I know how many beans go into a one-pound bag of Starbucks blend. At the Starbucks training camp in Seattle, I learned how to create a "home-away-from-home" experience for our guests. At Burger King University in Miami, I learned how to let customers have it their way.

On both corporate campuses, I was reminded of the importance of training programs for owners, managers, and employees at every position. Starbucks baristas get at least twenty-four hours of training in their first two to four weeks. There are classes in the history of coffee, drink preparation, coffee knowledge, customer service, and retail skills. On top of that, there is a four-hour workshop on how to brew the perfect cup of coffee. Baristas even get a crash course in Italian so they can explain the drink names to customers.

Starbucks training includes a focus on personal development. Baristas and other employees are taught "Star Skills" for building self-esteem. They are also coached on how to respond to customers. Starbucks managers go through a twelve-week training program that goes into the fine details of store operations, practices, and procedures. The fine details are plentiful in a company where standards are so exact that Starbucks roaster beans are tested in a blood-cell analyzer. Beans that don't make the grade don't go into the bag.

TRAIN TO GAIN

Mastering the details of an operation is usually not a problem for small-business entrepreneurs. Often they start out as one-person shops or with such a small team that everyone has to know how to perform every task. As your business grows, it becomes more and more important to pass knowledge and experience on to your employees.

Too often, entrepreneurs are so busy just keeping a business going and the cash flowing that they do not set up training programs for new people as they come on board. Yet study after study has shown that the most successful businesses are those that have thorough, updated training programs for their employees.

The Gallup Organization reports that well-trained, fully engaged employees tend to be more productive, more profitable, more customer-focused, safer, and less likely to quit.

Business owners and entrepreneurs often make the mistake of assuming that their employees will just pick up the skills and knowledge they need to do their job. That can be a costly error. Untrained or poorly trained employees can cause serious damage to your business and its reputation. Lawsuits and health and safety violations are also a potential danger when your employees haven't been properly schooled.

Protecting your business isn't the only reason to put in a training program. Most employees welcome a thorough, step-by-step process for learning about their jobs and the company. They see the training program as your investment in them, so they become more fully engaged in the mission and their roles.

Employees who have been well trained also tend to stay on the job longer. So it's a mistake to think of training as an expense. I consider it an investment in the company, our people, and our security. I've seen it pay real dividends.

As our business grows, we constantly reassess our employee training programs. I always try to look ahead to the skills my employees may need a year or two down the road so we can prepare them. We share our vision of the future with our team members so they understand where they fit in. That knowledge builds their confidence and motivates them to keep learning and growing with us.

COACHING SKILLS

Because of my background in sports, I think of employees as my teammates, so training is like coaching for me. Human resource pros have told me that this is often the best way to approach training. When you coach employees to improve their skills and boost their value in the workplace, they become more engaged, more excited, and more productive.

The best employees are those who feel valued and appreciated. If they see that there are opportunities to move up, they are less likely to move out. Your employees will thrive and your business will benefit when you take the time to invest in training programs that motivate and excite them while bringing them closer as a team.

I don't mind spending money on training employees, because it pays dividends later. That said, you certainly want to spend your money wisely when it comes to employee training. Our training programs are focused on the skills required of each individual while also making sure each employee understands the overall mission and his or her role in that mission.

Because our business interests are so diverse, I try to convey to our headquarters staff that they need to be on top of current events and the business world. Many members of our team are young and entrepreneurial, so I like to think of our offices as a real-world campus where people are eager to learn and looking for the leading edge.

Much of the training we do is informal, and that is a strategy. We don't want it to be like grinding through a business economics class. We want it to be a dynamic and intriguing process, so we try to make it fun and exciting too. I've found that it helps if I lead the charge because then everyone buys in to it. It's no surprise, the best time to do training is during our employee retreats to Hawaii or other spots where we can have fun in the sun while also building up our strength as a team.

Major companies often have their own training schools on a corporate campus. Small companies have introductory classes and continuing training programs in-house. No matter what size your business is, you should have some methods of measuring the effectiveness of your training programs. Experts say that training works only if you follow up, repeat the key messages, and offer encouragement on a regular basis.

When I am in the office, I often have lunch with everyone who is available to join us. We also go on retreats to establish informal social networks that encourage employees to train one another in ways that reinforce formal training programs. New employees at Magic Johnson Enterprises and the Magic Johnson Foundation meet with me and other top executives so they understand our values and our mission. I give them an understanding of where we've been, where we are, and where we are going.

Then our human resource staff provides them with the training they need to do their jobs. At the end of each training period, we ask for feedback so we can learn what works and what doesn't work for the newcomers or those moving up in our businesses.

GET WITH THE PROGRAM

Your employee training program should be more than quick introductions to coworkers, an office tour, and the awarding of an ID card and a restroom key. Our training programs often benefit from suggestions by team members who identify critical areas of importance and the most efficient processes for high-level performance.

I try to treat all our employees equally well and to give everyone all the training they need to master their jobs, but there is at least one team member whom I might have been a little tougher on than others.

When my son André decided to come work at Magic Johnson Enterprises, he received a special training session designed for TBS: The Boss's Son. I informed him that my other employees would be watching to see if he pulled his own weight. So would I.

André responded like a champ, and that sent a signal to

everybody else that he wanted to grow and learn with the rest of us. At age fifteen, André worked at the Magic Johnson Theatre in Los Angeles. He cleaned the bathrooms. He wasn't happy with that assignment, but he did it. I told him that if he ever hoped to be in management, he needed to know how to stack the candy and pop the popcorn too. Just like his dad.

André's early commitment to job training and professional growth paid off. Today, he is manager of business development for Magic Johnson Enterprises. He is responsible for identifying new partnerships, managing existing business ventures, and facilitating growth of the company. Among his many responsibilities, André manages our film and television projects as well as our prestigious Canyon-Johnson Urban Fund, LLP, playing a key role in the development of Canyon-Johnson's latest initiative, the Canyon-Johnson Urban Communities Fund.

Then again, my own adventures in training programs have not always served as a model for future generations. One of the more infamous incidents occurred after I went through training at Burger King University in Miami. I decided that I needed field experience too. So I requested training in a drive-through bay at my Magic Burger King in Birmingham.

I wanted to experience the pressure of that position, and I got my wish. Regular customers at my Burger Kings were used to the fact that when they drove up to place their orders in the drive-through lane, the first recorded message they heard was my voice greeting them. Still, they were not prepared to drive up and see me handing them their meals.

Oh my gosh! It's Magic!

It was fun to see their reactions. I'm always happy to pose for photographs and sign autographs. Yet our Birmingham Burger King experienced a traffic jam in the drive-through during my training visit.

I flunked the speed-of-service test—badly.

Customer Care

**Focus on the customer, and
you will never go wrong.**

Early in the life of Canyon-Johnson Urban Funds my competitive drive kicked in when we made a bid for a Los Angeles office building. There were other groups stalking this property, but I was determined to beat them to it. I set up a meeting with the majority owner. Then I checked him out.

He was known as a tough businessman, a hard-nosed negotiator who was also a stickler about everyone being on time. No problem there; I was so wound up to do this deal that I got to our meeting place an hour and a half early. I sat in the waiting room going over my presentation.

Finally, he walked out in a custom suit that looked bulletproof. He gripped my hand as if we were going to wrestle for the deal. Still clamped, he looked me in the eyes and gruffly launched into his prepared opening:

"Mr. Johnson, I just want to begin by telling you a story . . ."

Uh-oh, he's already made up his mind and we've lost this deal, I thought.

His voice seemed to harden as he continued: "I took my son to a Lakers game back in your rookie season many years ago . . ."

This could get ugly fast.

". . . and one of our friends got us into the locker room, where we found ourselves standing next to your teammate, who was already dressed and leaving."

Uh-oh, I know where this is going.

"I asked one of your teammates if he would sign an autograph for my son, but he brushed right by us and out the door."

I took a deep breath and tried to figure out how to make a smooth retreat. He locked on to my hand and kept going.

"You walked up just then, stepped up to my son, and said, 'Would you like my autograph? We could do a photograph too if you'd like.' "

He then tightened his grip on my hand, pulled me toward him, and put his other hand on my shoulder.

"Today my son is a lawyer and one of your biggest fans," he said. "And today, my friend, you have a deal!"

With that he gave me one last squeeze, turned around, and walked out. We got that building and turned a deal that resulted in a multimillion-dollar profit for our fund and its investors.

CUSTOMER SERVICE

I can't tell you how many times I've met with CEOs, corporate presidents, or board chairmen who were once fans in the stands or just someone I said hello to in an airport. Time and again, I'm reminded that how you treat people *always* matters.

I'm not putting down my teammates. Anybody can have a bad night. There may well be people out there who caught me on a bad night or at a bad time too, but I've always tried to be accommodating.

As a player, I went to the dinners and fund-raisers that my teammates skipped because I enjoyed interacting with fans. I come from a big family and I like being around people, so it is natural for me. I owe a lot to those who support my team and my businesses. I appreciate them. When I do something for a fan or a customer, I don't think about there ever being a payoff down the road, yet it is amazing how often there is.

SERVING IT UP

Entrepreneurs and business owners usually have little or no control over the market forces that impact their profits and their losses. Sometimes you just can't compete on price against the bigger players. Other times someone may have a better product or service. Your ace in the hole—always—is how well you treat your customers.

Consumer spending is particularly sensitive to changes in customer satisfaction, according to the National Quality Research Center at the University of Michigan, which developed the American Customer Satisfaction Index. When customers are not happy, they don't come back.

It can cost your company five times as much money to attract a new customer as to keep an existing one happy. The cost of one disgruntled customer is magnified because each of them typically complains about your business to at least seven other potential customers.

Treating your customers right, then, is one of the least expensive and most rewarding ways to put your business ahead of the competition. Small businesses that put a premium on customer service are more likely to thrive than those that put more emphasis on low prices, according to the National Federation of Independent Business.

Customer service is a focus of big business too. *BusinessWeek* reported that the office supply giant Staples saw its customer satisfaction rankings increase 5 percentage points after it refocused on employee training. Home Depot allocated $30 million for a program to give store workers bonuses based on their internal customer service scores. Nordstrom saw its profits go up 10 percent in one quarter after it responded to customer surveys and began offering styles requested by women shoppers, according to the *BusinessWeek* report.

Naturally, as more and more businesses catch on to the value of top-notch customer service, the bar is set higher and higher and it becomes all the more important that your business offer an exceptional level of it. I constantly remind our team members that our goal is to exceed all expectations. We pay attention to what our customers say in direct comments, phone calls, e-mails, and surveys, and we make adjustments based on feedback from many sources.

My joint venture with 24 Hour Fitness was launched by a mother's lament that she couldn't find a workout place that provided babysitting services. One day after church, I was talking about staying fit with another member of the congregation, a single mom, and she said there weren't any family-friendly health clubs in the Ladera–Baldwin Hills neighborhood where she could go and have someone watch her kids when she worked out.

Thanks to her comment and my response, parents in urban neighborhoods across the country can get fit knowing that their kids are safe and having fun at Magic Johnson 24 Hour Fitness centers.

HEALTHY OBSESSION

My focus on customer service has created some great opportunities, so I obsess about it—in a healthy way. I still stop by our theaters, restaurants, coffee shops, and other businesses to see how our customers are being treated. Of course, it is a little difficult for me to play "secret shopper" myself, but I have been known to send in less recognizable members of our teams to check things out. I always try to look at things from the customer's point of view and ask what we can do to meet their needs and anticipate them too.

Whether it is Lexus, Starbucks, or Best Buy, when you look at the companies that stand out in any field, the thing that often puts them over the top is outstanding customer service. It is no coincidence that I have partnerships, franchises, joint ventures, and other relationships with many of the companies that are ranked at the top of customer satisfaction surveys. I want to be associated with those companies so that I can learn from them.

Lexus has long ranked at the top of customer service surveys in the automobile industry. The luxury brand goes the extra mile by providing loaner cars for customers whose cars are being serviced and paying for some repairs even after warranties have expired. One of its most recent customer service innovations is a live Internet chat room set up to handle questions from potential buyers, customer complaints, and service issues.

Starbucks is also ranked high for customer service. My Starbucks restaurants are "Magicized" for our urban neighborhood customers with music and products suited to their tastes and needs. CEO Howard Schultz recently appointed his own chief creative officer, whose primary job is to improve the Starbucks experience for customers across the entire chain.

Magic Johnson Enterprises is also working with Best Buy to help it better serve minority customers and employees, but this top brand was already known for its focus on customer service. Best Buy enjoyed a huge leap in customer satisfaction when it launched its Geek Squad service to help customers who bring their computers and laptops into the store.

BusinessWeek also recognized the growing importance of customer service recently by launching its first rankings based on reader surveys and polls. The magazine found that companies that ranked high in customer satisfaction in its first survey also ranked high in employee satisfaction. Good service, then, is good for your entire business. Being accessible, receptive, and responsive is good for the soul—your corporate soul and your own soul. You can't buy the sort of goodwill that you get when you surprise people simply by showing that you are willing to listen to them and respond to their needs.

SIMPLE GESTURES

That lesson hit home again as I was putting this book together. It was one of those pleasant, brief exchanges that happen to me all the time. I went jogging near our home one Saturday morning a couple weeks before Christmas 2007. I took my usual route and had to stop for a traffic light when a distinguished man with three cute little girls came across the street smiling nervously.

He introduced himself as Dr. Hovan and said that he was from Arizona but in town for a medical conference. He then introduced his daughter and two nieces. They asked if they could take a picture with me, and I said sure. I bent down and put my arms around the three girls so we could all get in the frame.

Dr. Hovan tried to take the photograph, but his camera did not work.

"The button's stuck," he said.

He fiddled with the camera for a few minutes while I talked to the girls about their shopping trip and their school. The nieces said they'd been to my theater and my Starbucks, so we talked about that too. While we were talking, a few other people stopped and took pictures. Then a busload of foreign tourists pulled over, and a bunch more people piled out and started taking pictures.

I later told Cookie that my jog had turned into a street party.

Dr. Hovan got his camera working, so I posed again with his girls. Then I posed for more pictures. It didn't take all that long, and then I returned to my jog around the neighborhood without thinking much more about it.

A week or so later, I got a phone call from Bill Plaschke, a sports columnist with the *Los Angeles Times*. Bill came to L.A. shortly after I did, so I've known him a long time, though I hadn't heard from him in a while.

"I got an e-mail about you from a doctor in Arizona who ran into you in Beverly Hills a few days ago while you were jogging," Bill said.

It took me a second, but then I remembered Dr. Hovan and his daughter and nieces. I asked Bill if the photos had come out okay because he'd had trouble with his camera button. Bill said Dr. Hovan had sent him the pictures and said some nice things about our brief meeting that day. I told him it had been fun for me too and that it had turned into an impromptu party on the street.

Bill told me he was going to do a column about Dr. Hovan's e-mail and our encounter, but I got busy with Christmas parties and forgot about it. Then, on Christmas Day, Bill's column appeared in the newspaper. It wasn't a gift that I'd planned on, but it made a great day even better. It drove home the message that even the smallest effort to reach out and respond to people can bring greater rewards than you might imagine.

Lucky for Us,
Magic Has Been Our Gift That Keeps on Giving
By Bill Plaschke, sports columnist, *Los Angeles Times*

The busy Arizona doctor was idly rummaging through photos of a recent Los Angeles visit when one snapshot made him stop.

It had been the most apprehensive click of the trip.

It had been a dreaded intrusion into the life of a famous man on a famous street.

The doctor was scared to ask for it, scared to snap it, and even more scared when the camera stuck and he couldn't snap it.

Yet, look, here it was.

And, oh my.

Do you see the smiling giant swathed in white?

Do you see the three little girls cuddled underneath him?

Can you feel the kindness of the expression, the generosity of the spirit?

Could you see how the man is African American, and the three children are of different ethnicities, yet it looked like they were of the same family?

The doctor looked at the photo again, recalled the events surrounding its creation, then e-mailed it to a stranger who writes for a Los Angeles newspaper.

Upon opening the attachment, the image becomes immediately familiar in its wonder, its hope, its daily promise of a miracle.

"I know it sounds crazy," said the doctor, "but this looks like the photo of an angel."

The real magic is in how we have somehow managed to take Earvin Johnson for granted.

Nearly a dozen years after his last game as a Laker, we have become accustomed to seeing him cutting the ribbon on an inner-city business, donating money to an inner-city school, selling hope to folks who had never been able to afford it.

We barely notice that, more than 11 years after scoring his last point, Johnson elicits more oohs and aahs these days with powerful urban investments in everything from movie theaters to Starbucks to Magic Johnson's T.G.I. Friday's.

We overlook the scarcity of a sports star who contributes without entourage or attitude, who still smiles at the world without asking for a smile in return, who hugs without prompting and it doesn't matter who.

We overlook the rarity of an athlete who contributes more to his community after his retirement.

And we forget that Magic Johnson is doing all this when we thought he would be dead.

He is arguably this town's greatest sports blessing, yet how often do we count him?

And then somebody named Michael Hovan from Scottsdale, Ariz., stumbles into Johnson on a Beverly Hills street on a December Saturday morning and ends up with a photo that makes us remember.

This is the story of that photo.

This may be a good day to hear it.

"Really, like a giant angel," said Hovan.

It was the second Saturday morning in December.

Hovan, in town for a medical conference, was shopping on Rodeo Drive with family that included his 9-year-old daughter Emily and two nieces.

Across the street, the girls saw a giant man in a white sweat suit whom they immediately recognized.

"It was Magic Johnson, and they started begging me to cross the street and take his picture," Hovan said.

The first thing that struck the doctor was, how are these little girls so familiar with an athlete whom they never saw play? How did they even know Magic Johnson?

Then he realized his nieces, who live in Southern California, know him from their father being a longtime Lakers fan. And his daughter knew him from watching him on the TNT studio basketball show, seeing his Magic Johnson Theatre and visiting one of his Starbucks.

"I thought, it's amazing how this man's impact spans generations," he said.

Having been ignored by his only other encounter with a pro athlete in his life—Johnny Bench once blew him off—Hovan turned down the girls' request.

"I didn't want them to experience the pain of being brushed off," he said. "And I didn't want them to change the opinion of one of their heroes."

Johnson had stopped at a crosswalk light, and the girls kept insisting, so Hovan finally gulped and walked over to him.

"The first thing I noticed was, he was all by himself, nobody around him," Hovan said.

The next thing he noticed was that Johnson didn't try to run, or hide. In fact, when Hovan shakily introduced himself and the girls, Johnson actually came to them.

"He bent down and hugged them," said Hovan. "He asked how they were doing. He put his arms around them and got ready for the picture."

At which point, the camera's button stuck. Of course it stuck. Isn't that always happening to common folk looking for photos of famous folk? The camera breaking just long enough to remind everyone of their place in life, the famous folk walking away in a . . .

"But that was the thing," said Hovan. "He didn't walk away. He stayed there and talked to the girls while I fidgeted with the camera."

While Hovan fidgeted, other pedestrians noticed the pausing Magic and hustled over for their own photos. Then a busload of foreign tourists abruptly pulled up and dozens disembarked to join the scrum.

"It was just awful, I felt so terrible, I held Mr. Johnson up just long enough for him to be swarmed," said Hovan.

Johnson stayed and waited until Hovan fixed the camera and took the photo, then stuck around to take care of everyone else, at which point the doctor noticed something else.

The entire time, Johnson never stopped smiling. He never stopped chatting. He embraced and engaged and touched everyone.

"He went far beyond any measure of responsibility that a public figure should feel," said Hovan. "He stayed far longer than was reasonable."

Surely there was a reality show camera around there somewhere?

"That was the interesting thing," said Hovan. "Nobody was with him. Nobody was watching. There was no reason he needed to stay there other than, he was just being himself."

Often children leave the company of their heroes as if they had just been dropped out of the heavens. Hovan's daughter and nieces walked away giggling as if they had just spent time with a friend.

"He transferred his sense of importance to the children, he made them feel just as big as him," said Hovan. "He was less intimidating than the Santa at the mall."

Hovan is not an avid basketball fan. He has not been to a live NBA game in 25 years.

"But you spend a couple of minutes with Mr. Johnson and you realize why he remains relevant," he said. "He's genuine. That smile you see on TV is him."

Hovan laughed.

"Most folks would never want to live next door to a pro athlete, but we left there thinking, Mr. Johnson would be a great next-door neighbor," Hovan said.

His daughter keeps that photo in a school binder.

Every day, it seems, somebody asks about it. Every day, she talks about her new friend.

You call Magic Johnson on his cell phone.

If he's available, he's answering it. If he's not available, it's his voice on the recorded message.

He doesn't have an electronic entourage, either.

He's there. He answers. You tell him the story about the doctor and the three little girls.

He pauses for a second.

"Wait a minute, was that the guy with the broken camera?" he says.

He laughs.

"Those were the cutest little girls," he says. "Did the photo come out? I know the man was worried about his camera. I told him not to worry. I wasn't going anywhere."

I wasn't going anywhere.

You ask him, how can one of the most important people in one of the most self-important cities in America not have anywhere to go?

"You have to understand, I love L.A., I love being our ambassador, I love bringing people together," he said. "It's funny, but I guess it still feels like I'm playing point guard, but in a different way, doing stuff more meaningful than winning."

He considers photos with strangers meaningful. He considers smiles and hugs in the middle of city streets to be important.

"I love being part of the fabric of a community that has given me so much," he said. "I embrace it."

These days, he is most proud of a statistic that has nothing to do with points or assists.

It's about the more than 30,000 minorities that have found employment in his businesses in 85 cities in 21 states.

"Somebody helped me," he said. "I want to help somebody else."

Plus, of course, he owns just less than 5% of the Lakers, which is actually one of the most low-key parts of his life, because he believes the organization should have one voice, and it's not him.

However, I just had to ask him about Kobe Bryant.

"He is going to stay, we are not trading him," he said. "I would rather take the risk of having him for two years and then letting him walk away for nothing . . . than trading him now for less value."

So Johnson helps run this town's biggest sports operation, he pours money into this town's neediest neighborhoods, he takes the time to giggle with this town's youngest visitors.

And he does it all while in a constant fight with HIV that essentially ended his career in 1991.

That is, by all accounts, amazing.

That we didn't even mention the virus until the final paragraphs of this story is perhaps even more amazing.

"It's dead in my body," he said of the virus.

If so, then it is a corpse that constantly inspires him.

"After 16 years with it, every day is a blessing," he said. "Every day, I want to get out there and fulfill my dreams and hopes. Every day, I just live."

On this Christmas Day, then, perhaps it is appropriate to give thanks that the Magic lives here, a year-round hulking swath of holiday cheer, like the man said, an angel among us.

Exit Strategies

Plan your exit from the day you enter.

Before there was McDonald's or Wendy's or, yes, even Burger King, there was Fatburger. Actually, it was "Mr. Fatburger" in the early days. Way back in 1947, a warm and wonderful lady named Lovie Yancey decided she wanted to open a hamburger stand. She'd had a restaurant in Tucson before moving to Los Angeles, but this time she wanted to focus on just hamburgers because she considered them "the fastest-selling sandwich in America."

Initially, Lovie had a partner, a construction worker named Charles Simpson who took some scrap lumber and built their three-stool Mr. Fatburger hamburger stand at Western Avenue and Jefferson Boulevard in Los Angeles. Lovie custom-made her big juicy burgers just the way her patrons wanted them. She liked to say that they didn't need anything else except maybe a few "fat fries" and a drink, because every burger was "a meal in itself." Still, one of Lovie's treats for the late-night and early-morning crowd was burgers with eggs on them.

This pioneering black woman entrepreneur became sole owner in 1952, when she dropped both Mr. Simpson and the "Mr." in the name of her burger stand. Over the years, Fatburger became an L.A. landmark. Lovie worked long days and nights to feed her customers.

Diners tended to stick around because she had a jukebox with great rhythm and blues, soul, and jazz records. Lovie's cozy little place became a hangout for entertainers and musicians, including the comedian Redd Foxx and the singer Ray Charles. She fed L.A.'s night shift. So many waiters, bartenders, bus drivers, street sweepers, and postal workers loved Fatburgers that she had to keep the place open practically around the clock.

Lovie opened a second Fatburger on La Cienega Boulevard in Beverly Hills in 1973. It became so popular with the Hollywood crowd and sports figures such as George Foreman—who rated Fatburgers the best he'd ever eaten—that some nights Lovie had to lock the doors because she couldn't fit any more people in the place.

I know this is true because there were many times that I was one of those hungry people knocking to get in. Shortly after I moved to Los Angeles in 1979, Fatburger became my home away from home. I discovered that Fatburgers had the biggest, juiciest burgers in L.A. Its turkey burgers were every bit as good as its hamburgers and, since they were custom-made to order, you could dress them up any way you wanted.

Lovie created a great brand. It wasn't just the food, it was the whole atmosphere. Going to Fatburger was like hanging out in my own mother's kitchen surrounded by family. The amazing thing was that all of her customers had the same warm feelings about her place.

When other fast-food burger places started cropping up, Lovie decided to franchise "The Last Great Hamburger Stand." By 1985 she had four company-owned Fatburgers and fifteen franchise sites. Fatburgers were especially big in California, where they became as much a part of the culture as the Hollywood sign.

Television and movie writers wrote Lovie's place into their scripts. Fatburgers popped up in episodes of *Sanford and Son* and in movies such as *The Fast and the Furious* and *Lethal Weapon 4,* where Mel Gibson stops shooting people long enough to have some of Lovie's famously fat fries. David Letterman once claimed "going to Fatburger" as one of the Top Ten things he'd miss most about Los Angeles.

MAKING AN EXIT

Lovie was a very smart businesswoman who built her simple hamburger stand into a beloved brand and a successful franchise business. Then she did what smart businesspeople do; she got out when the getting was good.

Fatburger's founder sold out to an investment group in 1990 and did very well for herself. Then she focused on the charity she had started in 1986 with a $1.7 million endowment at the City of Hope National Medical Center in Duarte. Lovie began her philanthropy in memory of her grandson, who had died of sickle-cell anemia. She passed away in January 2008 at the age of ninety-six, surrounded by her daughter, her grandchildren, and her great-grandchildren. She was a very special lady.

I got to know Lovie well. I was one of her best customers when I was young and single and often very hungry. I took my own kids there once I got married and started a family too. I even had Fatburger cater parties for my daughter.

Then I became an investor and, for a few years, one of the principal owners of the Fatburger chain. After Lovie sold her business, it changed owners a couple times but grew to nearly fifty stores. By the year 2000, its annual sales were $33 million. Since Fatburgers were so popular in urban communities, I wanted to build on the wonderful brand that Lovie had created.

In October 2001 I led a team of investors who purchased Fatburger Corporation with plans to expand it in a big way across the country.

Our president and CEO was Keith A. Warlick, who had helped Lovie build Fatburger and stayed with the chain through several owners over the years. Keith put his heart and soul into this business, and he had big plans for expanding globally.

I had known Keith for about as long as I'd been eating Fatburgers. He catered parties at our house. Keith is also a Michigan native, and we share the same entrepreneurial spirit. He had encouraged me to become the majority owner of Fatburger because he knew that I loved the brand and cared about its future. I wanted to see Lovie's creation continue to offer jobs for urban residents, as well as burgers.

Keith did too. He was passionate about it because he'd been with the company so long. Keith was eager to grow the company quickly. We wanted to expand on our base in Southern California, Washington, Nevada, and Arizona too, but our group's strategy was more deliberate.

We were having lunch one day in 2003, a couple years after I'd bought in to Fatburger, when Keith said something that struck me.

"I've been through all these owners, but I've never had the opportunity to own it myself," he said. "I've put my life into this brand, and I've always dreamed that I would own it myself one day."

Keith was frustrated. He had a vision for expanding Fatburger. He wanted to franchise more stores at a faster rate. My advisers and I preferred retaining ownership and moving forward at a slower pace. Yet I understood his frustration and I admired his passion. Next to Lovie herself, Keith had probably put more into the making of the Fatburger brand than any other individual.

This was the first time he'd confided his dream of owning the business. It made sense.

"Keith, I'll tell you what. I've never heard you say that before. If you can meet my price so that my investors come out okay, I will sell Fatburger to you," I told him.

I had invested in Fatburger because Lovie had created something special and I wanted to see it continue serving its loyal customers. Keith cared about it even more than I did because he had worked there so long. He shared his dream with me, and I bought in to it. I told him to put a deal together within the next few months.

He lined up investors, and we did the deal. Keith was happy. I was happy. My fellow investors were happy. Keith was able to pursue his dream, and the sale of the once local Fatburger chain freed me up to become a Burger King franchise owner, which enabled me to then trade up and become a major supplier to Burger King and other customers!

LOVE IT AND LEAVE IT

My former business adviser Michael Ovitz once told me, "Never fall in love with something you might have to sell." I am very passionate about my businesses. Still, emotions should not guide business decisions.

Every one of my undertakings serves my overall mission of providing economic boosts to urban communities and the people in them. I love my businesses, but before I buy them, I prepare myself to sell them, just as Lovie Yancey did when the timing was right for her.

Smart entrepreneurs always go into businesses knowing two things:

1. *What* they want to get out of the business
2. *When* they need to get out of the business

Too often, though, passionate entrepreneurs dive into a new undertaking without giving adequate thought to those two key considerations. A PricewaterhouseCoopers survey of business owners within five years of retirement found that 54 percent of them did not have an exit strategy. The figure was worse for CEOs of businesses with revenues under $10 million: 70 percent of them had no exit strategy.

Why is it important to have an exit strategy in place before you start a business venture? When you start with an end in mind, it helps you make smart decisions as you grow the business. Your exit strategy may have to be adjusted to shifts in the market and changes in your personal circumstances. Still, someday will be the perfect day to get out—and you need to have a plan for doing that.

You don't want to fall into the trap of suddenly deciding to sell your business because you are worn out or distressed. The only thing worse than that is to simply close the door and liquidate your assets, which can come with a heavy tax burden.

Savvy owners sell their enterprises while they are still growing and still moving toward a peak, rather than when they are in decline and worth less in the market. A thriving business sells at a premium.

It can take years to complete the sale of a business. Finding the right buyer, negotiating the terms, and working out all of the legal and tax ramifications takes considerable time, but you can reduce that by being prepared from the start to deal with the end.

Nearly 90 percent of those who sell businesses use the services of business brokers or investment bankers, but those professionals generally get involved only in deals worth $10 million or more. They also charge fees that will cut into your walk-away money, so be sure you hire an ethical firm and make certain that you know exactly what you are paying for. Some business brokerage firms charge an up-front fee of 1 percent of the sales price that is to come off the commission. At least twenty states have banned that practice.

If you hire a business brokerage firm, its representative should have a database of qualified buyers. The broker should qualify potential buyers and help you get your financial matters ready for the sale. You also should expect the broker to market your business and to write a professional offering memo. Since about three out of four business sellers end up financing at least 60 percent of the sale, particularly in times of tight credit, you will need to prepare for that too.

A good business and tax accountant can help guide your decisions based on your personal preferences, your circumstances, and market conditions. If you have children, your plan should provide for their education as well as help to secure their future and your retirement.

PLANNED DEPARTURE

I couldn't believe it the first time my business advisers told me that they wanted to talk to me about an exit strategy for one of my early endeavors. "We haven't even started the company yet, and you want to talk about getting out of it?" I asked.

They patiently explained to me that I should look at all of my business ventures as investments. They said I should put my money into them, expecting to one day take even more money out so that I could then either look for bigger and better opportunities or buy a boat and head out to sea for a comfortable retirement.

Having an exit strategy doesn't necessarily mean that you plan to retire or even get out of a business entirely. Sometimes your exit strategy might involve passing your business on to your children or your employees. You can also "exit" as the sole owner by taking a private company public so that you cash in on its value in the marketplace while still retaining shares.

Your strategy is based on your personal goals and the market. Your business plan and your life plan have to work together. You should enter into every business deal only after looking at where you are: whether you are just starting out with young children, looking at having kids in college, or nearing the point where you want to be able to enjoy the fruits of your labors more and work less.

If your goal is to pass your business on to family members or employees, planning ahead is critical. Such deals generally mean that you will stay involved in the business longer while slowly turning it over to them as they buy it.

GRACEFUL EXITS

I never enter into a business without knowing how, and approximately when, I am going to get out. In the early days of building my business interests, my exit strategies were usually five years out at the most. Now we look ahead ten to twenty years and even further, because we are building a corporation that will continue to benefit my family and urban communities long after I am gone.

The first step in any exit strategy is to work with a trusted and experienced team of accountants and lawyers to create a financial plan that determines how much income you will need to be comfortable when you retire. That figure will then guide your decisions on growing and eventually exiting your businesses.

Next, you should work to maximize your retirement savings at every opportunity. That means taking full advantage of retirement savings tools such as IRAs and 401(k)s or pension plans custom-designed for you. These tools allow you to put money away and deduct it from your taxes too.

It is also important to monitor constantly the value of your business interests in the market. You can hire valuation analysts to give you a precise number, but that can be an expensive process. Most financial advisers say that a good way to estimate the value of your business is to take your annual net cash figure and multiply it by three to five times.

When it comes time to exit, you will need to determine how the process of selling your business will work. You should minimize your tax exposure at every step, of course, so that you get to keep as much of your hard-earned money as possible. It is also important to have a good management team in place so that the transition goes smoothly for the new owner.

If you have a long-term exit strategy in place, you should be so well prepared that your lawyer can work out the final transaction without huge legal fees. Your accountant and your lawyer may advise you to sell over a long period to take advantage of tax benefits. You might also be advised to create trusts for your spouse, children, and other heirs.

By planning your exit strategy from the time you start a business, you will also avoid the sad scenario of the entrepreneur who one day gets fed up and just unloads his business for less than its true value, and then suffers a huge tax hit. Selling a business can be emotional, even traumatic, if you don't prepare for it. If you fail to plan your exit strategy, you can pretty much plan on failing. Yet you will walk out a winner if you prepare yourself and understand the legal and tax ramifications.

Philanthropy

Give to your community and
your business will benefit.

For nearly thirty years, the Franklin Villa housing project in Sacramento, California, was notorious for its crime, gang violence, and drugs. Most of the urban neighborhood's 1960s-era apartment buildings were boarded up and falling apart by the 1990s.

A local reporter once wrote that "only the desperate rented there." Like the sad urban landscapes I saw from our team bus as a player, Franklin Villa appeared to be a lost cause.

Gang wars and drug trafficking were so bad that mothers wouldn't let their children go outside even during the day. At one point, police put an armed checkpoint at the neighborhood's entrance to cut down on the violence and crime. Nearly every street corner was marked by a memorial for someone who had been killed. One Christmas, thieves broke into several apartments and stole all the children's presents.

Franklin Villa seemed barren of hope back then. In just one year, police responded to six thousand calls in that eight-block area. Many honest, law-abiding residents left or wrote it off. Fortunately, there were determined people such as City Council member Bonnie Pannell and Jackie Rose, the director of residence services in Franklin Villa.

In 2002, their grassroots group of activists began reclaiming their neighborhood from the gangs and from hundreds of absentee landlords who had taken money out but made no investment in the community. Their campaign tapped $85 million in public funds to tear down ramshackle apartment buildings and build new residences. Police patrols were increased, and pools and playgrounds were built, along with a neighborhood activity center.

In 2003 residents of the cleaned-up, safer, and rightfully proud community changed its name to Phoenix Park to signify its rebirth. Four years later, I was honored to join the continuing effort to improve the lives of residents in this urban community in south Sacramento.

We held a ribbon cutting that day to open the Magic Johnson Foundation's Community Empowerment Center in Phoenix Park. Because of the hard work done by community leaders and residents, we were able to bring computers and other learning tools worth hundreds of thousands of dollars into this once-dangerous neighborhood.

Now men, women, and children are free to use those tools to learn skills and train for careers in programs offered by the center. At our grand-opening ceremony, Sacramento officials proclaimed it a "Magic Day."

I agree, though it had nothing to do with me.

The real magic was performed by the determined men and women who transformed a violent community into a place where its residents of all ages are now free to pursue their dreams. I am honored that my foundation has been allowed to build upon their incredible accomplishment and those of other dedicated men and women across the country.

DIGITAL DIVIDE

When I spoke at the grand opening of the Phoenix Park Empowerment Center, I told community leaders and residents that our goal was to level the playing field for them by giving them access to the best technology. Children and adults can use the center to get their high-school diplomas, to train for jobs, and to take classes in everything from money management to computer programming.

The original intent of our centers was to bridge the "digital divide"—the gap between those people with effective access to digital and information technology and those without it—in underserved urban areas and rural communities. In recent years, we have expanded the centers to include educational and career programs to help residents master computer technology, complete their education, and establish careers.

Many young people take computer technology for granted because it's such a major part of their world, but imagine what it would be like to be shut out of that world because you or your family could not afford a computer. We saw that many were being left behind.

Our Empowerment Centers are designed to give them the skills they need to live and compete in a world dominated by information technologies. Acquiring computer skills is important outside the workplace too. The Internet has become a primary source of vital news, weather, and other information. It is also a tool for finding and building social networks and for getting access to goods and services. Studies have shown that those who do not have computers or computer training often feel cut off from the rest of society.

That feeling brought a former church pastor, Curtis Bowman of rural Hodges, South Carolina, into our Empowerment Center in Greenwood, South Carolina. He had worked for a printing company for "thirty-two years and four months." In his last few years on the job, his employers had bought computers to modernize their printing processes. "But they only taught us just what we needed to know to get the job done," Mr. Bowman said. "They showed us how to do two things—how to get into the computer to do what we had to do and how to get back out."

Mr. Bowman was sixty-five years old and had been retired from his printing job for three years when we opened an Empowerment Center in Greenwood in 2005. He was one of the first to sign up for six months of computer training.

"At Magic's place, I learned how to use the keyboard's home keys—Lord have mercy, can you believe they never taught me that at work?—and how to use Microsoft Word, get on the Internet, and make PowerPoint presentations," said Mr. Bowman, who plans to use his new computer skills when he returns to pastoring at his church.

PLUGGING IN

No one from the communities we serve pays for the services and programs at our centers. Many of them are in neighborhoods still struggling to overcome poverty, crime, and neglect. In one of our New York City centers, a former gang member's shank is framed on the wall. The gang member handed in the homemade weapon after an instructor told his gang and their rivals that if they caused any trouble in "Magic's house," they would never be allowed to come back.

Even though we invest $250,000 in computers and other supplies in each of our twenty Empowerment Centers, we have never had a problem with theft. We like to think that our respect for the communities we serve is reflected in that fact.

Our Empowerment Centers located across the country have provided training and assistance for more than 240,000 people. We equip each center with twenty to forty-five computer systems and software, and we provide training so that young people, parents, and grandparents can use them.

Seventy-five percent of the young people who use our centers report improved grades. We've also conducted classes so that 1,200 of them could get their GED high-school diplomas. More than 2,200 adults from our classes have entered the job market as Microsoft-certified systems engineers. We've helped more than four hundred families move from subsidized housing into their own homes.

Empowerment Centers are located in Harlem; Chicago; Cleveland; Los Angeles; Washington, D.C.; Bladensburg, Maryland; three rural South Carolina communities; Houston; Jacksonville and Miami, Florida; Lansing; Oakland; Sacramento; Seattle; Philadelphia; and New Orleans. Our current plan is to build a new flagship center in Los Angeles.

MAKING A DIFFERENCE

I wrote earlier of my goal to rebuild urban America one street corner at a time. We have been putting up commercial buildings, apartment complexes, Starbucks, 24 Hour Fitness centers, Magic Johnson Theatres, T.G.I. Friday's, and Burger Kings where they had never been before. Yet those efforts represent only the business side. We also provide health, educational, technological, and career programs through our nonprofit Magic Johnson Foundation.

Giving back is part of the culture I grew up in, whether it was through our church in Lansing or watching my father and mother help a neighbor in need. The Urban League, the United Negro College Fund, and the NAACP are traditional minority charities built, dollar by dollar, by working-class men and women. It's a fact that people who don't have much themselves are often the most giving of their money, their time, and their talent. Those who build wealth after starting with nothing often never lose the giving spirit.

Urban communities around the country share stories like that of Matel Dawson, Jr., a forklift operator at Ford Motor Company in Detroit who donated more than $1.3 million to charities, schools, and nonprofit groups—money he had earned while working double shifts every day.

Oseola McCarty, an eighty-seven-year-old Hattiesburg, Mississippi, resident, quietly saved her earnings from a lifetime of washing and ironing other people's clothes so that she could give $150,000 to start her own scholarship fund for needy African-American students at the University of Southern Mississippi.

Another black woman who grew up poor in Mississippi, Oprah Winfrey, has given hundreds of millions of dollars to people all over the world. In fact, African Americans give 25 percent more of their discretionary income to charities than whites, according to *The Chronicle of Philanthropy*.

In its reports on America's leading black philanthropists, *Black Enterprise* magazine has included radio host Tom Joyner, NBA star David Robinson, Tiger Woods, Sean "P. Diddy" Combs, Bill and Camille Cosby, Chris "Ludacris" Bridges, Warrick Dunn, Hank Aaron, and money manager Eddie Brown among those who give back in a big way.

We all have something to contribute, whether it is a cash donation to a charity or time spent mentoring a young person. Giving circles are a new method of philanthropy that builds on the tradition of communal giving. These informal charitable groups are made up of individuals who pool their resources so they can make their money count and make a difference.

There are at least four hundred of these informal grass-roots groups around the country, and according to the Giving Circles Network (www.givingcircles.org), they have donated hundreds of millions of dollars to a wide range of causes and charities. Another great resource is the National Center for Black Philanthropy (www.ncfbp.net) in Washington, D.C., which offers training programs in endowment planning, fund-raising, and management.

GIVING BACK

For every hour I spend working at Magic Johnson Enterprises, I probably spend three or four at the Magic Johnson Foundation or working for another charitable cause. I don't play golf, but I do hang out on golf courses for the American Heart Association. I also take part in sporting events, dinners, auctions, and other fund-raisers for the Boys & Girls Clubs of America, the Muscular Dystrophy Association, the Make-A-Wish Foundation, the Starlight Foundation, the Urban League, the City of Hope, Rust College, and the United Negro College Fund.

I created the Magic Johnson Foundation in 1991 to raise awareness of and funds for community organizations dealing with HIV/AIDS education and prevention programs. We teamed up with the AIDS Healthcare Foundation, the nation's largest HIV/AIDS medical provider, to open five HIV/AIDS clinics in Los Angeles, San Francisco, and Oakland, California; and in Jacksonville and North Miami Beach, Florida. The clinics provide specialists, medications, and services needed by residents in surrounding urban communities, whether they can afford them or not.

I've learned what works and doesn't work in our foundation's efforts to identify and meet those needs. It's every bit as challenging to run our nonprofit businesses as it is our other enterprises.

Still, philanthropy is more fun. To walk into that Empowerment Center in Phoenix Park and see kids and adults learning how to use state-of-the-art computers and the Internet is more gratifying than anything else I can imagine. There is nothing like going to a charity auction, holding up a handful of Laker tickets, and raising $80,000 in five minutes for a great cause—unless it's pulling in $125,000 in ten minutes, as we did recently at a New York City charity auction.

I would not be where I am today without the many helping hands that reached out to me back when I was just a kid from a working-class family in Lansing. Now I try to return the favor whenever and wherever possible. I recruit my business partners to join me so that we can do more together and maximize our efforts.

The work done at the Magic Johnson Foundation is every bit as important as that done at Magic Johnson Enterprises. One could not exist without the other, for the simple reason that you can't go in and profit from urban America unless you show that you are willing to give back to it.

These are savvy communities. Residents are well schooled in the ways of the world. If they see you making money in their neighborhoods, they rightfully expect you to repay their loyalty. I respect that, and we honor it. We also expect our business partners to join us in giving back, and they gladly do it.

The thought that philanthropy made good business sense never occurred to me until I saw how good deeds create goodwill within our organizations. The giving spirit is contagious for our business partners too; they often ask to join in our philanthropic programs. We have also found that our brand benefits greatly from that goodwill. Yet we reach out with our scholarships, health clinics, technology centers, job fairs, and other programs because it is the right thing to do. I urge you to do the same in any way you can, as often as you can.

Life/Work Balance

Your family and your health
should be priorities too.

This e-mail came to the Magic Johnson Foundation in the spring of 2008. When I saw where the message originated, it struck me that as diverse and as far-flung as the human race may be, we all share the same needs and concerns. Once again, I was reminded of just how blessed I am to still be here to live, love, and play on this planet.

Dear Sirs,
No one could deny that Magic Johnson is one of the very popular persons round the globe. He is my Superstar. However, since we in Papua, Indonesia, have no knowledge about our Superstar Magic Johnson, we really want to know how is his present health condition, and what is he doing now.

Thanks and regards,
Winny Mambu SH,
Facilitator of HIV AIDS
PAPUA, INDONESIA

I am doing just fine, Winny Mambu, and thanks for asking. Since it was discovered that I had HIV back in late 1991, my health has been a major focus for me and the people who care about me. Yet there are millions of others around the world infected with HIV and AIDS. We should care about them too because they are our family members, our loved ones, our neighbors, our friends, and our future.

Shortly after I was diagnosed with HIV, Cookie and I visited Elizabeth Glaser, who had contracted the virus through a blood transfusion while giving birth to her daughter. Despite the fact that she was fighting for her own life, Elizabeth founded the Elizabeth Glaser Pediatric AIDS Foundation and became a great resource and an inspiration to Cookie and me.

Before she died, she challenged me to "become the face of HIV/AIDS awareness" so that I could educate others and motivate at-risk people to get tested. Now I stand with millions of Americans and others from around the world whose lives have been touched by HIV/AIDS.

Though advances have been made, HIV/AIDS is still one of the greatest challenges facing our world—it knows no boundaries of race, nationality, sexuality, religion, or politics.

The African-American community is the hardest hit in the United States. AIDS remains the leading cause of death for blacks ages twenty-five to forty-four, according to the Centers for Disease Control and Prevention. Blacks make up just 13 percent of the population of the United States, but we account for 49 percent of all cases of HIV.

The first step is to get tested. Many free HIV-testing services exist, so cost is not a factor. Fear is often the greatest barrier to overcome. Yet having HIV and not being treated is the most frightening situation. Getting tested, paying attention to the results, and practicing safe sex is the only way we can treat the infection and stop its spread throughout our community.

That is why Cookie and I started the "I Stand with Magic"

campaign, a five-year, $60 million effort in partnership with the drug firm Abbott. Our goal is to cut AIDS rates among black Americans by 50 percent. Cookie overcame her shyness to join me in this campaign not only because of our personal experience but because the HIV rates among African-American women are twenty times those of Caucasian women. Black women account for 64 percent of all women with HIV.

Since we started this campaign, it has provided free HIV/AIDS testing to more than 21,000 Americans in sixteen cities. More than 85,000 have enrolled in our campaign at www.istandwithmagic.com. Cookie thought other black women might listen to her. If just one person hears her message and responds, it will be worth it.

The number one thing we have to do is change the mind-set and attitude in black America. If your partner does not want to get tested, you have to say no. Women have to take the lead role and refuse to have unprotected sex. Everyone needs to get tested. There is no excuse. My Magic Johnson Healthcare Centers provide free and confidential HIV testing, because enough is enough. Everyone can fight this terrible killer by practicing safe sex, getting tested, and encouraging others to do the same.

FIRST THINGS FIRST

There are thirty-two chapters in this book because that was the number I wore as a Los Angeles Laker. I wanted to acknowledge those days throughout the book because the goodwill and notoriety I earned as a player have paid dividends in my business career. Of course, none of that would have mattered if I had not stayed healthy, and that is the message I want to impart in this concluding but far from final chapter. There will be more books to come, I promise you, because I am going to live a long and productive life.

I want you to do the same.

It's as simple as this: Take care of yourself. Take care of your family. Without good health and loving relationships, your business success and the wealth you accrue will never be enough to fulfill you. You have to put together the whole package, and you have to take care of those aspects of your life too.

I wasn't so smart about taking care of myself during my playing days, and it took a toll on my career, ending it prematurely. That was sad, but I was able to get the medical care I needed to keep fighting. I am still fighting. I work long days even though I am still living with HIV more than fifteen years after being diagnosed.

The medications I take to combat HIV are the same as those available to everyone. I also follow an exercise regimen designed to keep me and my immune system strong. I take three pills twice a day. I run. I bike. I do a kickboxing workout. I also lift weights. I eat right too. Most important, I surround myself with people I care about and I let them know as much as possible that I love them too. Their positive influence keeps me positive, and I believe that is as important as any medications I could take.

I also team with Abbott Laboratories to sponsor World AIDS Day to promote awareness and testing for the virus, especially in minority communities where people have tended to resist being tested. My message to them is that they don't have to die. If they get tested, they can get the same medications I take. They can fight the virus, and they can live—if it is detected early enough and if they get help.

A WAKE-UP CALL

Most people face health challenges of some kind. African Americans face more than most, often because they have fewer health care options. That is one reason I formed a business alliance with

Aetna to help inform and educate minorities without health insurance or access to health care. If we can work together to improve health care education and convince people of the benefits of exercise and healthy eating, we can make a big difference.

It makes no sense for any entrepreneur to focus so intently on building a business or pursuing wealth that you neglect your health or your loved ones. That said, I'll be the first to tell you it is not easy to do it all. In the beginning of building my business career, I was a workaholic. Ten years ago, I was not the husband or the father that my family deserved. You can believe that Cookie and our children let me know about it too.

"Honey, you need to spend more time with the kids" was Cookie's first hint.

I got it. So I made a plan. Saturday officially became kids' day with Daddy. We go to the movies or the arcade or sometimes both. Ice cream is usually on the agenda too because my daughter loves it.

We were having wonderful times two months into our official observances of Saturdays with Daddy. Then we got home late one afternoon, and there stood my wife with her hands on her hips. This is usually a sign that all is not right in Cookie's world.

"You're doing a great job with the kids," she said. "Now what about me?"

I had messed up. I'd been taking bows, patting myself on the back, thinking that I was doing a super job with my kids, spending quality *and* quantity time with them. I'd dropped the ball when it came to my wife.

Cookie had a legitimate gripe. That happens occasionally. Men really are from Mars, or at least some planet other than the one that women come from. We often don't get things because we don't pick up on the same cues that women pick up on. Or we just don't pay enough attention.

Men tend to think that if they are taking care of business, then they are taking care of the family. *But I'm working for you so you can have a good life!* That may be true, but it covers only part of our responsibilities as husbands and fathers.

Yes, there is more, as Cookie let me know that Saturday afternoon many years back. Her concerns led to the creation of Friday Date Night for Mr. and Mrs. Johnson. Every Friday night, we go out to a movie and dinner, and that gives us time to focus on each other and catch up as boyfriend and girlfriend, husband and wife.

I'm so happy that we started doing that. It's been great for our relationship and for our emotional and mental health. Cookie will probably kick me for saying this, but our Friday nights together have also made me an even better businessman.

By spending more time with Cookie and the kids, I realized that I can still be an effective entrepreneur and business leader. I learned to give more responsibilities and decision-making powers to the members of our team. It's made them happier, me happier, and my family happier. Our business is thriving.

Cookie's ultimatums forced me to let someone else take the wheel, and our enterprises are better for it. Instead of always trying to be in control, I focused on building a strong team so I felt comfortable delegating responsibilities. I am a natural-born control freak, so it wasn't easy to do that. Yet I'm glad I did. It has probably added years to my life and certainly to my marriage. I have learned to trust that there are other passionate people who are capable of running things day to day while I take care of myself and my relationships.

My business calendar is now built around my family calendar. School plays, my kids' sporting events, vacations, and holidays go on the schedule first. Then I fill the rest in with work. Sometimes there are conflicts. There are occasions when I have to miss something with the family to honor a business commitment or to deal with a crisis. Still, my family knows I put them first.

The hard thing to realize for me and many passionate and driven entrepreneurs is that the time you spend away from the business can be as beneficial to it as the time you spend obsessing over every detail. Some CEOs play golf to refresh and recharge. Others climb mountains or go on safaris. You have to decide what sort of getaway works best for you.

Personally, I need water. Whether it's from a beach or on a boat, I need to go off and stare across the water and let my brain patterns ebb and flow with the currents. I won't lie to you and tell you that I don't think about business when I'm out there. I do. Yet the process is different. My mind unconsciously washes over all the minute details and puts things into perspective. I can't tell you how many hours I've spent just gazing off across the Pacific Ocean. Often, I will take that time to reflect on how far we have come and to celebrate those successes. Just as often, I'll be kicked back and lost in what seems like nothing at all when a solution to a problem or a vision or a new undertaking suddenly presents itself.

I've come to value those Zen-like moments because my schedule is so busy that I often don't have time to reflect or to ponder during the regular workday. Getting out on the water allows me to sit back and savor, and it gives my mind a chance to work things out. I highly recommend that you find your own methods of relaxing, recharging, and reflecting. If it works for me, it will work for you too.

THE FINAL BUZZER

I hope you have learned helpful things in this book that will enrich your life both financially and spiritually. Though I don't wear my faith on my sleeve, I am an advocate of prayer. When I look at where I started and how far I have come, there's no getting around the fact that many blessings have come my way. Challenges have presented themselves too, but I've had more breaks than anyone should expect. The greatest blessings to grace my life are the people who have cared for me, loved me, encouraged me, and set me straight when I needed it.

I encourage you to do the same for the people around you. Reach out to them. Teach them through your example. Show them that they can succeed if they work hard, stay on the straight path, and listen to those who are willing to guide them. My hope is that someday we can all do business together and, in the process, make the world a better place for us all.

Overtime

Because business changes and life are constantly steering me in new directions, I wanted to have new stories and anecdotes for you up to the minute the book was published. So as an added bonus, I give you chapter 33. When I laced up my sneakers at Michigan State, my number was 33—and I figured, why not do something special and unique—like add a final chapter 33 online.

Log on to www.magicjohnsonenterprises.com to see pictures of my business career, videos of me during the book-creation process, and updated tales on business and new beginnings. Have a question or want to post a message? We encourage that—hope to hear from you soon.

Earvin "Magic" Johnson

EARVIN "MAGIC" JOHNSON—known worldwide for his talent on the basketball court—has an equally impressive career off the court. As the chairman and chief executive officer of Magic Johnson Enterprises, Mr. Johnson has been a pioneer in revitalizing ethnically diverse urban areas by bringing brand-name businesses into underserved communities for more than twenty-five years. With a brand presence in eighty-five cities and twenty-one states, and a growing multimillion-dollar business empire, Mr. Johnson has become a respected businessman with a proven track record. He shares his passion for urban development and inspires audiences annually by headlining in more than one hundred speaking engagements nationwide. Mr. Johnson is also the chairman and founder of the Magic Johnson Foundation, Inc. Founded in 1991, the foundation is dedicated to developing programs and supporting community-based organizations that address the educational, health, and social needs of ethnically diverse, urban communities.